RHCE Linux

Second Edition

Kara J. Pritchard

RHCE Linux Exam Cram, Second Edition

© 2000 The Coriolis Group. All rights reserved.

Limits of Liability and Disclaimer of Warranty

The author and publisher of this book have used their best efforts in preparing the book and the programs contained in it. These efforts include the development, research, and testing of the theories and programs to determine their effectiveness. The author and publisher make no warranty of any kind, expressed or implied, with regard to these programs or the documentation contained in this book.

The author and publisher shall not be liable in the event of incidental or consequential damages in connection with, or arising out of, the furnishing, performance, or use of the programs, associated instructions, and/or claims of productivity gains.

Trademarks

Trademarked names appear throughout this book. Rather than list the names and entities that own the trademarks or insert a trademark symbol with each mention of the trademarked name, the publisher states that it is using the names for editorial purposes only and to the benefit of the trademark owner, with no intention of infringing upon that trademark.

The Coriolis Group, LLC
14455 N. Hayden Road
Suite 220
Scottsdale, Arizona 85260

(480)483-0192
FAX (480)483-0193
www.coriolis.com

Library of Congress Cataloging-in-Publication Data
Pritchard, Kara J.
    RHCE Linux/by Kara Pritchard.--2nd ed.
        p.   cm. -- (Exam cram)
    Includes index.
    ISBN 1-57610-828-7
    1. Linux.   2. Operating systems (Computers).   I. Title.   II. Series.
QA76.76.O63 P756 2000
005.4'469--dc21   00-064438
                                                          CIP

President and CEO
Keith Weiskamp

Publisher
Steve Sayre

Acquisitions Editor
Lee Anderson

Product Marketing Manager
Brett Woolley

Project Editor
Sybil Ihrig
Helios Productions

Production Coordinator
Kim Eoff

Cover Designer
Jesse Dunn

Layout Designer
April Nielsen

Printed in the United States of America
10 9 8 7 6 5 4 3 2 1

The Coriolis Group, LLC • 14455 North Hayden Road, Suite 220 • Scottsdale, Arizona 85260

ExamCram.com *Connects You to the Ultimate Study Center!*

Our goal has always been to provide you with the best study tools on the planet to help you achieve your certification in record time. Time is so valuable these days that none of us can afford to waste a second of it, especially when it comes to exam preparation.

Over the past few years, we've created an extensive line of *Exam Cram* and *Exam Prep* study guides, practice exams, and interactive training. To help you study even better, we have now created an e-learning and certification destination called **ExamCram.com**. (You can access the site at **www.examcram.com**.) Now, with every study product you purchase from us, you'll be connected to a large community of people like yourself who are actively studying for their certifications, developing their careers, seeking advice, and sharing their insights and stories.

I believe that the future is all about collaborative learning. Our **ExamCram.com** destination is our approach to creating a highly interactive, easily accessible collaborative environment, where you can take practice exams and discuss your experiences with others, sign up for features like "Questions of the Day," plan your certifications using our interactive planners, create your own personal study pages, and keep up with all of the latest study tips and techniques.

I hope that whatever study products you purchase from us—*Exam Cram* or *Exam Prep* study guides, *Personal Trainers*, *Personal Test Centers*, or one of our interactive Web courses—will make your studying fun and productive. Our commitment is to build the kind of learning tools that will allow you to study the way you want to, whenever you want to.

Visit ExamCram.com now to enhance your study program.

Help us continue to provide the very best certification study materials possible. Write us or email us at **learn@examcram.com** and let us know how our study products have helped you study. Tell us about new features that you'd like us to add. Send us a story about how we've helped you. We're listening!

Good luck with your certification exam and your career. Thank you for allowing us to help you achieve your goals.

Keith Weiskamp
President and CEO

Look for these other products from The Coriolis Group:

LPI General Linux I: Part 1 Exam Cram
By Emmett Dulaney

LPI General Linux I: Part 2 Exam Cram
By Emmett Dulaney and William Steen

General Linux I Exam Prep
By Dee-Ann LeBlanc

Sair Linux/GNU Installation and Configuration Exam Cram
By Michael Jang

In memory of my grandfather, Hershell Enlow (1926–1999).
Your strength has guided me where I am today
and will carry me forever.
—Kara J. Pritchard

❧

About the Author

Kara J. Pritchard is currently the Assistant Director for Program Development of the Linux Professional Institute, working on developing the standard base for Linux certification. As an independent consultant, Kara has been promoting the use of Linux in both corporate and educational facilities since late 1995 in the Illinois and St. Louis metropolitan areas.

Kara began participating in the Linux community in the fall of 1995, when she was introduced to the Southern Illinois Linux Users Group (SILUG), founded by her husband in 1994. With her husband, Kara founded the Linux Users of Central Illinois (LUCI) in 1997 and moved SILUG into an umbrella organization including multiple LUGs across southern Illinois. She now works with LUGs all over the world through her LUG Resource Project (**http://www.linuxusersgroups.org/**) sponsored as a Linux Evangelist by Linuxgruven. You can contact her at **kara@luci.org**.

Acknowledgments

First, credit goes to the Linux community of developers, supporters, and activists who have made Linux what it is today. May the source be with you!

I would like to thank the project editor, Sybil Ihrig of Helios Productions, and the copy editor, Catherine Oliver, for tackling the revision of this book for the second edition. I would also like to thank the Coriolis team for supporting the efforts behind Linux certification by publishing updated material for the RHCE exam, and for giving me the opportunity to be one of the pacesetters for this growing series of books dedicated to Linux and Linux certification.

An extra-special thanks goes to all the individuals who helped me piece together all the documentation and resources for this book: Clay P. Castleton, my Samba God; Randy Flood, RHCE2b.com founder; Rik, arnt, bam, lia, digital, shade, crab, and the rest of my IRC friends; the readers who took the time to send in comments, errata, and suggestions for the new edition; and Peter Childers, Randy Russell, and the rest of the Red Hat staff I've had the pleasure of working with over the past couple of years.

Thank you to my husband, Steven, for doing the technical editing of this book and for having introduced me to Linux in the first place. Without your patience and your tolerance for take-out food and wrinkled shirts, I'd never have finished this project.

Thanks and dedication belong most to my family. To my mother, father, and sister who have supported everything I've ever done; to my grandmother who's shown me I can accomplish anything I put my mind to; and, of course, to my cats, who lovingly stood on my keyboard and made me retype too much of this book.

—*Kara J. Pritchard*

Contents at a Glance

Table of Contents

Chapter 5
Installation 85

Introduction

Welcome to *RHCE Linux Exam Cram, Second Edition!* This book aims to help you get ready to take—and pass—the Red Hat certification exam RHCE 302. This Introduction explains Red Hat's certification programs in general and talks about how the *Exam Cram* series can help you prepare for Red Hat's certification exams.

Exam Cram books help you understand and appreciate the subjects and materials you need to pass Red Hat certification exams. *Exam Cram* books are aimed strictly at test preparation and review. They do not teach you everything you need to know about a topic (such as the ins and outs of building your own RPMs). Instead, I present and dissect the questions and problems I've found that you're likely to encounter on a test. I've worked from Red Hat's own training materials, preparation guides, and tests. My aim is to bring together as much information as possible about Red Hat certification exams.

Nevertheless, to completely prepare yourself for any Red Hat test, you should begin by taking the Self-Assessment included in this book (immediately following this Introduction). This tool will help you evaluate your knowledge base against the requirements for an RHCE under both ideal and real circumstances.

Based on what you learn from that exercise, you might decide to begin your studies with some classroom training, or you might pick up and read one of the many Linux guides available from Red Hat or third-party vendors. I strongly recommend that you also install and configure the software and tools that you'll be tested on, because nothing beats hands-on experience and familiarity when it comes to understanding the questions you're likely to encounter on a certification test. Book learning is essential, but hands-on experience is the best teacher of all—especially because two-thirds of the exam is hands-on.

The Red Hat Certified Engineer (RHCE) Program

The RHCE exam is made up of three parts:

➤ Installation and Configuration Lab Exam

➤ Debugging Lab Exam

> ➤ Written Exam

The three exams are taken on the same day and are each graded individually. The RHCE exam taker must receive a composite score of 80 percent on all three exams, with no single score dropping below 50 percent.

The best place to keep tabs on the RHCE program and its various certifications is on the Red Hat Web site. The current URL for the RHCE program is **http://www.redhat.com/training/rhce/courses/**. Red Hat's Web site changes frequently, so if this URL doesn't work, try using the Search tool on Red Hat's site with either "RHCE" or the quoted phrase "Red Hat Certified Engineer Program" as the search string. This will help you find the latest and most accurate information about the company's certification programs.

Taking a Certification Exam

Alas, testing is not free. Your exam could cost from $349 to $749 (depending on whether you participate in the training program or take the exam-only approach). Currently, exams are administered by Red Hat. To reach the Red Hat RHCE team, email **training@redhat.com**. Exams are also offered by Global Knowledge (**http://db.globalknowledge.com/catalog/certlisting.asp?code=RHCE**) and IBM Global Services (**http://www-3.ibm.com/services/learning/spotlight/linux.html**).

To schedule an exam, call at least 10 days in advance. Exam seats are limited and are often booked solid two months in advance. To cancel or reschedule an exam, you must call at least 2 days before the scheduled test time in order to receive any sort of refund. (For canceling 2 days in advance, you are billed 80 percent; for 3 to 10 days in advance, you are billed 50 percent; and for more than 10 business days in advance, you are given a full refund.) When calling Red Hat, please have the following information ready for the RHCE staff member who handles your call:

> ➤ Your name, organization, and mailing address.

> ➤ A method of payment. (The most convenient approach is to supply a valid credit card number with sufficient available credit. Otherwise, payments by check, money order, or purchase order must be received before a test can be scheduled. If the latter methods are required, ask your order taker for more details.)

On the day of the test, arrive at least 15 minutes before the scheduled time slot. You must bring and supply two forms of identification, one of which must be a photo ID.

All exams are completely closed-book. In fact, you will be required to stow anything you brought with you under your desk. You will be furnished with a blank sheet of paper, a pencil, and any other tools you might need for your exam. I suggest that you immediately write down on that sheet of paper all the information you've memorized for the test.

When you complete a Red Hat certification exam component, you will report to your instructor. Either the instructor will sign off on your lab exam, instructing you on the next step, or you will turn in your written exam and be excused for a break. All exam components are scored on a percentage basis.

How to Prepare for an Exam

Preparing for any Linux exam requires that you obtain and study materials designed to provide comprehensive information about Red Hat Linux and the specific exam for which you are preparing. The following list of materials will help you study and prepare:

➤ The Red Hat Linux 6.2 manuals (or online documentation found on Red Hat's Web site)

➤ The Linux Documentation Project (online resource found at **http:// www.linuxdoc.org/**)

➤ Red Hat Preparation Site (online resource found at **http://rhce2b.com/**)

In addition, you'll probably find the following training courses useful in your quest for Red Hat Linux expertise:

➤ *RHCE 300 Certification Training* —Red Hat Inc. (Durham, NC) offers an RHCE 300 Certification course. The course is a week-long adventure and includes a full day of examinations. Current perks of the course include daily catered lunches and all the soda and juice you can handle. You pay for it in the long run, however; the week-long course (which includes the exam fee) is currently priced at $2,498.

➤ *Other Red Hat Inc. Training* —Red Hat Inc. offers three additional courses to help you learn Red Hat Linux. They include RH033 (Introduction to Red Hat Linux I and II), RH133 (Red Hat Linux System Administration I and II), and RH253 (Red Hat Linux Networking and Security Administration). Each class is a four-day program, and prices range from $1,098 (RH033) to $2,198 (RH253).

➤ *Study guides* —Several publishers —including The Coriolis Group—offer Linux titles. The Coriolis Group series includes the following:

➤ *The Exam Cram series* —These books give you information about the material you need to know to pass the tests.

> ➤ *The Exam Prep series* —These books provide a greater level of detail than the *Exam Cram* books and are designed to teach you everything you need to know from an exam perspective. Each book comes with a CD that contains interactive practice exams in a variety of testing formats.

Together, the two series make a perfect pair. Check **ExamCram.com** for additional products from Coriolis.

You'll find that this book will complement your studying and preparation for the exam, either on your own or with the aid of the previously mentioned study programs. In the section that follows, I'll explain how this book works and why this book counts as a member of the required and recommended materials list.

About this Book

Each topical *Exam Cram* chapter follows a regular structure, along with graphical cues about important or useful information. Here's the structure of a typical chapter:

> ➤ *Opening hotlists* —Each chapter begins with a list of the terms, tools, and techniques that you must learn and understand before you can be fully conversant with that chapter's subject matter. The hotlists are followed by one or two introductory paragraphs to set the stage for the rest of the chapter.

> ➤ *Topical coverage* —After the opening hotlists, each chapter covers a series of topics related to the chapter's subject. Throughout this section, I highlight important topics or concepts as Exam Alerts, like this:

This is what an Exam Alert looks like. Normally, an Exam Alert stresses concepts, terms, software, or activities that are likely to relate to one or more certification test questions. For that reason, any information found offset in Exam Alert format is worthy of unusual attentiveness on your part. Indeed, most of the information that appears on the Cram Sheet appears as Exam Alerts within the text.

Pay close attention to material flagged as an Exam Alert; although all the information in this book pertains to what you need to know to pass the exam, I flag certain items that are really important. You'll find what appears in the meat of each chapter to be worth knowing, too, when preparing for the test. Because this book's material is very condensed, I recommend that you use this book along with other resources to achieve the maximum benefit.

In addition to the Exam Alerts, I have provided tips that will help build a better foundation for Red Hat Linux knowledge. Although the information might not be on the exam, it is certainly related and will help you become a better test taker.

TIP This is how tips are formatted. Keep your eyes open for these, and you'll become a Linux guru in no time.

➤ *Practice questions* —This section presents a series of mock test questions and explanations of both correct and incorrect answers.

➤ *Details and resources* —Every chapter ends with a section titled "Need to Know More?", which provides direct pointers to Red Hat and third-party resources offering more details on the chapter's subject. If you find a resource you like in this collection, use it, but don't feel compelled to use all the resources. On the other hand, I recommend only those resources that I use on a regular basis, so none of my recommendations will be a waste of your time or money. (But purchasing them all at once probably represents an expense that many network administrators and would-be RHCEs might find hard to justify.)

The bulk of the book follows this chapter structure slavishly, but there are a few other elements that I'd like to point out. Chapters 12, 13, and 14 represent what you should expect for the three elements of the RHCE 302 exam. Chapter 12 discusses objectives and elements involved during the Installation and Configuration Lab exam. Chapter 13 discusses methods for handling the Debugging Lab exam. Chapter 14 includes a sample written test that provides a good review of the material presented throughout the book to ensure that you're ready for the exam. Chapter 15 is an answer key to the sample test that appears in Chapter 14. You'll notice that no answer key is provided for the exams that appear in Chapters 12 and 13. This is because performance-based exams test your ability to accomplish a specific task, not necessarily how you accomplish it. Therefore, there is no specific right or wrong, yes or no answer. Additionally, you'll find a glossary that explains terms, and an index that you can use to track down terms as they appear in the text.

Finally, the tear-out Cram Sheet attached next to the inside front cover of this *Exam Cram* book represents a condensed and compiled collection of facts and tips that I think you should memorize before taking the test. Because you can dump this information out of your head onto a piece of paper before answering any exam questions, you can master this information by brute force—you need to remember it only long enough to write it down when you walk into the test room. You might even want to look at it in the car or in the lobby of the testing center just before you walk in to take the test.

How to Use this Book

If you're prepping for a first-time test, keep in mind that I've structured the topics in this book to build on one another. Therefore, some topics in later chapters make more sense after you've read earlier chapters. That's why I suggest you read this book from front to back for your initial test preparation. If you need to brush up on a topic or you have to bone up for a second try, use the index or table of contents to go straight to the topics and questions that you need to study. Beyond the tests, I think you'll find this book useful as a tightly focused reference to some of the most important aspects of Red Hat Linux and Linux networking services.

Given all the book's elements and its specialized focus, I've tried to create a tool that will help you prepare for—and pass—Red Hat's "Red Hat Certified Engineer" exam. Please share your feedback on the book with me, especially if you have ideas about how I can improve it for future test-takers.

Please send your questions or comments to The Coriolis Group at **learn@examcram.com** or to the author at **kara@luci.org**. Please remember to include the title of the book in your message; otherwise, I'll be forced to guess which book you're writing about. Also, be sure to check out the Web page at **http://www.examcram.com**, where you'll find information updates, commentary, and clarifications on documents for each book; you can either read this material online or download it for use later on.

Thanks, and enjoy the book!

Self-Assessment

I included a Self-Assessment in this *Exam Cram* book to help you evaluate your readiness to tackle RHCE certification. This Self-Assessment should also help you understand what you need to master the topic of this book—namely, RHCE 302. But before you tackle this Self-Assessment, let's talk about concerns you may face when pursuing an RHCE and about what an ideal RHCE candidate might look like.

RHCEs in the Real World

In the next section, I describe an ideal RHCE candidate, knowing full well that only a few real candidates will meet this ideal. In fact, my description of that ideal candidate might seem downright scary. But take heart: although the requirements to obtain an RHCE might seem formidable, they are by no means impossible to meet. However, you should be keenly aware that getting through the process takes time, requires some expense, and consumes substantial effort.

Introduced in the spring of 1999, the RHCE program is very young. Demand for this certification is growing, and the limited seating for the testing makes the RHCE even more valuable. However, if you're willing to tackle the process seriously and to do what it takes to obtain the necessary experience and knowledge, you can take—and pass—all the certification tests involved in obtaining an RHCE. In fact, Coriolis has designed its *Exam Crams* and companion *Exam Preps* to make it as easy for you as possible to prepare for certification exams. We've also greatly expanded our Web site, **http://www.examcram.com**, to provide a host of resources for various certifications.

The Ideal RHCE Candidate

Just to give you some idea of what an ideal RHCE candidate is like, following are some relevant statistics about the background and experience such an individual might have. Don't worry if you don't meet these qualifications—this is a far from ideal world, and where you fall short is simply where you'll have more work to do.

➤ Academic or professional training in network theory, concepts, and operations. This training includes everything from networking hardware and software to the Linux operating system, services, and applications.

➤ Two or more years of professional networking experience, including experience with Ethernet, modems, and other networking media. This experience must include installation, configuration, upgrading, and troubleshooting.

➤ Two or more years in a networked environment with hands-on experience with Red Hat Linux or other Linux distributions, such as Caldera, Debian, or SuSE. A solid understanding of each system's architecture, installation, configuration, maintenance, and troubleshooting is also essential.

➤ Familiarity with key Linux-based TCP/IP-based services, including HTTP (Web servers), DHCP, and DNS, plus familiarity with one or more of the following: FTP, Samba, Squid, NFS, or ipchains.

Put Yourself to the Test

The following series of questions and observations is designed to help you figure out how much work you must do to pursue Red Hat certification and what kinds of resources you might consult on your quest. Be absolutely honest in your answers, or you'll end up wasting money on exams you're not yet ready to take. There are no right or wrong answers, only steps along the path to certification. Only you can decide where you really belong in the broad spectrum of aspiring candidates.

Two things should be clear from the outset, however:

➤ Even a modest background in computer science will be helpful.

➤ Hands-on experience with Linux, Linux products, and Linux technologies is an essential ingredient to certification success.

Educational Background

1. Have you ever taken any computer-related classes? [Yes or No]

   If Yes, proceed to question 2; if No, proceed to question 4.

2. Have you taken any classes on Unix operating systems? [Yes or No]

   If Yes, you'll probably be able to handle Red Hat's architecture and system component discussions. If you're rusty, brush up on basic Unix concepts, especially virtual memory, multitasking regimes, user mode versus superuser mode operation, filesystems, and general computer security topics.

If No, consider some basic reading in this area. I strongly recommend a good general operating-systems book, such as *Essential System Administration*, by Æleen Frisch (O'Reilly & Associates, 1995, ISBN 1-56592-127-5). If this title doesn't appeal to you, check out reviews of other, similar titles at your favorite online bookstore.

3. Have you taken any TCP/IP-based networking concepts or technologies classes? [Yes or No]

If Yes, you'll probably be able to handle Red Hat Linux's networking terminology, concepts, and technologies (brace yourself for frequent departures from normal usage). If you're rusty, brush up on basic networking concepts and terminology, especially networking media, transmission types, the OSI reference model, and networking technologies such as Ethernet and WAN links.

If No, you might want to read one or two books in this topic area. The two best books that I know of are *Computer Networks*, *3rd Edition*, by Andrew S. Tanenbaum (Prentice-Hall, 1996, ISBN 0-13-349945-6), and *Computer Networks and Internets*, by Douglas E. Comer (Prentice-Hall, 1997, ISBN 0-13-239070-1).

Skip to the next section, "Hands-on Experience."

4. Have you done any reading on the Linux operating system or networks? [Yes or No]

If Yes, review the requirements stated in the first paragraphs after questions 2 and 3. If you meet those requirements, move on to the next section.

If No, consult the recommended reading for both topics. A strong background will help you prepare for the Red Hat exams better than just about anything else.

Hands-on Experience

The most important key to success on all types of certification exams is hands-on experience. If I leave you with only one realization after you take this Self-Assessment, it should be that there's no substitute for time spent installing, configuring, and using Red Hat Linux and its components, upon which you'll be tested repeatedly and in depth.

5. Have you installed, configured, and worked with:

   ➤ Linux? [Yes or No]

   ➤ Red Hat Linux? [Yes or No]

If Yes, make sure you understand the methods used in Red Hat Linux 6.2, the differences between Red Hat Linux 6.2 and other Red Hat Linux versions, and the differences between Red Hat Linux 6.2 and other vendor distributions (such as Caldera, SuSE, and Debian).

If No, you'll want to obtain a copy of Red Hat Linux 6.2 and learn how to install, configure, and maintain it. You can use this book to guide your activities and studies.

6. For any specific Linux product that is not itself an operating system (for example, the X Window System or Apache), have you installed, configured, used, and upgraded this software? [Yes or No]

If the answer is Yes, skip to the next section. If it's No, you must get some experience. Read on for suggestions on how to do this.

With the RHCE 302 exam, experience is a must, be it something as simple as Pine or as challenging as NFS or Apache.

 If you have the funds, or your employer will pay your way, consider taking a class from Red Hat Software, Inc., or from an Authorized Training Partner. In addition to classroom exposure to the topic of your choice, you get a copy of the Red Hat Linux version that is the focus of your course, along with the training materials for that class.

Before you even think about taking any exam, make sure you've spent enough time with the related software to understand how it can be installed and configured, how to maintain such an installation, and how to troubleshoot that software when things go wrong. This will help you in the exam as well as in real life.

Testing Your Exam-Readiness

Whether you attend a formal class on a specific topic to get ready for an exam or use written materials to study on your own, some preparation for the Red Hat Certified Engineer exam is essential. At $749 a try, pass or fail, you want to do everything you can to pass the exam on your first try. That's where the importance of studying comes in.

I've included practice objectives, goals, and exams in this book, so if you don't score that well on the first test, you can study more and then tackle the second test. If you still don't hit a score of at least 85 percent after the second test, you'll want to investigate practice-tests available from commercial vendors.

For any given subject, consider taking a class if you've tackled self-study materials, taken the test, and failed anyway. The opportunity to interact with an instructor and fellow students can make all the difference in the world if you can afford that privilege. For information about Red Hat classes, visit the Training and Certification page at **http://www.redhat.com/products/training.html**.

Onward, through the Fog!

After you've assessed your readiness, undertaken the right background studies, obtained the hands-on experience that will help you understand the products and technologies at work, and reviewed the many sources of information to help you prepare for a test, you'll be ready to take a round of practice tests. When your scores come back high enough to get you through the exam, you're ready to go after the real thing. If you follow this assessment regime, you'll know not only what you need to study but also when you're ready to make a test date. Good luck!

Red Hat Certification Exams

Terms you'll need to understand:

✓ Exhibit
✓ Multiple-choice question formats
✓ Careful reading
✓ Process of elimination

Techniques you'll need to master:

✓ Assessing your exam-readiness
✓ Preparing to take a certification exam
✓ Practicing (to make perfect)
✓ Making the best use of the testing software
✓ Budgeting your time
✓ Saving the hardest questions until last
✓ Guessing (as a last resort)

Exam taking is not something that most people anticipate eagerly, no matter how well prepared they might be. In most cases, familiarity helps ameliorate test anxiety. In plain English, this means that you probably won't be as nervous when you take your fourth or fifth Red Hat certification exam as you'll be when you take your first one. Granted, every certification exam—whether it's a Red Hat exam, a Caldera exam, or another certification program—will be different, but the preparation process will be similar and you'll become more comfortable with each experience.

Whether it's your first exam or your tenth, understanding the details of exam taking (how much time to spend on questions, the environment you'll be in, and so on) and understanding the exam software will help you concentrate on the material rather than on the setting. Likewise, mastering a few basic exam-taking skills should help you recognize—and perhaps even outfox—some of the tricks and gotchas you're bound to find in some of the exam questions.

This chapter, besides explaining the exam environment and software, describes some proven exam-taking strategies that you should be able to use to your advantage.

Assessing Exam-Readiness

Before you take your Red Hat exam, I strongly recommend that you complete the Self-Assessment included with this book (it appears just before this chapter, in fact). This assessment will help you compare your knowledge base to the requirements for obtaining an RHCE, and it will help you identify parts of your background or experience that might need improvement, enhancement, or further learning. If you get the right set of basics under your belt, obtaining Red Hat certification will be that much easier.

Once you've gone through the Self-Assessment, you can study those topics where your background or experience might not measure up to an ideal certification candidate. But you can also tackle subject matter for individual tests at the same time, so you can continue making progress while you're catching up in some areas.

Once you've worked through an *Exam Cram*, read the supplementary materials, completed the chapter tasks, and taken the practice test, you'll have a pretty clear idea of when you should be ready to take the real exam. I strongly recommend that you keep practicing until your scores top the 80 percent mark; 85 percent would be a good goal to give yourself some margin for error in a real exam situation (where stress will play more of a role than it does when you practice). Once you hit that point, you should be ready to go. But if you get through the practice exam in this book without attaining that score, you should keep taking practice tests and studying the materials until you get there. You'll find more information about how to study and prepare in the Self-Assessment section of this book, along with even more pointers on how to study and prepare. But now, on to the exam.

The Exam Situation

When you arrive at the testing center where you scheduled your exam, or at Red Hat's training facility, you'll need to sign in with an exam coordinator. He or she might ask you to show two forms of identification, one of which must be a photo ID. After you've signed in, you'll be escorted to your testing station, and you'll be asked to deposit below your desk any books, bags, or other items you brought with you. Typically, the room will be furnished with anywhere from half a dozen to a dozen computers.

You'll be furnished with a pen and pencil and a blank sheet of paper. You're allowed to write down any information you want on both sides of this sheet. Before the exam, you should memorize as much as you can of the material that appears on The Cram Sheet (inside the front cover of this book) so you can write that information on the blank sheet as soon as you are seated in front of the computer. You can refer to your rendition of The Cram Sheet any time you like during the test. Keep in mind, however, that most of the RHCE exams are performance based, not multiple choice. This means that you'll be facing time restrictions that you have to balance between your physical system time, task coordination, and more. So use your time wisely.

The exam situation will be staffed at all times by the instructor or exam coordinator, who will monitor the test takers and give instructions when necessary. In addition, the instructor is available as a last resort for help. Please note that asking the instructor for help does affect your score by a very large percentage (as much as 25 percent for one question). If you're running out of time and can't get past a specific portion of the exam, you might opt to take the point reduction to complete the exam. Depending on which part of the exam you begin, the instructor will have loaded or prepared the appropriate Red Hat certification exam setup. You'll be testing with a number of other students, and you'll all be asked to start at the same time.

All Red Hat certification exams allow a certain maximum amount of time in which to complete your work. The RHCE 302 Exam consists of three sections. The sections are presented in random order—meaning that one time the written exam might be first, another time the Installation Lab, and another time the Debugging Lab—so make sure you're prepared before entering the exam area. You might not be able to take advantage of the breaks in between exams to prepare for the next one. The exam takes a total of six hours: two and a half hours for each hands-on exam and one hour for the written exam.

Red Hat certification exams are performance based. Although this might sound quite simple, the exam comprises three elements, two of which, as I mentioned, are hands-on. You're given a task assignment for each section, as well as a nondisclosure agreement stating that you won't disclose the information and questions on the exam. In the debugging section, you'll be asked to fix a system with a problem that the instructor has set up. This section has two tasks with individual goals assigned to each task. You are graded for each goal you reach in each task.

The installation and configuration section of the exam is also hands-on. It also provides you with a task list of multiple scenarios, goals, and system processes to set up on an uninstalled, unconfigured machine.

The least stressful part of the exam is the written element, composed of 50 multiple-choice questions. Do not let the simplicity of a multiple-choice exam fool you, however. You might be asked to select the best or most effective solution to a problem from a range of choices, all of which technically are correct. In addition, you can almost guarantee that you'll be presented with questions that were not made available in any preparation material or even to those individuals who participated in the RHCE 302 preparation course. Taking the exam is quite an adventure, and it involves real thinking, skill, and time management. This book shows you what to expect and how to deal with the potential problems, puzzles, and predicaments.

Exam Layout and Design

For the multiple-choice exam, each question typically presents four or five options. The written exam is expected to change often (to fully test the exam taker), so you never know when you're going to get a curve ball. To get you comfortable with all types of questions, I've included some differently formatted question types in the end-of-chapter questions (the "Practice Questions" section in each chapter). For example, in this book, at least, you'll have to answer questions that have multiple correct answers, such as "What are three video configuration tools used in Red Hat 6.2?"

Exam-Taking Basics

The most important advice about taking any exam is this: Read each question carefully. Some questions are deliberately ambiguous, some use double negatives, and others use terminology in incredibly precise ways. The author has taken numerous exams—both practice and live—and in nearly every one has missed at least one question because she didn't read it closely or carefully enough.

Here are some suggestions on how to deal with the tendency to jump to an answer too quickly:

> ➤ Make sure you read every word in the question. If you find yourself jumping ahead impatiently, go back and start over.

➤ As you read, try to restate the question in your own terms. If you can do this, you should be able to pick the correct answer(s) much more easily.

➤ When returning to a question after your initial read-through, read every word again—otherwise, your mind can fall quickly into a rut. Sometimes revisiting a question after turning your attention elsewhere lets you see something you missed, but the strong tendency is to see what you've seen before. Try to avoid that tendency at all costs.

➤ If you return to a question more than twice, try to articulate to yourself what you don't understand about the question, why the answers don't appear to make sense, or what appears to be missing. If you chew on the subject for awhile, your subconscious might provide the details that are lacking, or you might notice a "trick" that will point to the right answer.

Above all, try to deal with each question by thinking through what you know about Red Hat Linux and Linux in general—the characteristics, behaviors, facts, and figures involved. By reviewing what you know (and what you've written down on your information sheet), you'll often recall or understand things sufficiently to determine the answer to the question.

Question-Handling Strategies

Based on exams the author has taken, some interesting trends have become apparent. In the multiple-choice element, for questions taking only a single answer, usually two or three of the answers will be obviously incorrect, and two of the answers will be plausible—but, of course, only one can be correct. Unless the answer leaps out at you (if it does, reread the question to look for a trick; sometimes those are the ones you're most likely to get wrong), begin the process of answering by eliminating those answers that are most obviously wrong.

Things to look for in obviously wrong answers include spurious menu choices or utility names, nonexistent software options, and terminology you've never seen. If you've done your homework for an exam, no valid information should be completely new to you. In that case, unfamiliar or bizarre terminology probably indicates a totally bogus answer.

Numerous questions assume that the default behavior of a particular utility is in effect. If you know the defaults and understand what they mean, this knowledge will help you cut through many Gordian knots.

Budget your time by making sure that you've completed one-fourth of the questions one-fourth of the way through the exam period (or the first 12 or 13 questions in the first 14 or 15 minutes) and completed three-quarters of them three-quarters of the way through (36 or 37 questions in the first 45 to 47 minutes).

If you're not finished when 55 minutes have elapsed, use the last 5 minutes to guess your way through the remaining questions. Remember, guessing is potentially more valuable than not answering because blank answers are always wrong, but a guess might turn out to be right. If you don't have a clue about any of the remaining questions, pick answers at random, or choose all a's, b's, and so on. The important thing is to submit an exam for scoring that has an answer to every question.

Mastering the Inner Game

In the final analysis, knowledge breeds confidence, and confidence breeds success. If you study the materials in this book carefully and review all the exam-prep questions at the end of each chapter, you should become aware of those areas where additional learning and study are required.

Next, follow up by reading some or all of the materials recommended in the "Need to Know More?" section at the end of each chapter. In addition, check out some of the online resources listed in Chapter 4. The idea is to become familiar enough with the concepts and situations you find in the sample questions that you can reason your way through similar situations on a real exam. If you know the material, you have every right to be confident that you can pass the exam.

After you've worked your way through the book, take the practice written exam in Chapter 14. This will provide a reality check and help you identify areas you need to study further. Before scheduling a real exam, make sure you follow up and review materials related to the questions you miss on the practice exam. Only when you've covered all the ground and feel comfortable with the whole scope of the practice exam should you take a real one.

 If you take the practice written exam and you don't score at least 85 percent correct, you'll want to practice further.

Armed with the information in this book and with the determination to augment your knowledge, you should be able to pass the certification exam. However, you need to work at it, or you'll spend the exam fee more than once before you finally pass. If you prepare seriously, you should do well. Good luck!

Additional Resources

A good source of information about Red Hat certification exams comes from Red Hat itself. Because its products and technologies—and the exams that go with them—change frequently, the best place to go for exam-related information is online.

If you haven't already visited the Red Hat Certified Engineer site, do so right now. The RHCE home page resides at **http://www.redhat.com/training.html**.

Note: This page might not be there by the time you read this, or it might have been replaced by something new and different, because things change regularly on the Red Hat site.

The options on the home page's menu point to the most important sources of information in the RHCE pages. Check out the Certification Choices option to read about the various certification and training programs that Red Hat offers.

These are just the high points of what's available in the Red Hat certification and training pages. As you browse through them—and I strongly recommend that you do—you'll probably find other informational tidbits mentioned that are every bit as interesting and compelling.

Coping with Change on the Web

Sooner or later, all the information about the Red Hat Certified Engineer and training pages, and the other Web-based resources mentioned throughout this book, will go stale or be replaced by newer information. In some cases, the URLs you find here might lead you to their replacements; in other cases, the URLs will go nowhere, leaving you with the dreaded "404 File not found" error message. When that happens, don't give up.

There's always a way to find what you want on the Web if you're willing to invest some time and energy. Most large or complex Web sites—and Red Hat's site qualifies on both counts—offer a search engine. As long as you can get to Red Hat's site (it should stay at **http://www.redhat.com** for a long while yet), you can use this tool to help you find what you need.

The more focused you can make a search request, the more likely it is that the results will include information you can use. For example, you can search for the string "training and certification" to produce a lot of data about the subject in general, but if you're looking for the installation guide for Red Hat 6.2 you'll be more likely to get there quickly if you use a search string similar to the following: "Installation Guide Red Hat 6.2".

Finally, feel free to use general search tools—such as **http://www.google.com**, **http://www.search.com**, **http://www.altavista.com**, and **http://www.excite.com**—to search for related information. The bottom line is this: If you can't find something where the book says it is, intensify your search.

General Linux Information

Terms you'll need to understand:

✓ Open source software (OSS)

✓ Copyright

✓ Free software

✓ Usenet

✓ Minix

Techniques you'll need to master:

✓ Describing the history and development of open source software

✓ Describing the history and development of Linux

✓ Finding resources to help you learn and use Linux

Open source software (OSS) and Linux in general have come a long way since Linus Torvalds began his hobbyist project called "Linux" back in 1990. In order to understand Linux at all, you must learn both the history and the general concepts behind the development of OSS and Linux. So before you get engrossed with all the technical details of Linux, let's discuss where it started and how it developed. This chapter will help you understand where Linux came from, what it's all about, and where to look when you need more information.

Understanding Open Source Software

OSS (open source software) is software whose source code is available to the public. Having publicly available source code doesn't necessarily mean that there are no copyright issues, however. In fact, OSS typically is copyrighted with restrictions meant to preserve its open source status, authorship, and control. OSS is usually developed by the mass effort of programmers all over the world. Universities, government agencies, and not-for-profit organizations (as well as individual programmers) develop OSS.

Although companies and individuals had released their software source code for years, the actual label "open source" wasn't used until early 1998. On one early February day, a group of individuals met to discuss Netscape Communications' January 1998 announcement that it was going to release the source code for its popular Web browser, Netscape Navigator. The members of this group included Todd Anderson, Chris Peterson (of the Foresight Institute), Jon "maddog" Hall and Larry Augustin (of Linux International), Sam Ockman (from the Silicon Valley Linux Users Group), and Eric S. Raymond.

These individuals recognized the impeccable timing that would be needed to respond to Netscape Communications' actions. The Linux and "free software" community would need to react appropriately to seize the opportunity to gain corporate recognition for the open development process. After brainstorming about tactics, the corporate community, and Netscape Communications' recent actions, this community finally agreed on the "open source" label. Peterson had suggested this title instead of "free software."

Many things have happened to the open source community since it adopted the term "open source" instead of "free software." Shortly after the announcement regarding the new movement toward OSS, a feverish debate between hackers all over the world began about the use of the new term. In fact, even Richard Stallman, founder of the GNU project, considered using the new term, if only for a little while. By the end of that February, however, the roar died down over the "open source" label issue. All attention was diverted back to the corporate world as both

Netscape Communications and O'Reilly and Associates had agreed to begin referring to OSS in their press releases and on their Web sites.

At the end of March, Netscape Navigator's source code was made freely available, spawning a massive download over the Internet. Within a few hours of its release, hackers all over the world began returning code fixes and enhancements.

In April, the press began its stream of non-technical coverage of open source software for the public's benefit. *Salon* magazine interviewed Eric S. Raymond (commonly referred to as "ESR" in the Linux community) and published an article on the details of OSS.

May was an exciting month for the open source community. Corel announced that it was going to port WordPerfect and its office products to Linux. In addition, Sun Microsystems and Adaptec were the first two large, established vendors to join Linux International.

OSS began to heat up in July when an article was published in *Forbes* magazine. The focus of the article? An interview with Linus Torvalds himself.

The number of open source projects continued to escalate into the end of the year. In October, Microsoft helped give an exciting end to Linux's first year. In response to its impending antitrust case, Microsoft released a formal statement claiming that Linux's existence proved that Microsoft didn't in fact have an operating-system monopoly. The year closed up with a bang after IDG announced that the Linux market share had increased by 212 percent in 1998.

Today "open source" has been adopted as a mainstream term by the majority of technology vendors. Vendors that use open source projects today in their commercial businesses include Apple Computer, Inc., Compaq, Corel Corporation, IBM, SGI, and Sun Microsystems.

The Free Software Foundation (FSF)

Before the OSS project began, the Free Software Foundation (FSF), founded to help protect and pursue the rights of free software, was already established. The FSF, which supports the free software movement, is currently a tax-exempt charity that raises funds to work on the GNU Project.

According to the FSF, free software is a matter of liberty, not price. The FSF says that to understand the concept, you should think of "free speech," not "free beer." The FSF believes that free software is the freedom for the user to run, copy, distribute, study, change, and improve software.

The GNU Project

The GNU Project was started in 1984 to develop a completely free Unix-like operating system. GNU's founder, Richard Stallman (also fondly known by his email handle RMS), is the best one to explain its beginnings, so here (quoted verbatim) is his original post to Usenet in September 1983. He explains his plans for the GNU Project:

```
From CSvax:pur-ee:inuxc!ixn5c!ihnp4!houxm!mhuxi!eagle!mit-
vax!mit-eddie!RMS@MIT-OZ
From: RMS%MIT-OZ@mit-eddie
Newsgroups: net.unix-wizards,net.usoft
Subject: new UNIX implementation
Date: Tue, 27-Sep-83 12:35:59 EST
Organization: MIT AI Lab, Cambridge, MA


Free Unix!

Starting this Thanksgiving I am going to write a complete Unix-
compatible software system called GNU (for Gnu's Not Unix), and
give it away free to everyone who can use it. Contributions of
time, money, programs and equipment are greatly needed.

To begin with, GNU will be a kernel plus all the utilities
needed to write and run C programs: editor, shell, C compiler,
linker, assembler, and a few other things. After this we will
add a text formatter, a YACC, an Empire game, a spreadsheet,
and hundreds of other things. We hope to supply, eventually,
everything useful that normally comes with a Unix system,
and anything else useful, including on-line and hardcopy docu-
mentation.

GNU will be able to run Unix programs, but will not be identi-
cal to Unix. We will make all improvements that are convenient,
based on our experience with other operating systems. In par-
ticular, we plan to have longer filenames, file version num-
bers, a crashproof file system, filename completion perhaps,
terminal-independent display support, and eventually a Lisp-
based window system through which several Lisp programs and
ordinary Unix programs can share a screen. Both C and Lisp will
be available as system programming languages. We will have
network software based on MIT's chaosnet protocol, far superior
to UUCP. We may also have something compatible with UUCP.

Who Am I?
I am Richard Stallman, inventor of the original much-imitated
EMACS editor, now at the Artificial Intelligence Lab at MIT. I
```

have worked extensively on compilers, editors, debuggers,
command interpreters, the Incompatible Timesharing System and
the Lisp Machine operating system. I pioneered terminal-
independent display support in ITS. In addition I have implemented one crashproof file system and two window systems for
Lisp machines.

Why I Must Write GNU

I consider that the golden rule requires that if I like a
program I must share it with other people who like it. I cannot
in good conscience sign a nondisclosure agreement or a software
license agreement.

So that I can continue to use computers without violating my
principles, I have decided to put together a sufficient body of
free software so that I will be able to get along without any
software that is not free.

How You Can Contribute

I am asking computer manufacturers for donations of machines
and money. I'm asking individuals for donations of programs
and work.

One computer manufacturer has already offered to provide a
machine. But we could use more. One consequence you can expect
if you donate machines is that GNU will run on them at an early
date. The machine had better be able to operate in a residen-
tial area, and not require sophisticated cooling or power.

Individual programmers can contribute by writing a compatible
duplicate of some Unix utility and giving it to me. For most
projects, such part-time distributed work would be very hard to
coordinate; the independently-written parts would not work
together. But for the particular task of replacing Unix, this
problem is absent. Most interface specifications are fixed by
Unix compatibility. If each contribution works with the rest of
Unix, it will probably work with the rest of GNU.

If I get donations of money, I may be able to hire a few people
full or part time. The salary won't be high, but I'm looking
for people for whom knowing they are helping humanity is as
important as money. I view this as a way of enabling dedicated
people to devote their full energies to working on GNU by
sparing them the need to make a living in another way.
For more information, contact me.

```
Arpanet mail:
  RMS@MIT-MC.ARPA
Usenet:
  ...!mit-eddie!RMS@OZ
  ...!mit-vax!RMS@OZ
US Snail:
  Richard Stallman
  166 Prospect St
  Cambridge, MA 02139
```

The FSF's main project is the GNU project. Linux is composed of the Linux kernel and many GNU programs and utilities. Some popular GNU tools that are used frequently are Bash, CVS, ed, Emacs, finger, GCC, ghostview, the Gimp, gzip, ispell, mtools, screen, and tar. These are just a few of the existing GNU programs available, however. In fact, the GNU tools are often available for other commercial versions of Unix as well.

Due to the large number of GNU tools that are used within Linux, and those that help make the Linux distribution, some Linux advocates and evangelists differ in their opinions of what to call Linux. Many GNU evangelists insist on calling Linux "GNU/Linux" or "Lignux." Personally, I simply call it "Linux." However, I do credit the GNU tools for making Linux work. Therefore, as in the debate about how to pronounce Linux (lie-nucks, lih-nucks, or lee-nooks), I have no preference about what you call Linux.

Note: Some components of Linux were incorporated from various versions of Unix. For instance, the X Window System was actually derived from BSD.

The GNU General Public License (GPL)

The General Public License (GPL) is the license that most open source projects use for their software. Developed in the late 1980s, the GPL has not been revised since its publication in 1991. The GPL is quite extensive, and many of its users interpret the document in different ways. The GPL's text is included in this book's Appendix. Read it for a better understanding of the foundation of the open source community.

 Although you aren't tested on this information in the RHCE Exam 302, you are required to have working knowledge of it.

History of Linux

Linus Torvalds started Linux as a hobbyist project in 1990. Torvalds, a college student from Finland, began the project after purchasing a computer to run Minix, a Unix-like operating system that was included in Andrew Tanenbaum's textbook *Operating Systems: Design and Implementation*. Shortly after, Torvalds decided to learn more about some of the low-level features of the Intel 80386 processor, and he then began working on what would eventually develop into the Linux kernel.

Within two months of starting the project, Linus released kernel 0.01 shortly after he posted this to the comp.os.minix newsgroup:

```
From: torvalds@klaava.Helsinki.FI (Linus Benedict Torvalds)
Newsgroups: comp.os.minix
Subject: What would you like to see most in minix?
Message-ID: <1991Aug25.205708.9541@klaava.Helsinki.FI>
Date: 25 Aug 91 20:57:08 GMT

Hello everybody out there using minix -

I'm doing a (free) operating system (just a hobby, won't be big
and professional like gnu) for 386(486) AT clones. This has been
brewing since april, and is starting to get ready. I'd like any
feedback on things people like/dislike in minix, as my OS re-
sembles it somewhat (same physical layout of the file-system (due
to practical reasons) among other things).

I've currently ported bash(1.08) and gcc(1.40), and things seem to
work. This implies that I'll get something practical within a few
months, and I'd like to know what features most people would want.
Any suggestions are welcome, but I won't promise I'll implement
them :-)

        Linus (torvalds@kruuna.helsinki.fi)

PS. Yes - it's free of any minix code, and it has a multi-threaded
fs. It is NOT protable [sic] (uses 386 task switching etc) and it
probably never will support anything other than AT-harddisks as
that's all I have :-(
```

Nearly three years after Torvalds started this project, Linux 1.0 was released. By this time, several Linux distributors had begun packaging the Linux kernel with basic support programs, the GNU utilities and compilers, the X Window System, and other useful programs. The mass numbers of Linux kernel hackers had managed to develop all the things expected from a current Unix system, including preemptive multitasking, virtual memory, shared libraries, TCP/IP support, NFS (Network File System), Ethernet, and so on.

In 1995, the Linux 1.2 kernel was released. The new kernel supported kernel modules, the PCI bus, kernel-level firewalls, non-TCP/IP networking protocols, and so on. By this time, Linux had become as stable as any commercial version of Unix on the x86 platform, and it was even being ported to the DEC Alpha, Sun SPARC, and SGI MIPS platforms.

In 1996, the Linux 2.0 kernel was released. Version 2 saw the preliminary support for SMP (symmetric multiprocessor) machines. It also was fully functional on multiple platforms, including the x86, Alpha, SPARC, Motorola 68K, PowerPC, and MIPS platforms.

In 1999, the latest stable kernel, version 2.2, was released. The 2.2 kernel fully supports the SMP machines, and it more fully supports multiple platforms, including the 64-bit platforms. In addition, version 2.2 is significantly faster than previous versions.

In summer of 2000, the newest stable kernel, version 2.4, will be released. There will be a lot of new features, including tighter firewalls and more hardware support.

History of Red Hat

Red Hat was started in early 1994 when two entrepreneurs, Bob Young and Mark Ewing, decided to venture into beginning a commercial Linux distributor. In just one short year, Red Hat's distribution of Linux was taking the market by storm and was even voted desktop operating system of the year by *InfoWorld*. In 1997, Red Hat won another *InfoWorld* award when its distribution of Red Hat Linux version 5 was named network operating system of the year. Red Hat won this award again in 1999 with Red Hat Linux 5.2, in addition to being voted "LinuxWorld Favorite" by the open source convention, LinuxWorld. This was a feat no other software product had achieved in the *InfoWorld* awards history.

In September 1998, large technology firms began to invest in Red Hat. Some of the first included Intel Corporation and Netscape Communications. In addition to technical firms, venture capital firms decided to invest. The first two were Benchmark Capital and Greylock Management. Red Hat's investment base continued to grow, and the company eventually filed to enter the stock market as RHAT in June 1999.

Red Hat has expanded, changed, and adapted many times in its short six years. Since beginning as simply a packager of Linux, Red Hat has gained many important developers for the project, including Alan Cox. Since its extremely successful initial public offering (Nasdaq: RHAT) in August 1999, Red Hat has hired such primary kernel developers as David Miller, Ingo Molnar, and Stephen Tweedie. In addition, Red Hat is quickly expanding its installation base by being the most popular Linux distribution to be sold and supported by mainstream vendors such as IBM, Compaq, Dell, and Hewlett-Packard. Before these vendors began shipping Linux, however, many Linux vendors, including VA Linux Systems and Penguin Computing, were already shipping Red Hat Linux-configured machines.

Linux Resources

When you get stuck, your computer breaks, or you just want to learn about something, the best skill you can learn is RTM (Read The Fine Manual). Many good online resources are available. In fact, some Web sites and Linux vendors (such as Red Hat) host very helpful mailing lists. Here are some of the many online resources for general Linux information, vendors, distributors, software, projects, news, downloads, and newsgroups.

General Information and HOWTOs

➤ http://linuxkb.cheek.com/—Linux Knowledge Base

➤ http://www.isc.org/—Internet Software Consortium

➤ http://www.lintraining.com/—Linux Certification resource site

➤ http://www.linux.com/—Linux information

➤ http://www.linux.org/—Linux Online

➤ http://www.linuxdoc.org/—The Linux Documentation Project

➤ http://www.linux-howto.com/—Linux HOWTOs

➤ http://www.linuxstart.com/—Linux resource site

➤ http://www.redhat.com/services/training/—Site for the Red Hat Certified Engineer Program

➤ http://www.rhce2b.com/—RHCE (Red Hat Certified Engineer) resource site

➤ http://www.ssc.com/glue/—Groups of Linux Users Everywhere (GLUE)

➤ http://www.ssc.com/linux/—Linux resources Web site

➤ http://www.tux.org/—General Linux information

➤ http://www.tuxedo.org/—Portal for Eric Raymond's projects and papers

➤ http://www.w3.org/—World Wide Web Consortium

Linux Vendors

➤ http://www.aslab.com/—ASL, Inc., a Linux hardware provider

➤ http://www.cheapbytes.com/—CheapBytes online store

➤ http://www.eLinux.com/—eLinux.com

➤ http://www.infomagic.com/—Info Magic

➤ http://www.linuxcare.com/—Linuxcare

➤ http://www.linuxcentral.com/—Linux Central

➤ http://www.linuxgeneralstore.com/—Linux General Store

➤ http://www.linuxmall.com/—The Linux Mall

➤ http://www.lokigames.com/—Loki Entertainment Software

➤ http://www.lsl.com/—Linux System Labs

➤ http://www.penguincomputing.com/—Penguin Computing

➤ http://www.valinux.com/—VA Linux Systems

Linux Distributors

➤ http://www.caldera.com/—Caldera Systems, Inc.

➤ http://www.debian.org/—Debian Project home page

➤ http://www.linux.corel.com/—Corel Corporation

➤ http://www.mandrake.com/—Site for Linux-Mandrake

➤ http://www.mklinux.org/—MkLinux

➤ http://www.phatlinux.com/—Phat Linux

➤ http://www.redhat.com/—Red Hat, Inc.

➤ http://www.slackware.com/—Slackware

➤ http://www.stormix.com/—Stormix Technologies Inc., Storm Linux

➤ http://www.suse.com/—SuSE Inc.

➤ http://www.turbolinux.com/—TurboLinux

Software Information

➤ http://squid-cache.org/—Site for the Squid Web proxy cache

➤ http://www.abisource.com/—Site for the AbiSource project, which is developing an open source office suite, beginning with AbiWord

➤ http://www.adobe.com/—Adobe Systems Inc., Adobe Acrobat and Adobe Acrobat Reader

➤ http://www.apache.org/—The Apache Software Foundation, maker of the Apache Web server

➤ http://www.applix.com/—Applix, Inc.

➤ http://www.dosemu.org/—DOS Emulator

➤ http://www.estinc.com/—Enhanced Software Technologies, Inc. (maker of BRU backup software)

➤ http://www.gimp.org/—Site for the GIMP (GNU Image Manipulation Program)

➤ http://www.informix.com/informix/solutions/linux/—Informix Software

➤ http://www.interbase.com/—Interbase

➤ http://www.mozilla.org/—Information about the Mozilla open source Web browser

➤ http://www.myxa.com/elm.html/—Elm (Electronic Mail for Unix) email reader

➤ http://www.netscape.com/—Netscape Communications

➤ http://www.realaudio.com/—Site for RealAudio and related streaming-media products

➤ http://www.sendmail.org/—The Sendmail Consortium

➤ http://www.software.ibm.com/data/db2/linux/—IBM's DB2 Universal Database for Linux

➤ http://www.stardivision.com/—Site for StarOffice, Sun Microsystems' cross-platform office suite

➤ http://www.tuxedo.org/~esr/fetchmail/—Site for the fetchmail remote-mail retrieval and forwarding utility

➤ http://www.vim.org/—VIM home page

➤ http://www.vmware.com/—VMware, Inc., maker of VMware software, which lets you run multiple computing environments on a single PC

➤ http://www.xemacs.org/—XEmacs home page

➤ http://www.washington.edu/pine/—Pine Information Center; site for the Pine (Program for Internet News and Email) email program

Project Information

➤ http://www.beowulf.org/—The Beowulf Project

➤ http://www.fsf.org/—Free Software Foundation

➤ http://www.gnome.org/—The GNOME Project, maker of the GNOME desktop environment, development platform, and office applications

➤ http://www.jargon.org/—Mirror of the Jargon File Resources site

➤ http://www.kde.org/—KDE (K Desktop Environment)

➤ http://www.kernel.org/—Linux kernel Web site

➤ http://www.kernelnotes.org/—The KernelNotes Project (Linux kernel information)

➤ http://www.li.org/—Linux International

➤ http://www.lpi.org/—Linux Professional Institute

➤ http://www.opensource.org/—The Open Source Initiative (OSI)

➤ http://www.rpm.org/—Red Hat Package Manager

➤ http://www.xfree86.org/— The XFree86 Project, which produces XFree86, an implementation of the X Window System

Linux News

➤ http://www.freshmeat.org/—Freshmeat, more News for Nerds

➤ http://www.linuxjournal.com/—*Linux Journal*

➤ http://www.linux-mag.com/—*Linux Magazine*

➤ http://www.linux-radio.com/—Site for the Linux radio show

➤ http://www.linuxresources.com/—Linux Resources Online

➤ http://www.linuxtoday.com/—*Linux Today*

➤ http://www.linuxworld.com/—*LinuxWorld*

➤ http://www.lwn.net/—*Linux Weekly News*

➤ http://www.slashdot.org/—*Slashdot,* "News for Nerds"

➤ http://www.ssc.com/lg/—*Linux Gazette*

➤ http://www.thelinuxshow.com/—Site for *The Linux Show*

Download Sites

➤ ftp://metalab.unc.edu/—Popular FTP site

➤ ftp://ftp.caldera.com/—Caldera Systems, Inc.

➤ ftp://ftp.debian.org/—Debian

➤ ftp://ftp.gnu.org/—Official GNU FTP site

➤ ftp://ftp.kernel.org/—Linux kernel

➤ ftp://ftp.linux.org/—Popular sites

➤ ftp://ftp.redhat.com/—Red Hat

➤ ftp://ftp.xfree86.org/—FTP site for The XFree86 Project's XFree86 (implementation of the X Window System)

➤ http://www.binaries.org/—Download site for software binaries

➤ http://www.linuxberg.com/—Popular download site

Newsgroups

➤ comp.os.linux.announce

➤ comp.os.linux.answers

➤ comp.os.linux.hardware

➤ comp.os.linux.misc

➤ comp.os.linux.redhat

➤ comp.os.linux.setup

➤ comp.os.linux.x

➤ linux.redhat.announce

➤ linux.redhat.list

Practice Questions

Question 1

Who developed Linux?

- ○ a. Linus Torvalds
- ○ b. Richard Stallman
- ○ c. Bob Young
- ○ d. None of the above

Answer a is correct. This is a tricky question because both answers a and d would be correct by today's definition. Technically, Linux is developed by thousands of individuals, not just one. However, though a very large community helps to develop Linux today, the original developer was Linus Torvalds.

Question 2

What is the GPL and what is its purpose?

The GPL is the General Public License. Its purpose is to protect the copyright and the open source or free-software characteristics that the author of a software package wishes to keep. This license prevents other authors, companies, and so on from using the software source, making modifications, and redistributing it without redistributing the code as well.

Question 3

Who founded the FSF and began the GNU Project?

- ○ a. Linus Torvalds
- ○ b. Richard Stallman
- ○ c. Bob Young
- ○ d. None of the above

Answer b is correct. Richard Stallman founded the FSF and began the GNU Project.

Question 4

Who founded Red Hat?

Red Hat was a cooperative project between two entrepreneurs, Bob Young and Mark Ewing.

Question 5

What online resource can you use for documentation and links for help with Linux-related programs, hardware, and more?

- ○ a. **http://www.microsoft.com**
- ○ b. **http://linuxdoc.org/**
- ○ c. **http://www.compaq.com**
- ○ d. **http://www.slashdot.org**

Answer b is correct. All of these sites offer interesting Linux information of sorts; however, the best place to find help and documentation for your Linux issues is the Linux Documentation Project, found at **http://www.linuxdoc.org/**.

Question 6

Red Hat is the primary developer of Linux.

- ○ a. True
- ○ b. False

Answer b is correct. Linux is developed by teams, companies, and programmers from all over the world. Red Hat does have staff members who develop parts of Linux, but it's not their main business. Rather, Red Hat helps the community by packaging, testing, bug fixing, developing, and supporting different parts of Linux.

Question 7

What is the FSF?

The FSF is the Free Software Foundation. It was founded by Richard Stallman to promote and support free software development and developers.

Question 8

What does GNU stand for?

○ a. Greek Noble Unix

○ b. Genius Native Unix

○ c. Geek Needed Unix

○ d. GNU's Not Unix

Answer d is correct. Although some of the other answers could be accurate, they aren't what GNU stands for. GNU stands for GNU's Not Unix.

Need to Know More?

 Dibona, Chris, Sam Ockman, Mark Stone, eds. *Open Sources*. O'Reilly & Associates, 1999. ISBN 1-56592-582-3. This entire book focuses on the roots of open source software, including where it came from and where it is going.

 http://www.fsf.org/—This Web site covers information regarding both the GNU Project and the Free Software Foundation. Visit the page **http://www.fsf.org/gnu/gnu-history.html** to learn more about the GNU Project. Visit the page **http://www.fsf.org/fsf/fsf.html** to learn more about the Free Software Foundation.

 http://www.opensource.org/—This Web site covers information and projects that are associated with open source software.

 http://www.redhat.com/—This Web site contains information about Red Hat Software, Inc. To learn more about Red Hat Software, follow the "About" link (**http://www.redhat.com/about/**).

Red Hat
Prerequisites

Terms you'll need to understand:

✓ Filesystem

✓ Partition

✓ Shell

✓ Filter

✓ Compile

✓ Source

Techniques you'll need to master:

✓ Partitioning hard disks

✓ Using the mkfs tool to build filesystems

✓ Using the fsck tool to check and repair filesystems

✓ Manipulating text files

✓ Compiling a kernel

✓ Reading shell scripts

✓ Reading a log file

✓ Starting and stopping services

✓ Using the tar and cpio programs to back up and restore files

Before pursuing your dream of becoming a Red Hat Certified Engineer (RHCE), or just becoming a Linux power user, you should have extensive knowledge of Linux, Linux tools, and TCP/IP networking basics. These prerequisites are also required if you take part in the Red Hat Certified Engineering training program, which is scheduled for the four days before you take your exam. This chapter will discuss many of the general Linux and Unix concepts that you need to be familiar with before tackling your RHCE preparation.

Unix Basics

Linux is a Unix-like operating system. Therefore, it's essential for you to know basic Unix commands in order to become an RHCE. You must have working knowledge of Unix concepts such as the filesystem hierarchy, filesystem mounting and administration, basic shell configuration, and basic file operations. You must also be familiar with filters, wildcards, vi, and other tools for manipulating and editing files.

Unix Filesystem Hierarchy and Structure

Unix filesystems are structured in a directory tree. Although these structures differ slightly in each flavor of Unix system, the directories I describe here are standard on Linux.

The main directory, called the *root directory*, is denoted with a simple forward slash (/). All directories on a Unix system are subdirectories of the root. Directly under the root directory are the following subdirectories:

➤ */bin*—The typical location for executable and binary files for Unix commands and utilities. It also contains executables used by users.

➤ */dev*—The device directory. The /dev directory contains files divided into subdirectories that contain files for a specific device and special files that we'll discuss later in this chapter. These directories are named based on the type of device files they contain. Some examples of these directories are hda1 (for the first IDE hard drive), fd0 (for the floppy disk), and cdrom, which is a symbolic link created to the CD-ROM device that Red Hat was installed from, if it was installed via CD-ROM.

➤ */etc*—The location for configuration files and—what's more important—for the system boot scripts. These boot scripts are located under the /etc/rc.d/ directory. The services that run at bootup are located under /etc/rc.d/init.d/.

It is rumored that this method will be changing in upcoming versions of Red Hat Linux to reflect Debian's locations for the boot scripts. Therefore, these files might be represented under /etc/init.d rather than /etc/rc.d/init.d. This is still different from other distributions and other commercial versions of Unix, which place these files under /sbin/init.d/.

➤ */sbin*—The location of some system configuration and system administrator executable files. Most of your general administration commands—such as **lilo, fdisk, fsck,** and **route**—are located here.

➤ */home*—The location of the home directories for your general users. Under /home, each user can set up his or her own email, public_html, and personal files.

➤ */lost+found*—The system's directory for placing lost files that are found (or created) by disk errors or improper system shutdowns. At boot, programs such as fsck find the inodes, which have no directory entries, and reattach them as files in this directory. In addition to the root filesystem, there should be one /lost+found directory located on every filesystem created on the system. If no lost+found directory exists, the fsck program will create it.

➤ */mnt*—The default mount directory. Under /mnt, you mount your devices such as CD-ROMs and floppy disks.

➤ */proc*—Your process directory. Under /proc, you'll find information about running processes, as well as system configuration information such as interrupt usage, I/O port use, and CPU type.

➤ */tmp*—A default directory created to house temporary files. This is a good directory to keep an eye on if you're trying to limit disk space.

➤ */usr*—The location for subdirectories for local programs and executables for user and administrative commands. The /usr directory contains the binaries for X, games, your shared libraries, and more. Essentially, /usr will contain just about everything that isn't necessary for booting the system.

➤ */var*—The location for your spooling, logging, and other data (the "var" is short for "various"). Common applications that use /var for spooling and logging are mail, printing, and cron.

➤ */opt*—The location for optional packages. Many programs, such as Applixware (from VistaSource) and KDE, install packages in this directory.

➤ */usr/local*—The location where the administrator can install programs on the system. This is usually reserved for system-related programs. Linux distributions don't use this directory heavily because most Linux distributions come packaged with the most popular utilities, and such packages don't need to be installed by the administrator.

Mounting Filesystems and Devices

You can mount devices, partitions, and separate disks to directories (called *mount points*) within the filesystem. To read from a device, such as a floppy disk or a CD-ROM, you use the **mount** command. The **mount** command's syntax is: **mount** *–t type /dev/device mountpoint* . For example, to mount a CD-ROM drive, type

```
mount -t iso9660 /dev/cdrom /mnt/cdrom
```

To access the CD-ROM drive, simply change into the /mnt/cdrom directory, and then type **ls** to display a list of files found on the CD-ROM.

Your default filesystem types and mount points are set in /etc/fstab. The fstab file sets the default device, mount point, filesystem type, type of mount, and filesystem dump and **fsck** order options. Here is an example of an fstab file:

```
/dev/hda3       /              ext2      defaults         1  1
/dev/hda1       /boot          ext2      defaults         1  2
/dev/hda4       swap           swap      defaults         0  0
/dev/fd0        /mnt/floppy    ext2      noauto           0  0
/dev/cdrom      /mnt/cdrom     iso9660   noauto,ro,user   0  0
```

Settings in /etc/fstab also allow you to use the defaults when you're mounting filesystems manually. For instance, rather than typing

```
mount -t iso9660 /dev/cdrom /mnt/cdrom
```

you'd simply type

```
mount /dev/cdrom
```

or even

```
mount /mnt/cdrom
```

and **mount** automatically mounts the CD-ROM, based on the defaults in your /etc/fstab file.

To mount filesystems with settings other than the defaults, or to mount filesystems that aren't listed in the /etc/fstab file, you need to specify the type, device, and mount point. For instance, to mount separate partitions on a single drive, such as an msdos partition, you can type

```
mount -t msdos /dev/hda1 /dos
```

To access this partition, simply change into the /dos directory, treating it like any local filesystem. The **t** option after the **mount** command is used to specify the type.

Filesystem Administration Commands

The Unix filesystem is unique because in order for it to function properly, it must be structured, formatted, partitioned, checked, and mounted and unmounted cleanly. With this in mind, you must understand the basics of administration tools such as fdisk, mkfs, and fsck.

fdisk

The administration tool fdisk, which has a command-line interface, is used to partition your hard drive. After you become accustomed to using the interface, you'll see that it allows quick and simple partitioning. Running fdisk opens a screen that looks similar to this:

```
Using /dev/hda as default device!
The number of cylinders for this disk is set to 1240.
This is larger than 1024, and may cause problems with:
1) software that runs at boot time (e.g., LILO)
2) booting and partitioning software from other OSs
                e.g., DOS FDISK, OS/2 FDISK)

Command (m for help):
```

Pressing the **m** key at the command prompt gives you a list of command options, as shown here:

```
Command (m for help): m
Command action
    a    toggle a bootable flag
    b    edit bsd disklabel
    c    toggle the dos compatibility flag
    d    delete a partition
    l    list known partition types
    m    print this menu
    n    add a new partition
    o    create a new empty DOS partition table
    p    print the partition table
    q    quit without saving changes
    t    change a partition's system id
```

```
u    change display/entry units
v    verify the partition table
w    write table to disk and exit
x    extra functionality (experts only)
```

As you can see from the list in this code block, you use the **p** option to print the partition table. The output will look something similar to the following code block if you have three partitions, including one FAT32, one Linux native, and one Linux swap. Also, this code is reporting for a 10GB IDE drive:

```
        Disk        /dev/hda: 255 heads, 63 sectors, 1240 cylinders
Units = cylinders of 16065 * 512 bytes

   Device Boot      Start       End    Blocks   Id  System
/dev/hda1    *          1       765   6144831    b  Win95 FAT32
/dev/hda2             766      1015   2008125   83  Linux native
/dev/hda3            1016      1024     72292+  82  Linux swap
```

You can edit these partitions by using the fdisk command options. The **d** option deletes a partition, prompting you for the partition number. The **n** option adds a new partition, prompting you for primary or extended, and the number. The **t** option changes the type of partition from the current type to a new type (for instance, changing a Linux native to Linux swap). The **l** option gives you a list of supported types and their codes. The **q** option quits fdisk without saving changes, and the **w** option writes the table to disk and exits.

mkfs

The administration tool mkfs is used to build a Linux filesystem on a device, usually a hard-disk partition. The mkfs tool is simply a front end for the various filesystem builders available for Linux. Typical usage of mkfs looks like this:

```
mkfs  [ -V ] [ -t fstype ] [ fs-options ] filesys [ blocks ]
```

The following list explains the typical options used with mkfs as well as some additional options available:

➤ **-V**—Produces verbose output, including all filesystem-specific commands that are executed. This is useful only for testing.

➤ **-t fstype**—Specifies the type of filesystem to be built. If the type isn't specified, the default filesystem type (currently ext2) is used.

➤ **fs-options**—Specifies filesystem-specific options to be passed to the real filesystem builder.

➤ **-c**—Checks the device for bad blocks before building the filesystem.

➤ **-l filename**—Reads the list of bad blocks from the file name.

➤ **-v**—Produces verbose output.

➤ **filesys**—Is either the device name (for example, /dev/hda1 or /dev/sdb2) or the mount point (for example, /, /usr, or /home) for the filesystem.

➤ **blocks**—Is the number of blocks that will be used for the filesystem.

fsck

The administration tool fsck is used to check and repair Linux filesystems. It is typically used like this:

```
fsck [ -AVR ] [ -s ] [ -t fstype ] [ fs-options ] filesys
```

The following list explains the options used in the previous snippet of code as well as a few extra options available:

➤ **-A**—Walks through the /etc/fstab file and tries to check all filesystems at once.

➤ **-R**—Skips the root filesystem when you're checking all filesystems with the -A flag.

➤ **-V**—Produces verbose output.

➤ **-s**—Serializes fsck operations.

➤ **-t fstype**—Specifies the type of filesystem to be checked. If the -A flag is specified, only filesystems that match fstype are checked.

➤ **fs-options**—

➤ **-a**—Repairs the filesystem automatically without any questions (use this option with caution).

➤ **-r**—Repairs the filesystem interactively (asks for confirmation).

➤ **filesys**—Indicates either the device name or the mount point.

Basic Shell Configuration

When you're using the bash shell, two files are located in your /home directory: .bash_profile and .bashrc. The .bash_profile file contains initialization scripts that are executed at login. Here is an example of a generic .bash_profile file:

```
# .bash_profile

# Get the aliases and functions
```

```
if [ -f ~/.bashrc ]; then
            .~/.bashrc
fi

# User specific environment and startup programs

PATH=$PATH:$HOME/bin
BASH_ENV=$HOME/.bashrc
USERNAME=""

export USERNAME BASH_ENV PATH
```

The .bashrc file contains execution scripts that are run each time a new shell is opened. Here is an example of a generic .bashrc file:

```
# .bashrc
# User specific aliases and functions

alias rm='rm -i'
alias cp='cp -i'
alias mv='mv -i'

# Source global definitions
if [ -f /etc/bashrc ]; then
        . /etc/bashrc
fi
```

Basic File Operations

For obvious reasons, you must be skilled at using basic Unix commands and filters to be a Unix administrator. Table 3.1 lists several basic commands, gives an example of the context to use each command, and explains what each command does.

Filters

Some of Unix's most popular filters manipulate files into specific output. They include **cat**, **grep**, **wc**, **tail**, **head**, and **sort**. Using **cat** on a file concatenates the contents of the file into standard output. Here's an example of using **cat**:

```
cat filename
```

The grep tool is very popular for searching files for a specific term or string. The output of the **grep** command displays only the lines that contain the term or

Table 3.1	Basic Unix commands.	
Command	**Example**	**Explanation**
cp	**cp file1 file2**	Is the Unix command to copy a file. The example copies file1 to file2.
mv	**mv file1 file2**	Is the Unix command to move a file. The example moves file1 and renames it to file2.
ls	**ls**	Prints the directory listing. You can run **ls** directly from the directory from which you want a file listing. Some special options for **ls** include **-l** (include details) and **-a** (show hidden files).
more	**ls -a l more**	Prints the output of a file or command page by page. The example prints the file, listing one page at a time.
less	**ls -la l less**	Is similar to **more** (but **less** allows for backward movement in a file); prints the output from a command page by page.
cd	**cd /etc**	Is the Unix command to change a directory. The example changes into the /etc directory.
pwd	**pwd**	Prints the full name of the current directory you're in.
tar	**tar -xvf filename.tar**	Is a Unix compression utility. The example gives the appropriate options to extract verbosely the filename.tar file.
rm	**rm dead.letter**	Deletes a file. The example deletes the dead.letter file.

string that was grepped. The grep tool can be used by itself, or it can be used to filter the output of another filter, such as **cat**. For example, both

```
cat filename | grep error
```

and

```
grep error filename
```

would search the contents of the specified file name for the word "error."

The **wc** filter is helpful when you need to count the number of bytes (-c), words (-w), or lines (-l) from the output of a file. The following snippet of code **cats** the file name, pipes it through grep, prints the lines that contain the term "error," and counts the number of lines of output by piping the output through **wc -l**:

```
cat filename | grep error |wc -l
```

The **tail** filter is commonly used to print logs and other large files. Simply running the code

```
tail /var/log/messages
```

prints the last 10 lines of /var/log/messages. However, to run a continuous output of a log, you use the -f option. For instance, running

```
tail -f /var/log/messages
```

prints a running log of the /var/log/messages file.

The opposite of **tail**, called **head**, prints the first part of a message file. To print the first 10 lines of a log, for instance, type **head -n 10 /var/log/messages**.

File Name Wildcards

When you're using the commands and filters discussed so far, it's often useful to use wildcards. Wildcards—such as *, ?, [ ] , and { }—are useful to select or work with multiple files that contain similar characteristics in their file names.

 Wildcards are commonly referred to as "file globs," as "globs," or by the verb "globbing." With Linux, globbing is implemented in the shell, unlike DOS, where each program implements its own globbing. For more information about globbing, read the man page (man 7 glob).

For the examples in the rest of this section, I'll use the list of files shown here:

```
$ls
file            file3           12file
1file           file4           file34
2file           file5file
```

The asterisk (*) character is used to represent any number of characters in a file name. Specifying **file*** returns all files with file names that begin with "file" and end with any character sequence. On the other hand, ***file** returns any file name that ends in "file." Here's **file*** in action:

```
$ls file*
file3           file34
file4           file5file
```

The question-mark (?) character is used to represent a single character. Specifying **file?** requests any file name that starts with "file" and ends with any other single character. On the other hand, **??file** requests any file name with two random characters that are followed by "file." Here's how to use **file?**:

```
$ls file?
file3
file4
```

Closed brackets ([ ]) are used to specify a range of characters. Specifying **file[abc]** requests the file names filea, fileb, and filec. Another example, **[169]file**, requests the file names 1file, 6file, and 9file. This example shows the use of square brackets:

```
$ls file[123]
file3
```

You'll notice that **file[123]** yields only file3. In our original list, file1 and file2 don't exist.

Curly brackets ({ }) are used to specify a range of characters, much like closed brackets; however, when you use curly brackets, multiple character strings can be separated by commas. For instance, **file{1,34,ab}** returns file names file1, file34, and fileab. Another example, **file{ab,s,ing}34**, requests fileab34, files34, and fileing34. This example shows the use of curly brackets in a string:

```
$ls file{1,2,3,34}
file3
file34
```

Basic vi Usage

Text editing is one of the most popular uses of any operating system, and vi is one of the most useful and popular text editors for Unix. With vi, you can create and edit any text file.

The vi text editor uses different modes to help you edit files. When you open or create a file with vi (by entering **vi filename**), you're in command mode. In command mode, single keys on your keyboard have special commands. For example, pressing the **i**, **a**, or **o** keys places you in insert mode. In insert mode, you can insert text directly into the file. To return to command mode, press the Esc key.

In command mode, you can also quickly move around in your document without using the cursor keys; this allows you to keep your hands on the home row, and it speeds up your editing. The **j** key acts as your down cursor and jumps down a line. The **k** key acts as your up cursor and jumps up one line. The **h** and **l** keys act as your left and right cursor keys, respectively. These *movement* commands are subject to *quantity* commands. For instance, **10j** jumps your cursor down 10 lines, and **5l** moves the cursor right by 5 characters. Other helpful movement commands are **w** (next word), **G** (end of file), **$** (end of line), and **0** (zero, beginning of line).

Command mode also offers you the opportunity to write (save), abandon (without saving), and exit the vi editor. To enter these commands, you always begin by pressing the colon key (:) to enter command mode. Issuing the **:w** command writes your changes to the file. Entering the **:q** command quits vi. You can execute these commands at the same time by issuing the **:wq** command. In addition, you can use the exclamation-point key (!) to force the command that you're using to execute. The **:w!** sequence writes to a read-only file, and **:q!** quits without saving changes.

Actual text editing uses both command and insert modes. When using vi, remember that you can combine all commands with quantity, movement, and other action commands to raise productivity and simplify editing.

Table 3.2 shows some basic vi editing commands.

Note: Remember that commands are case sensitive! Lowercase l moves the cursor right one character, but capital L moves the curser to the last position in the window. In addition, most commands are subject to movement and quantity commands.

Table 3.2	vi editing commands.
Command	**Description**
a	Appends text after the cursor
A	Appends text at the end of the line
c	Change (input command) (for example, **cw** - changes the word)
C	Changes to the end of the line
d	Delete (input command) (for example, **dw** - deletes the word)
D	Deletes to the end of the line
dd	Deletes the whole line
o	Opens the line below the current line and inserts text
O	Opens the line above the current line and inserts text
p	Puts yanked or deleted text after the cursor
P	Puts yanked or deleted text before the cursor
r	Replaces the character with the next character typed
s	Deletes the current character and inserts unlimited text
u	Undoes the last change
x	Deletes the character at the cursor
yy	Yanks (or copies) line

Here are some commands and their actions:

➤ **w**—Jumps a word.

➤ **dw**—Deletes a word.

➤ **cw**—Changes a word.

➤ **10w**—Jumps 10 words.

➤ **10W**—Jumps 10 words and ignores all punctuation.

➤ **/**—Invokes a search.

➤ **/word**—Searches for the word "word" in a document.

➤ **n**—Finds the next occurrence of "word" in the document.

➤ **:s**—Invokes a search-and-replace for the current line.

➤ **:s/word/newword/**—Replaces the first occurrence of "word" with "newword" in the current line.

➤ **:%s/word/newword/**—Replaces the first occurrence of "word" with "newword" in the entire document.

➤ **:%s/word/newword/g**—Replaces every occurrence of "word" with "newword" throughout the entire document.

Kernel Basics

Basic kernel configuration and rebuilding knowledge is essential to becoming an RHCE. You should be extremely familiar with the tools and files required to rebuild your kernel. The kernel is the most rapidly changing part of any Linux distribution. One of the reasons for the rapid development of the Linux kernel is the two-track development system that Linux has used since kernel version 1. The version number of the Linux kernel is always in the form *major.minor .patchlevel*, where the *minor* number indicates whether the kernel is stable or in development. Stable kernels are indicated by an *even* minor number. For example, 1.0.9, 1.2.13, 2.0.36, and 2.2.5 are all stable kernels, whereas 1.1.12 and 2.3.8 are both development kernels. Stable kernels are updated less frequently and are tested before they are released. Development kernels are released as frequently as possible to allow testing and to allow all developers to synchronize their kernel source trees with Linux's official tree.

Development kernels aren't guaranteed to compile, much less work properly. They usually do work well, so many sites that need one or more not-quite-perfect features in the development kernels will use them for production systems. (For example, many sites with SMP systems ran the 2.1.x kernels for greatly improved performance.) Real work is often being done with systems that run development kernels, so the kernel developers tend to receive excellent bug reports, and this fuels the fast development cycle.

You can always retrieve the Linux kernel source via anonymous FTP from **ftp:// ftp.kernel.org/pub/linux/kernel/** or from one of its many mirrors. There are directories for each kernel major.minor version. Each directory contains a file that indicates the latest release of that version. For example, a directory listing of the v2.4 directory shows the following:

```
-r--r--r--   1 korg    korg  0 Jun  23 21:53 LATEST-IS-2.4.0-test2
```

Another quick way to determine the latest kernel version is to run the **finger @finger.kernel.org** command. Doing so should give you output like that shown here:

```
[zeus.kernel.org]
  The latest stable version of the Linux kernel is:    2.2.16
  The latest beta version of the Linux kernel is:      2.4.0-test2
  The latest prepatch (alpha) version *appears* to be: 2.4.0-test3/pre4
```

After you've determined the version of the kernel source that you need, get the file linux-*x.y.z*.tar.gz or linux-*x.y.z*.tar.bz2 (where *x.y.z* is the version number). The file with the .bz2 extension is compressed with bzip2, and the file with the .gz extension is compressed with gzip. Generally, the bzip2-compressed file is much smaller (usually around 15 to 20 percent smaller) than the gzip-compressed file.

If you already have a version of the kernel source available, you might prefer to retrieve all the patch-*x.y.z*.gz or patch-*x.y.z*.bz2 files from the versions between your current kernel version and your goal kernel version. For example, if you already have the source for kernel 2.0.34 and you want to install 2.0.36, you'll need patch-2.0.35.bz2 and patch-2.0.36.bz2, or the equivalent gzip-compressed patches.

Unpacking the Kernel Source

After you have the kernel source tar file, you need to unpack it. The canonical location for the kernel source is /usr/src/linux, and many programs expect the kernel source to be there. (For example, /usr/include/linux is a symbolic link to /usr/src/linux/include/linux.) To keep track of which kernel versions you have installed, you should create a directory for the kernel called /usr/src/linux-*x.y.z* (where *x.y.z* is the version number), and make /usr/src/linux a symbolic link to that directory. For example, to prepare to unpack the Linux 2.2.16 kernel source, use the commands shown here:

```
cd /usr/src
mkdir linux-2.2.16
rm -f linux
ln -s linux-2.2.16 linux
```

Note: This example assumes that /usr/src/linux either doesn't exist or is a symbolic link. If it's a directory, you should move it to somewhere like /usr/src/linux.old.

Then, to install the sources, execute

```
bzip2 -cd linux-2.2.16.tar.bz2 | tar -xvf -
```

for the bzip2-compressed version, or

```
gzip -cd linux-2.2.16.tar.gz | tar xvf -
```

for the gzip-compressed version. With GNU tar, which is the default tar supplied on Linux, the equivalent commands for bzip2 and gzip (respectively) are:

```
tar -Ixvf linux-2.2.16.tar.bz2
tar -zxvf linux-2.2.16.tar.gz
```

Patching a Kernel

If you have any patches to apply, the standard procedure is to change directories into your kernel source directory (usually by typing **cd /usr/src/linux**). Then, run the command

```
bzcat patchfile.bz2 | patch -p1 -E -s
```

for patches compressed by bzip2, or

```
zcat patchfile.gz | patch -p1 -E -s
```

for patches compressed with gzip.

The **-p1** option tells the patch to ignore the top-level directory referred to by the patch (usually "linux," but it could be anything in unofficial patches). The -E option tells the patch to remove any files that are zero length ("empty," hence the "-E") after the patch is applied. The -s option tells the patch to produce output only if an error occurs. Normally, the patch is rather verbose, so to see exactly what file is being updated, leave off the -s option. With some versions of GNU patch, you can get even more information with the –**verbose** command-line option.

Building the Kernel

After the kernel source is unpacked, change directories into the kernel source directory, and then run one of these commands: **make config**, **make menuconfig**, or **make xconfig**. The **config** target presents you with a list of options for the kernel in the form of questions. The **menuconfig** and **xconfig** targets are menu-driven interfaces for the configuration process, the former with a text interface and the latter with an X interface. The **menuconfig** and **xconfig** options are certainly easier than the simple **config** options, but they don't work properly with compiling development kernels. The **config** option is considered the standard way to configure the kernel because it has been available since the beginning of Linux kernel development.

If you choose the **make config** route, you're presented with a series of questions, one for each of the kernel configuration options. The possible answers are generally **y** to turn the item on (or include the driver), **n** to turn the item off (or skip the driver), **m** to make the driver as a kernel module, or **?** to get help on that option. After running **make config**, you must prepare to compile the source code by using **make dep**, followed by **make clean**.

Next, you need to compile your kernel. To compile, you have two options: **make zImage** and **make bzImage**. Because **make zImage** limits the kernel to booting within the first 640K of disk space, I recommend that you use the **make bzImage** option to allow larger kernels. With either of these commands, you can then manually add your kernel to LILO within /etc/lilo.conf and have the option to boot your old kernel, in case your new one doesn't work properly.

The methods for **make zImage** and **make bzImage** are x86-based commands only. On other architectures (such as Alpha), you can use **make boot**, which works on the x86 platform as well.

After successfully building your kernel, you must run **make modules** and **make modules_install**. Doing so builds and installs the loadable modules that you configured for your kernel. After these commands have finished successfully, copy your new image to the /boot directory, and then add the appropriate lines to lilo.conf. An example of lilo.conf is shown here:

```
boot=/dev/hda
map=/boot/map
install=/boot/boot.b
prompt
timeout=50
image=/boot/vmlinuz-2.2.16
        label=linux
        root=/dev/hda2
        read-only
other=/dev/hda1
        label=dos
        table=/dev/hda
image=/boot/vmlinuz-2.0.36-3
        label=linux-2.0.36
        root=/dev/hda2
        read-only
```

This lilo.conf example is set to boot two separate Linux images and one other. The first image is the default boot that points to the new kernel image (renamed to vmlinuz-2.2.16). The "other" section points to the first partition, which happens to be a DOS partition. The third boot option is the old kernel image.

Note: Systems that use SCSI drives to boot also require an initrd image specified in the lilo.conf file. This option is discussed further in Chapter 8.

When you're finished editing your lilo.conf file, run the **lilo** command to load and save your changes. Then reboot your computer and enjoy your new kernel.

Understanding Bourne Shell Scripts

Shell scripts are sets of commands—either stored in a file or typed at the command line—that perform multiple operations on a file or files (which must be executable to run). To make a file executable, you can use **chmod +x** or **chmod 755** *filename*.

The kernel uses specific "signature" bytes, called *magic*, of an executable file to determine how to execute that file. For example, if the first two bytes of an executable file are "#!", the kernel knows that the file is a script. The kernel then reads to the first new-line character in the file, and uses the line as the name of the script interpreter to run. If the kernel sees

```
#!/bin/sh
```

as the first line of a script, it runs /bin/sh with the script name as an argument. The kernel also knows the file magic for various other types of binary executable files (ELF, various forms of a.out, COFF from various other Unix systems, and so on). This functionality can be further extended using the binfmt_misc module in the 2.2.x and higher kernels.

If you scan a shell script, you typically find comments, which help to explain what a command or section of the script is doing. All comments written within a shell script are noted with a hash mark (#) at the beginning of a line, as shown here:

```
#!/bin/sh
# This is a sample comment for a shell script.
if [ -x file ]; then echo foo; fi
```

When you're doing any sort of programming or scripting, it's a good habit to supply comments. A few months, or in some cases just a few days, after you've written your code, comments will help you (and others who need to read it) decipher what you've written.

Using Constructs

Typical scripts contain **if, else, elif, case,** and **for** constructs. The **if** construct supplies a conditional argument. All **if** constructs are closed with a **fi** line, as shown here:

```
if foo ; then
        do something
fi
```

The **else** construct is used in conjunction with **if**. The **else** construct gives an alternate outcome in case the first **if** condition isn't true, as shown here:

```
if foo ; then
        do something
else
        echo "It's not foo."
fi
```

The **elif** construct, shown here, offers the script a choice of conditions and responses:

```
if foo; then
        do something
elif bar ; then
        do somethingelse
else
        echo "sorry, can't do that"
fi
```

The **case** construct allows the script to switch between statements depending on a pattern match. **case** constructs are ended with an **esac** line. Unlike **elif**, **case** requires a pattern match. In some init scripts, such as the init scripts in /etc/rc.d/init.d, **case** is used heavily. Here's an example from /etc/rc.d/init.d/named:

```
# See how we were called.
case "$1" in
  start)
        # Start daemons.
        echo -n "Starting named: "
        daemon named
        echo
        touch /var/lock/subsys/named
        ;;
  stop)
        # Stop daemons.
        echo -n "Shutting down named: "
        killproc named
        echo "done"
        rm -f /var/lock/subsys/named
        ;;
  status)
        status named
        exit $?
        ;;
  restart)
        /usr/sbin/ndc restart
        exit $?
        ;;
  *)
        echo "Usage: named {start|stop|status|restart}"
        exit 1
esac
```

The **for** construct allows loop iteration to occur. The **for** construct is ended with a **done** line, as shown here:

```
for foo in start stop
        do /etc/rc.d/init.d/named $foo
done
```

Using Variables

Shell scripts, much like programs, use *variables* for argument communication. Variables are sequences of letters, digits, or underscores that must begin with either a letter or an underscore. To retrieve the contents of the variable, you must prepend a $ to the variable name, as shown next.

```
for foo in one two three; do
     echo $foo
done
```

You can also export variables to be used in child processes within the script. You do so with the **export** keyword. Essentially, **export** tells the shell to make this variable an environment variable. The environment is passed to each child process of the script.

Using The **test** Command

One of the most powerful commands in shell scripting is **test(1)**. The **test** command is an external command that is called by the shell, as shown here:

```
if test expression ; then
     do something
fi
```

The command **test** is symbolically linked to [. The functionality of **test** is built into most modern shells, including bash. When [is used in a script, it has to be closed with a] to be valid, as shown here:

```
if [ expression ] ; then
     do something
fi
```

Using the end bracket was implemented to instill good programming habits.

The **test** command uses some special options to make various types of tests, as shown in Table 3.3.

You can also use **test** to compare numbers or strings, as shown in Table 3.4.

Table 3.3 Options for the test command.	
Option	**Explanation**
[-w filename]	Is the specified file writeable?
[-r filename]	Is the specified file readable?
[-x filename]	Is the specified file executable?
[-s filename]	Is the specified file's size greater than zero?

Table 3.4 Uses for the test command.	
test String	**Description**
test n1 -eq n2	Are the numbers equal?
test n1 -ne n2	Are the numbers not equal?
test n1 -gt n2	Is the first number greater than the second?
test s1 = s2	Is the first string equal to the second?
test s1 != s2	Is the first string not equal to the second?

Administration Basics

As a Linux administrator, you should be familiar not only with Unix, shell, and kernel basics, but also with other tools and programs. Home directories, file-location default directories, daemons, logging, and backing up and restoring files are all concepts you should be familiar with.

Home Directories

When a user account is created, it automatically has a home directory assigned. This directory is /home/*username*. The /home/*username* directory contains default files, such as .Xdefaults, .bashrc, and .bash_profile. These files are copies from a default file location, typically found at /etc/skel (skeleton files).

Superusers are users who have increased file access and control. The standard superuser is *root,* where user id (UID) is set to 0. However, programs such as sudo can also provide limited superuser privileges to other users.

Daemons

A *daemon* process is one whose parent process is process ID 1 (for example, the **init** process). Linux uses daemons to perform routine tasks, such as monitoring system resources.

For a list of the daemons you're running, you can execute **ps -aux**, which reports a process status. To see which daemons are being loaded at bootup, you can type **ntsysv**. The daemons that are checked with an asterisk (*) are being loaded at bootup. The init scripts for these daemons are located under /etc/rc.d/init.d/. You can use the init scripts to start, stop, or restart your daemons.

Managing these daemons, as well as managing networking services, is simplified by using the ntsysv program to select which daemons to start at bootup. In addition, you can use **inetd**, the "Internet super-server" daemon. The **inetd** daemon uses /etc/inet.conf. This file consists of networking services that are listening to incoming connections on specific ports. A sample section of an inetd.conf file follows:

```
# These are standard services.
#
ftp       stream  tcp nowait   root    /usr/sbin/tcpd   in.ftpd -l -a
telnet    stream  tcp nowait   root    /usr/sbin/tcpd   in.telnetd
gopher    stream  tcp nowait   root    /usr/sbin/tcpd   gn
```

Services that aren't to be used are simply commented out of the inetd.conf file, as shown here:

```
#cfinger stream    tcp    nowait root    /usr/sbin/tcpd    in.cfingerd
```

The format of these lines uses service **stream** versus **dgram,** the **tcp** versus **udp,** the **wait** versus **nowait[.max],** and the **user[.group]** program arguments.

The cron Program

The cron program allows you to run jobs at specific intervals. The cron program uses your crontab file to configure which programs to run, and when. To set up a crontab file for an individual user, the user types **crontab -e** to edit the crontab file. The user crontab is automatically placed in /var/spool/cron/crontabs/. An example crontab entry looks like this:

```
# run example cron job
01 2 3 4 5   $HOME/bin/daily.job
```

Lines in the crontab file have six fields. The first field specifies the minute of the hour that the indicated executable is to be run (0 through 59). The second field specifies the hour of the day that the executable should be run (0 through 23). The third field specifies the day of the month (0 through 31). The fourth field specifies the month of the year (0 through 12). The fifth field specifies the day of the week (0 through 7). The final field specifies the program to be run.

 Using an asterisk (*) in place of any of the six first fields indicates "every."

In addition to individual user crontab files, there's a system crontab file. It's found in /etc/crontab. An example of a system crontab file looks like this:

```
SHELL=/bin/bash
PATH=/sbin:/bin:/usr/sbin:/usr/bin
MAILTO=root

# run-parts
01 * * * * root run-parts /etc/cron.hourly
02 4 * * * root run-parts /etc/cron.daily
22 4 * * 0 root run-parts /etc/cron.weekly
42 4 1 * * root run-parts /etc/cron.monthly
```

With the default root crontab setup, the crontab points to a directory in each line. When each line is run, every script in the directory is run. For instance, the first entry runs every script in /etc/cron.hourly at the first minute of every hour, and the second entry runs every script in /etc/cron.daily every day at 4:02 A.M. The third entry runs every script in /etc/cron.weekly every Sunday at 4:22 A.M., and the fourth entry runs every script in /etc/cron.monthly the first day of each month at 4:42 A.M.

The most important information you have to evaluate services, connections, and problems with your Linux box is your system logs. The daemon that logs these messages is called syslogd. To view your logs, you can **cat** the files or, even better, **tail** them. You can find most of your log files under /var/log/. Important system messages can be found in the file /var/log/messages, whereas logs containing mail information are in /var/log/maillog.

Backing Up and Restoring Files

To be a good Unix administrator, you should be in the habit of backing up important files regularly. Two typical programs that are used to make archives of a system are tar and cpio. The tar program is the tape archive utility. It stores and retrieves data from an archive. To make an archive with tar, use

```
tar -cvf filename.tar file
```

You can save this output file (filename.tar) in the example to floppy disk, tape, writable CD, or even another hard drive. To restore or extract the files by using tar, use

```
tar -xvf filename.tar
```

The cpio program is the "copy in-out" program. It's similar to tar; however, it can use archives in a number of formats, including the tar format. When extracting files from an archive, cpio reads the archive as standard output.

Practice Questions

Question 1

> Which is a valid format for mounting a CD-ROM after a typical Red Hat installation using **mount**?
>
> ○ a. **mount /dev/cdrom**
>
> ○ b. **mount /mnt/cdrom**
>
> ○ c. **mount –t iso9660 /dev/cdrom /mnt/cdrom**
>
> ○ d. All of the above

Answer d is correct. A default Red Hat Linux installation automatically sets up your /etc/fstab file to include the default settings for your CD-ROM drive by mounting /dev/cdrom (shown in answer a) to the mount point /mnt/cdrom (shown in answer b) with the iso9660 filesystem type (shown in answer c). Therefore, answers a, b, and c mount your CD-ROM device to the /mnt/cdrom mount point.

Question 2

> What are the appropriate Hex codes for setting Linux swap and Linux native partition types in fdisk?
>
> ○ a. 82 and 85
>
> ○ b. 83 and 85
>
> ○ c. 82 and 83
>
> ○ d. 84 and 85

Answer c is correct. When you're setting partition types, don't randomly guess. Enter l at the command prompt to see a list of Hex codes that fdisk supports.

Question 3

> What command do you use to rename a file?
>
> ○ a. **rename**
>
> ○ b. **mv**
>
> ○ c. **nn**
>
> ○ d. **cp**

Answer b is correct. The **mv** command allows you to move a file from one place to another, which allows you to move it from its current name to a new name as well. Answers a, c, and d are incorrect because **rename** and **nn** aren't real Unix commands, and although answer d can copy a command to a new name, it leaves the old name. This choice would work, but it isn't the best answer.

Question 4

> What is the difference between mkfs and fsck?

Both mkfs and fsck are filesystem tools. The mkfs tool is used to create Linux filesystems, whereas the fsck tool is used to check and repair Linux filesystems.

Question 5

> What can you execute to count the number of lines in a file?
>
> ○ a. **lc**
>
> ○ b. **wc -l**
>
> ○ c. **cl**
>
> ○ d. None of the above

Answer b is correct. The **wc** command is the word count command. The -l option tells it to count the lines. Answers a and c are incorrect because they aren't valid commands.

Question 6

> What's the difference between the **less** and **more** commands?

The **less** and **more** commands are both filters. If you pipe the output of a file or a command through either of these filters, you get the output one page at a time. The difference, however, lies in their functionality. For example, **less** is a more powerful tool than **more**; **less** allows you not only to view the output one page at a time, but also to scroll up and down through the file. **less** also allows you to search through the file using standard vi commands.

Question 7

> What command lists the last 10 lines of a file?
>
> ○ a. **grep**
> ○ b. **cat**
> ○ c. **head**
> ○ d. **tail**

Answer d is correct. The **tail** command lists the last 10 lines of a file. Answer a is incorrect because **grep** is a filter. Answers b and c display the contents of a file; however, **cat** lists all contents of the file, and **head** lists the first 10 lines. Therefore, they are incorrect.

Question 8

> Entering the command **ls foobar?** could give you which output? [Check all correct answers]
>
> ❑ a. foobarbaz
> ❑ b. foobazbar
> ❑ c. foobar?
> ❑ d. foobarz

Answers c and d are correct. The ? wildcard means that the missing character is a single-character wildcard. Using a ? in a file name is valid, so the ? wildcard found both foobar? and foobarz to be valid. Answers a and b are incorrect because they have more than one character after the requested file name.

Question 9

Where can system and mail logs be found in Red Hat Linux?

○ a. /log

○ b. /logs

○ c. /var/adm/syslogs

○ d. /var/log

Answer d is correct. On some systems that were set up by an expert, or by administrators accustomed to another flavor of Unix, you might find symbolic links from some of the other options to /var/log.

Question 10

Which vi commands can be used to move you into insert mode? [Check all correct answers]

❑ a. **I, i, A**

❑ b. **a, i, O**

❑ c. **0, a, i**

❑ d. **I, A, O**

Answers a, b, and d are correct. I and i are used to insert text at the beginning of the line and at the cursor, respectively. A and a are used to append at the end of the line and append after the next letter, respectively. O and o are used to open the line above the current line and open the line below the current line, respectively. Answer c is incorrect because a zero (0) is used instead of the letter O. Although you might not encounter the 0 vs. O trick on your RHCE exam, it can easily play tricks on you when you're trying to administer a console where 0 and O appear to be the same character.

Need to Know More?

 Frisch, Æleen. *Essential System Administration*. O'Reilly & Associates, 1995. ISBN 1-56592-127-5. This book gives you many of the basics required for using Unix-style operating systems, commands, filesystems, and so forth.

 Lamb, Linda and Arnold Robbins. *Learning the vi Editor*. O'Reilly & Associates, 1998. ISBN 1-56592-426-6. This book is an excellent aid for learning all the capabilities of and methods for using the vi text editor.

 Maxwell, Scott E. *Linux Core Kernel Commentary*. The Coriolis Group, 1999. ISBN 1-57610-469-9. This book explains the processes and development of the Linux kernel.

 Newham, Cameron, and Rosenblatt, Bill. *Learning the Bash Shell*. O'Reilly & Associates, 1998. ISBN 1-56592-347-2. This book gives all the details about operating and programming in a bash environment. Refer to Chapter 2 to learn about editing the command line and to Chapter 3 for writing bash scripts.

 Robbins, Arnold. *vi Editor Pocket Reference*. O'Reilly & Associates, 1999. ISBN 1-56592-497-5. This book is an excellent resource for command lists and usage of vi.

 Siever, Ellen. *Linux in a Nutshell*. O'Reilly & Associates, 1997. ISBN 1-56592-167-4. This book gives you a general look at Linux, with a focus on globbing in Chapter 6, vi in Chapter 8, and general commands in Chapters 12 and 13.

 http://www.kernel.org/—The Linux kernel homepage. This site hosts Linux kernel developments and information.

 http://www.linuxdoc.org/—The Linux Documentation Project. This site links to many Linux-related FAQs and HOWTOs.

Red Hat
Advanced Prerequisites

. . . .

Terms you'll need to understand:

✓ Queue

✓ Daemon

✓ Protocol

✓ Octet

✓ Supernetting

✓ Routing

✓ Permissions

Techniques you'll need to master:

✓ Partitioning disks

✓ Printing with Unix

✓ Networking with TCP/IP

✓ Routing with TCP/IP

✓ Configuring network services

The RHCE 302 exam is designed to certify the advanced Linux or Unix engineer and system administrator of Red Hat Linux. Anyone who participates in the program should have intermediate to advanced working knowledge of computer hardware, printing, networking, TCP/IP networking, network services, and network security. This chapter will cover these areas.

Hardware

The RHCE 302 certification exam is based on Red Hat 6.2 running on Intel hardware. You should be aware that Red Hat also runs on a number of other hardware platforms such as Alpha and SPARC. For this exam, you should be well versed in Intel and Intel-clone architectures. A firm knowledge of Interrupt Request (IRQ) settings, hard disk subsystems, and basic disk partitioning is a must.

Intel Architectures

Intel IA-32 (x86) and the clones from AMD, Cyrix, and others (also known as *IBM compatibles*) are based on Complex Instruction Set Computing (CISC) central processing units (CPUs). CPUs process low-level commands called *instruction sets*. The time required to carry out these instruction sets is based on the CPU's speed and architecture. Compared to Reduced Instruction Set Computing (RISC) CPUs, CISC CPUs use more complex instruction sets and have fewer registers with which to execute them, making them less efficient. Some RISC processors are used in these popular computer systems: Alpha, Hewlett-Packard's PA-RISC, Sun Microsystems' SPARC, SGI's MIPS, and IBM's PowerPC. Over the years, Intel and Intel clones have become the industry standard for computing hardware. Many once-proprietary hardware vendors are adapting the Intel architecture for their systems, providing greater compatibility and affordability.

The base of the Intel personal computer (PC) is the *motherboard*. Motherboards typically have sockets and slots integrated directly on the board for the CPU, the random access memory (RAM), and the Peripheral Component Interconnect (PCI) and Industry Standard Architecture (ISA) buses. Unlike older x86 boards, new motherboards integrate the serial (communication) and parallel ports, along with the Integrated Drive Electronics (IDE) and floppy controllers.

IRQ Settings

The PCI (and related Accelerated Graphics Port, or AGP) bus is the most popular expansion bus used in current PC systems. Most PC motherboards have both ISA and PCI bus slots available. The differences between ISA and PCI buses lie in the way they handle IRQ and input/output (I/O) addressing and in their data-transfer speed.

The ISA bus's settings, such as IRQ and I/O, are hard-wired directly on the card. This arrangement does not allow the operating system to query the bus, so you cannot change configurations without changing jumper settings on the card. Plug-and-play ISA cards are an exception, but they require special configuration tools. The ISA bus has these characteristics:

➤ It is limited by the maximum clock speed of approximately 8MHz.

➤ Its maximum data-transfer rate is 8Mbps.

➤ It is limited by the 16-bit data width and 20-bit address width.

The PCI bus, however, allows the BIOS to control IRQ and I/O addressing. The operating system can directly query the PCI bus, so you can control the settings from within the operating system. The PCI bus has these characteristics:

➤ It is faster than the ISA bus, allowing a maximum clock speed of 66MHz.

➤ Its maximum data-transfer rate is 132Mbps.

➤ It has a 32-bit data width and a 32-bit address width.

Serial ports on Intel and Intel-clone computers generally have standard I/O and IRQ settings. Table 4.1 lists the standard settings for serial ports.

Note: Linux sees an AGP card as another PCI card, but it's run at 100MHz. AGP is used almost exclusively for graphics cards.

Hard Disk Subsystems

Two of the most common hard disk subsystems used in current Intel hardware are IDE (Integrated Drive Electronics) and Small Computer Systems Interconnect (SCSI). IDE drives have the controller located directly on the piece of hardware, and they use an IDE bus that is typically integrated on the motherboard. Most Intel motherboards have two IDE buses. Each bus supports one master and one slave drive, limiting the number of IDE devices to four.

Table 4.1 Standard serial ports.			
Linux Serial Port	**DOS COM Port**	**I/O**	**IRQ**
ttyS0	com 1	3F8	4
ttyS1	com 2	2F8	3
ttyS2	com 3	3E8	4
ttyS3	com 4	2E8	3

SCSI devices use a controller that is separate from the drive itself. These controllers are run on SCSI cards (also called *SCSI adapters*) and are connected to the computer through the ISA or PCI slots. SCSI devices are not limited to master and slave drives, as are IDE devices. SCSI devices are limited only by the number of devices that the SCSI card supports. Typical cards can support anywhere from 7 to 30 devices; however, higher-quality cards are reported to support over 100 devices.

Performance factors differentiate the qualities of IDE and SCSI devices. Typical SCSI devices can transfer data from a range of 10Mbps through 160Mbps, and typical IDE devices from a range of 8Mbps through 100Mbps. Both systems' speed rates depend on the device and the controller card.

Disk Partitioning

Another must for understanding Linux is understanding hard-drive partitioning. *Partitioning*, which we briefly looked at in Chapter 2, is a mechanism used to segment a single physical disk into multiple logical disks. These logical disks appear as a contiguous section of physical blocks.

An entire hard disk does not have to be partitioned completely. You can save the remaining space for future allocation, or use it as a gap to allow for resizing partitions.

 Moving and resizing partitions is tricky and can easily corrupt your filesystem. Before altering your partition table, always back up your data.

The number of partitions created on a drive is typically determined by the particular machine's needs. Separate partitions are suggested for separate operating systems to use and, in Linux's case, for swap space. However, it is generally recommended that you assign separate partitions (or even separate hard disks) for mounting separate filesystems, such as /home, /var, /var/log, and root, for large-disk installations or active workstations.

Printing

Red Hat uses the printer spooling systems that were originally developed for BSD (Berkeley Systems Distribution) Unix. Linux can maintain multiple printers at multiple sites as well as multiple print queues. Some basic printing commands you'll use include **lpr**, **lpq**, **lprm**, **lpd**, and **lpc**, described in Table 4.2.

Table 4.2   Basic printing commands.

Command	Description
lpr	Adds jobs to the print queue
lpq	Lists jobs currently in print queues
lprm	Removes jobs from the print queue
lpd	Is the printer daemon that sends data from the spool to the printer
lpc	Is the administrative interface for printing

To add a printer to your system via direct parallel connection, first ensure that the printer is physically connected properly. Make sure that the lpd server is started at boot-time (check by running **ntsysv**). Edit /etc/printcap, and add an entry for the new printer. Create your spooling directory in mkdir /var/spool/newps. Make sure your print spool's permissions are set to 755 (we'll go into more detail on permissions later in this chapter). Create the printer's accounting file with the **touch** command. You can then start the printer in its queue by using the **lpc** command, as shown here:

```
#touch /var/adm/lp_acct/ps3
#chown daemon /var/adm/lp_acct/ps3
#chmod 755 /var/adm/lp_acct/ps3
#lpc up ps3
```

The spooling system on Linux can also print to remote printers. To add a remote printer, simply edit /etc/printcap, adding lines similar to the following:

```
#remote printer setup
remlp|print on remote line printer:\
        :lp=:rm=remote:rp=lp2:sd=/var/spool/remlp
```

Note: The above /etc/printcap entry has no references about the details of the printer itself. This is because the host will manage the job after it's sent.

This entry sets up the remote printer named remlp. Not specifying the **lp=** field tells us that this entry is for a remote printer. The **rm=** field points us to the destination system (here, we've named it "remote"). The **rp=** field holds the name of the target printer. The **sd=** field selects the spool directory that the printer will use.

Networking with TCP/IP

A Linux box without a network is like a typist without hands. Therefore, a Linux administrator who wishes to obtain the RHCE certificate must have a good understanding of networking concepts such as Transmission Control Protocol/Internet Protocol (TCP/IP), network ports, and networking services.

TCP/IP Fundamentals

The most important networking protocol used in today's networks is TCP/IP. It is the fundamental set of protocols used to establish the Internet as well as the majority of the world's wide area networks. Networking is one of Linux's star features, making it more popular every day for business networks, Internet Service Providers (ISPs), manufacturing facilities, and network companies.

TCP/IP and the Open Systems Interconnection (OSI) Model

The TCP/IP architectural model of computer-to-computer communication is based on the Open Systems Interconnection (OSI) model. The OSI model consists of seven layers, whereas the TCP/IP model has only four. Here is a list of the OSI model's layers:

➤ Application layer

➤ Presentation layer

➤ Session layer

➤ Transport layer

➤ Network layer

➤ Data Link layer

➤ Physical layer

Compare those with the TCP/IP model's layers:

➤ *Application layer*—Handles TCP/IP network daemons and applications. This layer performs the jobs of the OSI model's Presentation, Session, and Application layers.

➤ *Transport layer*—Handles all the data routing and delivery issues, including session initiation, error control, and sequence checking. This layer covers the OSI model's Transport layer and part of the Network layer.

➤ *Internet layer*—Handles all the data addressing, transmission, and the IP packet. This layer covers part of the OSI model's Network layer.

➤ *Network Access layer*—Specifies the procedures for transmitting data over the network, including how to access the physical medium. Also called the Network Interface layer. (This is used for many protocols, including Ethernet and FDDI, the Fiber Distributed Data Interface.)

TCP and User Datagram Protocol (UDP) Protocols

TCP is not the only protocol used in TCP/IP networking. Some applications, such as the Network File System (NFS), use a sibling protocol called UDP (User Datagram Protocol). Both protocols allow the application to contact a service on a specific port. However, UDP doesn't establish a connection; rather, it sends single packets to the service.

Internet Control Message Protocol (ICMP) Packet Types

Internet Control Message Protocol (ICMP) is used by the kernel code to send error messages to other hosts. There are several ICMP packet types, and some can carry multiple messages. Some valid types are echo-reply, destination-unreachable, source-quench (deprecated, but NT still sends them for some reason), redirect, echo-request, router-advertisement, router-solicitation, time-exceeded, parameter-problem, timestamp-request, timestamp-reply, address-mask-request, and address-mask-reply.

The destination-unreachable packet can carry one of 14 messages. These include network-unreachable, host-unreachable, protocol-unreachable, port-unreachable, fragmentation-needed, source-route-failed, network-unknown, host-unknown, network-prohibited, host-prohibited, TOS-network-unreachable, TOS-host-unreachable, communication-prohibited, and host precedence-cutoff.

The redirect packet can carry one of four messages: network-redirect, host-redirect, TOS-network redirect, and TOS-host-redirect.

The time-exceeded packet (also known as ttl-exceeded) can carry one of two messages: ttl-zero-during-transit and ttl-zero-during-reassembly.

The parameter-problem packet can carry one of these two messages: ip-header-bad and required-option-missing.

Understanding Ports

Network services are each assigned (or bound to) a port. Ports are TCP's and UDP's abstraction of a service endpoint. There are 64K (or 65,536) possible ports available for use. All ports under 1,024 (low-number ports) are considered *privileged* ports. This means that only the root can bind to them. However, 1,024 and above are *unprivileged* ports, meaning that any user can bind to them.

Every networking program should look into the /etc/services text file to get the port number (and protocol) for its service. The /etc/services file provides a mapping between names for Internet services and their underlying assigned port numbers and protocol types. Table 4.3 lists some standard services from a sample /etc/services file (the table does not list all the services found in /etc/services).

Table 4.3	Some of the services in the /etc/services file.		
Service	**Port/Protocol**	**Alias**	**Comments**
echo	7/tcp	N/A	N/A
echo	7/udp	N/A	N/A
netstat	15/tcp	N/A	N/A
ftp	21/tcp	N/A	N/A
ssh	22/tcp	N/A	N/A
telnet	23/tcp	N/A	N/A
smtp	25/tcp	mail	N/A
name	42/udp	nameserver	N/A
whois	43/tcp	nicname	# usually to sri-nic
finger	79/tcp	N/A	N/A
http	80/tcp	N/A	# www is used by some # broken progs, http is more # correct
www	80/tcp	N/A	
pop-3	110/tcp	N/A	# PostOffice V.3
auth	113/tcp	ident	# User Verification
nntp	119/tcp	usenet	# Network News Transfer
imap	143/tcp	N/A	# imap network mail protocol
exec	512/tcp	N/A	# BSD rexecd(8)
login	513/tcp	N/A	# BSD rlogind(8)
who	513/udp	whod	# BSD rwhod(8)
printer	515/tcp	spooler	# BSD lpd(8)
route	520/udp	router routed	# 521/udp too
mount	635/udp	N/A	# NFS Mount Service
nfs	2049/udp	N/A	# NFS File Service
irc	6667/tcp	N/A	# Internet Relay Chat

IP Addressing

The most important concept to understand in TCP/IP networking is IP addressing. An *IP address* is a numeric identifier assigned to each machine on an IP network. An IP address is a software address, not a hardware address (hardware addresses are hard-coded into the machine or the network interface card).

IP Numbers

An IP address is made up of 32 bits. These bits are separated into four 8-bit sections called *octets*. (Each octet contains four bytes of information and specifies either the network or the machine node.) Every machine on a subnet has the same network address but individual node addresses.

You can display an IP address in three ways. The first and most common method is dotted decimal. An example of the dotted decimal notation is 130.57.30.56. The second way is using the binary system. If you convert 130.57.30.56 to binary, it is 10000010.00111001.00011110.00111000. The third way is the hexadecimal system. If you notate 130.57.30.56 using hexadecimal, it is 82 39 1E 38.

Note: Throughout this section—and the entire book—IP addresses are written using the dotted decimal format.

IP Classes

There are three classes of IP networks: Class A, Class B, and Class C. Different classes are used depending on network size. The Class A network is used for a collection of a small number of networks with a large number of nodes. The Class B network is rarely used in a network, but can be used in a large network where numerous Class C networks are unmanageable and a Class A network is too large. The Class C network is used for a collection of a very large number of networks that have few nodes.

A Class A network uses the addressing format Net.Node.Node.Node, allowing you to have up to 127 networks and 16,777,216 nodes per network. IP addresses for Class A networks range from 1.0.0.0 to 127.0.0.0.

Note: Class A networks are no longer being assigned because none is available to assign. In fact, some Class A networks are already being carved up into smaller networks.

Being assigned a Class A network gives you all network addresses under the Net address. For instance, a company that owns the 12.0.0.0 Class A set of IP addresses has every IP address from 12.0.0.0 to 12.255.255.255.

A Class B network uses the addressing format Net.Net.Node.Node. This allows you to have up to 16,384 networks and 65,534 nodes per network. IP addresses for Class B networks range from 128.0.0.0 to 191.0.0.0. Being assigned a Class B network gives you all network addresses under the Net.Net. assignment. For instance, a company that owns the 130.1.0.0 Class B network owns every IP address from 130.1.0.0 to 130.1.255.255.

The Class C networks are the most common network class used today. They allow you to have up to 2,097,152 networks, but you are limited to having only 254 nodes per network. IP addresses for Class C networks range from 192.0.0.0 to 223.0.0.0. Being assigned a Class C network gives you all network addresses under the assigned Net.Net.Net.Node address. For instance, an administrator or company who owns the 200.0.2.0 Class C network owns every IP address from 200.0.2.0 to 200.0.2.255.

You might be wondering what happens with network addresses above 223.255.255.255. Well, there are other classes of networks: Class D and Class E. Class D is used for multicast packets. These packets include the addresses from 224.0.0.0 to 239.255.255.255. A multicast transmission is used when a host wants to broadcast to multiple destinations, such as when a host is attempting to learn all the routers on its network. The Class E range of addresses is 240.0.0.0 through 255.255.255.255. These numbers are reserved for future use. You should not assign either Class D or Class E addresses to nodes on your network.

Network addresses are controlled by an official Internet organization called the Network Information Center (NIC), also referred to as InterNIC. Its Web site is located at **http://www.internic.net**.

The Internet Assigned Numbers Authority (IANA) has reserved the following three blocks of the IP address space for private networks:

➤ 10.0.0.0 through 10.255.255.255

➤ 172.16.0.0 through 172.31.255.255

➤ 192.168.0.0 through 192.168.255.255

These addresses can be used on any internal private network free of charge. However, these addresses aren't publicly routable.

Note: Classless InterDomain Routing, or CIDR (discussed in the next section), has mostly made the Class A, B, and C system technically irrelevant. Regardless, the classes terminology is still widely used.

Supernetting IP Classes

In 1992, a new adaptation to the IP classes was proposed. The idea was to *supernet* multiple classes in order to reserve IP numbers. Otherwise, IP addresses would be wastefully assigned (for example, a Class B address might be assigned when only two Class Cs' worth of addresses was required), and we would run out of IP addresses quickly. Therefore, Classless InterDomain Routing (CIDR) was invented.

Using supernetting, the class subnet masks are extended so that a network address and a subnet mask can, for example, specify multiple Class C subnets with one address. For example, if you need about 500 addresses, you can supernet two Class C networks together. Table 4.4 shows supernetted subnets.

It is expected that CIDR will have enough IP addresses available for the next few years, until IPv6 is implemented. IPv6 uses 128-bit addresses, which would comfortably allow over 340 trillion trillions of unique IP addresses.

Subnets

To create a subnet, you split IP addresses into two parts: a network and a host. Typically, the destination network is derived from the network part of the IP address; therefore, hosts with identical IP network numbers should be found within the same network.

Every subnet is assigned a *netmask* (also referred to as a *subnet mask*): the number of bits interpreted as the subnet number. For instance, a Class C network number of 192.168.1.0 has a netmask of 255.255.255.0, whereas a Class B network number, such as 176.16.0.0, has a netmask of 255.255.0.0.

Network Configuration

The **ifconfig** command is used to configure the kernel-resident network interfaces. It is used at boot-time to set up network interfaces as necessary. The first interface you'll have to set up is the loopback interface (**lo**), as shown here:

```
#ifconfig lo 127.0.0.1
```

Table 4.4 Supernetting subnets.	
Subnet/Result	Description
193.60.220.0	Class C subnet address
193.60.221.0	Class C subnet address
193.60.220.0	Supernetted subnet address
255.255.252.0	Subnet mask
193.60.220.255	Broadcast address

To view the configuration of the interface, run **ifconfig lo**, as shown here:

```
$ ifconfig lo
lo        Link encap:Local Loopback
          inet addr:127.0.0.1 Mask:255.0.0.0
          UP LOOPBACK RUNNING MTU:3924 Metric:1
          RX packets:677619 errors:0 dropped:0 overruns:0 frame:0
          TX packets:677619 errors:0 dropped:0 overruns:0 carrier:0
          collisions:0 txqueuelen:0
```

The loopback interface has been assigned a netmask of 255.0.0.0 because 127.0.0.1 is a Class A address.

The second interface you need to set up is the Ethernet interface. As with the loopback interface, you set this one up with **ifconfig** (and in nearly the same manner):

```
$ifconfig eth0 207.239.117.252 netmask 255.255.255.0

$ifconfig eth0
eth0    Link encap:Ethernet HWaddr 00:10:4B:63:05:94
        inet addr:192.168.117.252 Bcast:192.168.117.255
        Mask:255.255.255.0
        UP BROADCAST RUNNING MULTICAST MTU:1500 Metric:1
        RX packets:6236605 errors:1 dropped:0 overruns:0 frame:1
        TX packets:6449859 errors:0 dropped:0 overruns:0 carrier:11
        Collisions:25319
        Interrupt:17 Base address:0x6100
```

For the eth0 interface, the broadcast address is automatically set, in this case to 207.239.117.255. The maximum size of Ethernet frames that the kernel generates for this interface (message transfer unit) has been set to 1,500.

After setting up your **ifconfig** configuration, you must add a routing entry that points to the network that can be reached through eth0, as shown here:

```
#route add -net 192.168.117.0 dev eth0
```

You can use the **route** command to verify that you have the correct routing entries. To check your routing table, use the **route -n** command, as shown here:

```
Kernel IP routing table
Destination      Gateway    Genmask          Flags Metric Ref Use Iface
192.168.117.254  0.0.0.0    255.255.255.255  UH    0      0   0   eth0
192.168.117.0    0.0.0.0    255.255.255.0    U     0      0   0   eth0
127.0.0.0        0.0.0.0    255.0.0.0        U     0      0   0   lo
0.0.0.0          192.168.117.1 0.0.0.0       UG    0      0   0   eth0
```

When you're establishing this route, you might want to set up host-name resolution. To do so, use the /etc/hosts file. (If you don't use DNS or NIS for address resolution, you must put all hosts in the /etc/hosts file.) The /etc/hosts file has three fields. The first is the IP address, the second contains the fully qualified domain name, and the third contains any aliases for the name. Table 4.5 shows a sample /etc/hosts file.

Configuring the Domain Name Service (DNS)

To configure the use of the BIND name service for host lookups, you have to tell the resolver library which name servers to use. The file used to specify the name server is called resolv.conf, as shown here:

```
search example.net
nameserver 0.0.0.0
```

If the resolv.conf file is empty, the resolver assumes that the name server is on your local host.

The **search** option specifies the local domain. Therefore, if the name server can't find the name "sites," it looks for "sites.example.net," as specified in the /etc/hosts file just shown. The **nameserver** option specifies the IP address of the name server, which in this case is localhost, or 127.0.0.1.

Network Tools

Some additional tools that are helpful when you're working with networks and their inevitable problems are ping and traceroute. The **ping** command sends an

Table 4.5   Sample /etc/hosts file.

IP Address	Domain	Alias (If Applicable)
127.0.0.1	localhost	localhost.example.net
192.168.156.252	web1.example.net	web1
192.168.156.253	sites.example.net	sites
192.168.156.254	www.example.org	

ICMP echo request to the specified IP address. It reports the time it takes to get
a response from the requested machine, as shown here:

```
#ping 192.168.156.253
PING 192.168.156.253 (192.168.156.253): 56 data bytes
64 bytes from 192.168.156.253: icmp_seq=0 ttl=255 time=0.4 ms
64 bytes from 192.168.156.253: icmp_seq=1 ttl=255 time=0.2 ms
64 bytes from 192.168.156.253: icmp_seq=2 ttl=255 time=0.2 ms
64 bytes from 192.168.156.253: icmp_seq=3 ttl=255 time=0.2 ms

-- 192.168.156.253 ping statistics --
4 packets transmitted, 4 packets received, 0% packet loss
round-trip min/avg/max = 0.2/0.2/0.4 ms
```

The **traceroute** command is used exactly as its name implies. You use it to trace
the route between you and the requested machine. The snippet shown here is an
example of output of **traceroute** to the domain pritchard.example.net:

```
#traceroute pritchard.example.net
traceroute to pritchard.example.net (256.23.140.37), 30 hops max, 40
byte packets
 1 192.168.117.1 (192.168.117.1) 1.374 ms 0.896 ms 0.834 ms
 2 10.1.1.1 (10.1.1.1) 8.552 ms 6.476 ms 6.440 ms
 3 192.168.194.33 (192.168.194.33) 18.956 ms 18.906 ms 18.837 ms
 4 ord1-core1-s5-0-0.example.net (192.168.52.41) * 26.367 ms *
 5 192.168.10.93 (192.168.10.93) 24.911 ms 24.301 ms 25.962 ms
 6 core2.example.net (192.168.4.45) 62.657 ms 54.196 ms *
 7 border7-fddi-0.example.net (192.168.98.51) 48.723 ms 219.232 ms
 8 North.example.net (192.168.211.18) 36.319 ms 61.095 ms *
 9 pritchard.example.net (192.168.140.37) 63.738 ms 66.498 ms
   63.625 ms
```

IP Routing

IP routing is the process of a packet finding the appropriate host by traveling
through a sequence of hosts from an original host to a destination host. Three of
the protocols used in IP routing are:

➤ *Address Resolution Protocol (ARP)*—Used to map IP addresses to Ethernet
addresses

➤ *Reverse Address Resolution Protocol (RARP)*—Used to permit hosts to find out
their IP addresses at boot-time

➤ *Routing Information Protocol (RIP)*—Used to dynamically adjust routes inside
a small network

Routes

Routes are specific paths set up for packet information to travel from the source to its destination. Three types of routes are static, dynamic, and default routes.

Static routes are used for small- to medium-sized networks. These networks tend to be very simple because they do not have several redundant paths to destinations. Static routes are established by issuing **route** commands at boot-time.

Dynamic routes differ from static routes; with dynamic routes, the optimal path to destinations is determined as requested and then updated as necessary. Dynamic routing is typically used by either the routed daemon or the gated daemon.

Default routes are established between your immediate host and its host, between the host's host and its host, and so on. For instance, if a packet's destination is 10.248.89.7, and the internal router's routing-table entries include 192.168.0.1 and 10.168.1.0, then the packet is sent to the default route (typically 0.0.0.0). The default route is assigned a gateway, which redirects the packet to the router's host. If the host's router doesn't have the 10.248.89.x routing-table entry, the packet is forwarded to the host's host, and so on. Each of these exchanges is called a *hop*. After 30 hops, if the packet hasn't reached its destination, it dies. This scenario is called a ttl-exceed.

Networking Services

After working with networks for an extended period of time, you'll become familiar with a variety of networking services. Some of these popular services include Network File System (NFS), sendmail, POP3 and Internet Message Access Protocol (IMAP), File Transfer Protocol (FTP), Domain Name Service (DNS), Dynamic Host Control Protocol (DHCP), Samba, the Hypertext Transport Protocol Daemon (httpd), Network Information Service (NIS), and inetd.

NFS

The Network File System (NFS) service allows filesystems that physically reside on one computer system to be used by other computers on the network. These connections appear as local disks to remote users. NFS configuration files can be found in /etc/fstab and /etc/exports. NFS uses several daemons to handle its services. These services are started at boot-time in the /etc/rc.d/init.d/nfs scripts.

Some of these services include:

➤ *nfsd*—Handles filesystem exporting and file-access requests from remote systems. This daemon gets run multiple times as more remote systems use the services.

➤ *biod*—Performs NFS block I/O operations for client processes.

➤ *rpc.mountd*—Handles mount requests from remote computers.

➤ *rpc.lockd*—Manages file locking for both client and server systems.

➤ *rpc.statd*—Handles lock crash and recovery services for both client and server systems.

➤ *portmap*—Facilitates the initial connection between local and remote servers.

Note: Current versions of Red Hat use the kernel nfsd (knfsd). Simple nfsd is a kernel module.

sendmail

The sendmail program is the most popular mail transport agent (MTA) for Linux. The sendmail program does the physical sending and receiving of user and system email. You use sendmail in conjunction with a mail delivery agent (MDA) and a mail user agent (MUA). The MDA receives the incoming mail from sendmail and delivers it to the appropriate user. A typical Red Hat Linux installation uses procmail as the MDA for sendmail. Some other commonly used MDAs include mail.local and deliver. After the MDA has delivered the mail, the user uses an MUA to retrieve it. Some popular Unix MUAs include Pine, Elm, mutt, and mailx. Going the other direction, a user uses his MUA (Pine) to send mail directly to the MTA (sendmail).

POP3 and IMAP

POP3 (Post Office Protocol 3) and IMAP (Internet Message Access Protocol) are protocols that allow a user to retrieve her mail from the mail server to her mail reader. POP3 pulls mail from the mail spool, one message at a time, to a local spool. The user can then opt to delete all the messages on the mail spool or leave them all there. IMAP, however, reads the mail messages directly from the spool without copying the messages to the local spool. The user can then change, delete, and create folders, and so forth, on her local mail reader. When she does so, the changes are automatically applied to the mail spool.

FTP

FTP (File Transfer Protocol) is used to transfer files between systems over a network. For a user to connect to a system via FTP, either the user must supply a valid username and password, or the system must be able to accept anonymous users.

DNS

DNS (Domain Name Service) is used to translate domain names, such as redhat.com, to IP addresses, such as 199.183.24.134. Your DNS zones are managed by various registrars.

DHCP

DHCP (Dynamic Host Control Protocol)—a descendant of the boot protocol (bootp)—automatically assigns IP addresses to a client on a local network. DHCP uses User Datagram Protocol (UDP) while the client sends a DHCPDISCOVER message as a broadcast packet to the network.

The DHCP server receives this packet and assigns (either statically or dynamically) an IP address to the client. The DHCP server sends to the client a DHCPOFFER packet that contains an address and the lease time, as well as other pertinent networking information (such as address, netmask, gateway, name servers, and so on). The client then issues a DHCPREQUEST for the specified address. The server responds to this with the DHCPACK (which agrees with the client and starts the lease time).

This procedure differs from that used with bootp. In bootp's case, bootp sends the address without managing the lease time.

The Internet Software Consortium (ISC) dhcpd uses /etc/dhcpd.conf for configuration files and /etc/dhcpd.leases for lease information.

SMB

Samba is a server for the Server Message Block (SMB) protocol, which is the default file-sharing and printer-sharing protocol that all versions of Windows, OS/2, and Lan Manager use. Samba allows alternative operating systems to use a Unix or Linux box as a file or print server. Samba consists of two daemons: smbd (the Samba server) and nmbd (the NetBIOS name server). Clients use nmbd to find other hosts on the network. Configuration files are located in /etc/smb.conf and /etc/smbusers.

httpd

httpd (Hypertext Transport Protocol Daemon) is the HTTP (or World Wide Web) server. On Red Hat, the default httpd is Apache. Apache is a free Web server that was originally derived from the National Center for Supercomputing Applications (NCSA) HTTP server. The configuration files are located in /etc/httpd/conf/.

NIS

NIS (Network Information Service), originally called *Yellow Pages*, was developed by Sun Microsystems to simplify filesystem administration by maintaining the files in a central database. The clients contact the database server to retrieve information. Two basic NIS utilities include ypcat (which displays an NIS database) and ypmatch (which searches an NIS database).

inetd

This is the Internet services daemon that listens for service requests on network connections and then starts up the appropriate daemon to respond to the particular request.

Network Security

All Unix and Linux administrators should know the basic methods for securing their systems, including monitoring users and groups, setting file permissions properly, using umask, and using shadow passwords.

Monitoring Users and Groups

One of the most time-consuming duties of a Red Hat system administrator revolves around monitoring users and groups. Some basic administration tasks include monitoring services used, user accounts, and even software use.

Among other things, you'll need to monitor unneeded services. To see which services are automatically started at boot-time, run **ntsysv**. If any services that you don't use are checked, simply uncheck them. Doing so stops them from being started at boot-time. You can also stop services you're currently running (for example, **nfs**) by running **/etc/rc.d/init.d/nfs stop**.

Using common sense when you're assigning user accounts can save you many headaches later. For instance, set up guidelines when users choose their passwords; they shouldn't be the same as their usernames, nor should they be any type of English word. It's best to have a mixture of numbers and alphabetical characters, using upper- and lowercase. Also, allow shell access to only those users who need it. For instance, if a user is simply pulling his mail from the account, set his shell access to /usr/bin/passwd (or something similar). Doing so forces the user to change his password instead of allowing him to have shell access.

Another good area to monitor is software usage; keep an audit of the software you're running. Many times, unauthorized users exploit popular software, such as sendmail or BIND, and then gain root access to your system. Keep up to date by using the most current versions of your software.

Setting File Permissions Properly and Using umask

Every file, program, and directory is set up with file permissions. Executing an **ls** -l command in a directory prints the list of files, including details, as shown here:

```
-rw-rw-r--  1 kara   kara    7688 Jan 13 14:32 pick
drwxr-xr-x  9 kara   kara    1024 Mar 27 12:15 public_html
-rw-r--r--  1 root   root  434898 May 7 1998 termcap
-rw-r--r--  1 root   root    3313 Apr 30 1998 wgetrc
```

The first group of characters represents the permissions for the file. The permissions are noted (when you are using **ls -l**) by a string of 10 characters, **drwxrwxrwx** and combinations thereof. When a particular character is replaced by a hyphen (-), the permission assigned to that character is not granted. These characters are split into four groups. The first character is represented by a **d**, which stands for a directory. Therefore **drwxr-xr-x** indicates a directory, whereas -rw-rw-r-- indicates a file name. The remaining nine characters are split into three groups, **rwx rwx rwx**. The first group pertains to the owner, the second to the group, and the third to everybody else. The **r** in each case stands for readable, the **w** for writable, and the **x** for executable. Table 4.6 shows an example of permission settings.

Table 4.6 Permissions.	
Permission String	**Explanation**
-rwx------	Readable, writable, and executable by the owner only
-rwxr-x--	Readable, writable, and executable by the owner; readable and executable by the group
-rwxr-x--x	Readable, writable, and executable by the owner; readable and executable by the group; executable by the public

· ·

When you are assigning or referring to permissions of a file, the **r**, **w**, and **x** characters are assigned numeric values of 4, 2, and 1, respectively. You then add these values together per group to get the permission values (for example, **rwx** = r+w+x = 4+2+1 = 7; **r-x** = r+0+x = 4+ 0 +1 = 5). Table 4.7 shows permission strings and their numerical values.

Therefore, a file with **-rw-r--r--** file details has permissions set to 644. By default, all files are created with file permissions of 666. These permissions are adjusted per user by their default umask. A *umask* sets the file permissions by subtracting the user's umask from the default 666. For example, if a umask is set to 022, the files created within that shell and its subprocesses are set to 644 (666-022).

To set the umask within a shell, use the **umask** command. Here's an example:

```
#umask 022
```

For files that need to have their permissions changed—such as to be executable or to limit access to the owner and the group—you use only the **chmod** command. Here's an example:

```
#chmod 777 filename
```

This code sets the file name to have 777 permissions (**-rwxrwxrwx**), and the world can read, write, and execute them. However,

```
#chmod 770 filename
```

causes the owner and group—but not anyone else—to be able to read, write, and execute the file name.

By default, when a user account is created, that account is given its own user ID and group. To add users to other groups, edit the /etc/group file. The following is an excerpt from an /etc/group file:

```
luci::402:steve,kara,jburke
egypt::499:alan,barb
steve:x:500:
```

Table 4.7	Permission values.
Permission String	**Numerical Permission Value**
-rwx------	7-0-0
-rwxr-x---	7-5-0
-rwxr-x--x	7-5-1

In this example, files that have specified access to the group named luci give users steve, kara, and jburke access. On the other hand, alan and barb do not have access because they are assigned to the egypt group, not to luci, and vice versa. To set a specific group to use a file, use the **chgrp** command. For instance,

```
#chgrp luci index.html
```

sets the group ownership of index.html to the luci group. The index.html file has 664 permissions, is owned by steve, and has the luci group assigned to it. Therefore, steve and users in the luci group (steve, kara, and jburke) can read and write to that file, whereas everybody else can only read the file. The following code changes the group ownership of the index.html file to luci; this change is verified with the **ls –l** command:

```
#chgrp luci index.html
#ls -l index.html
-rw-rw-r-- 1 steve  luci    3709 Mar 22 17:57 index.html
```

Using Shadow Passwords

Shadow passwords have several purposes. First, the password field of /etc/passwd is removed (replaced by an x). The file /etc/shadow then contains the password hash. The permissions on the shadow file make it unreadable by anyone but root (and, on some distributions, the shadow group). As a result, extracting password hashes to run through crack or any other similar password-guessing program is more difficult as compared to running the program on a system that doesn't use shadow passwords. The shadow file contains password aging information as well.

You can convert a system to shadow passwords by running the pwconv program. If necessary, you can later convert it back by using pwunconv. The change should be transparent to all programs that use Pluggable Authentication Modules (PAM). You can control password aging with the change program.

Practice Questions

Question 1

What hardware architectures are currently supported by Red Hat? [Check all correct answers]

❏ a. Macintosh

❏ b. Alpha

❏ c. IBM-compatible

❏ d. SPARC

Answers b, c, and d are correct. Currently, Red Hat, Inc., offers official supported versions of Red Hat Linux for the Alpha, IBM-compatible, and SPARC architectures.

Question 2

What is the printing daemon?

○ a. **lpd**

○ b. **lpr**

○ c. **lpq**

○ d. **lpc**

Answer a is correct because **lpd** is the line printer daemon. Answer b is incorrect because **lpr** is the command that adds jobs to the queue. Answer c is incorrect because **lpq** lists the current jobs in the queue. Answer d is incorrect because **lpc** is the administrative interface for printing.

Question 3

What permission allows a file to be readable by the owner, group, and user, while allowing only write access to the owner and group?

○ a. 644

○ b. 750

○ c. 755

○ d. 774

Answer d is correct. Permissions of 774 give a file -**rwxrwxr--** permission attributes. This means that the file is **rwx** by owner, **rwx** by group, but only **r** by user. Answer a is incorrect because 644 allows **rw** by owner, **r** by group, and **r** by user. Answer b is incorrect because 750 allows **rwx** by owner, **r-x** by group, and no access by user. Answer c is incorrect because 755 allows **rwx** by owner, **r-x** by group, and **r-x** by user.

Question 4

Why do you need DNS?

You need DNS for domain name resolution. DNS is used to convert IP addresses to domain names, and domain names back to IP addresses. This process allows you to connect to the Internet with a domain name (such as **www.coriolis.com**) instead of having to remember 209.140.152.4.

Question 5

NFS is used to read filesystems on a Linux server with Windows clients.

○ a. True

○ b. False

Answer b is correct. Although NFS is required for setting up a network filesystem, it isn't used to read filesystems on a Linux server from a Windows client. In fact, you must set up Samba on the Linux server to be able to read Linux filesystems from your Windows client over a network.

Question 6

> To see the route between your machine and a remote machine, which of the following could you use?
>
> ○ a. **/usr/sbin/tracert**
>
> ○ b. **/usr/bin/traceroute**
>
> ○ c. **/bin/ping**
>
> ○ d. None of the above

Answer d is correct. Answer a is incorrect because the **tracert** command is used on Windows computers to trace a network route. Answer b is incorrect because, although the **traceroute** command is used on Linux to trace a route, the command is located in the /usr/sbin directory, not in /usr/bin. Answer c is incorrect because **ping** is used to send ICMP echo request packets to network hosts.

Question 7

> You must use a DNS server to ping **www.redhat.com**.
>
> ○ a. True
>
> ○ b. False

Answer a is correct. If you aren't using a DNS server, you have to ping the IP address of **www.redhat.com**.

Question 8

> What are the three classes of IP networks, and how do they differ?

The three classes of IP networks are the A, B, and C classes. These are based on 32-bit addresses, written in the xxx.xxx.xxx.xxx format. Class A networks are the largest class of network and include all addresses in a class (such as 204.0.0.0 through 204.255.255.255). Class B networks include addresses in a range such as 204.4.0.0 through 204.4.255.255. Class C is the most widely used network class. It is assigned in a 255-node range (for example, from 204.4.25.0 through 204.4.25.255).

Question 9

> Which of the following is a single valid Class C private network range?
>
> ○ a. 192.168.0.0 through 192.168.255.255
>
> ○ b. 10.0.0.0 through 10.255.255.255
>
> ○ c. 192.168.0.0 through 192.168.0.255
>
> ○ d. 10.1.0.0 through 10.1.255.255

Answer c is correct because it includes the full Class C address space for the 192.168.0 netblock, including the address nodes from .0 through .255. Answer a is incorrect because it indicates 255 Class C networks (equivalent to a Class B). Answer b is incorrect because it indicates a Class A network. Answer d is incorrect because it indicates a Class B network.

Question 10

> What are the seven layers in the OSI model?
>
> _____

The seven layers are Application, Presentation, Session, Transport, Network, Data Link, and Physical.

Need to Know More?

 Albitz, Paul and Cricket Liu. *DNS and BIND*. O'Reilly & Associates, 1998. ISBN 1-56592-512-2. This book covers implementation and usage of DNS and BIND.

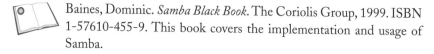 Baines, Dominic. *Samba Black Book*. The Coriolis Group, 1999. ISBN 1-57610-455-9. This book covers the implementation and usage of Samba.

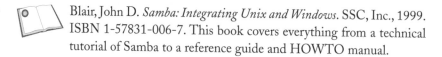 Blair, John D. *Samba: Integrating Unix and Windows*. SSC, Inc., 1999. ISBN 1-57831-006-7. This book covers everything from a technical tutorial of Samba to a reference guide and HOWTO manual.

 Costales, Bryan and Eric Allman. *Sendmail*. O'Reilly & Associates, 1997. ISBN 1-56592-222-0. This book covers all of the technical aspects of compiling, configuring, and using sendmail.

 Frisch, Æleen. *Essential System Administration*. O'Reilly & Associates, 1995. ISBN 1-56592-127-5. This book gives you many of the basics required for using Unix-style operating systems, commands, filesystems, and so forth.

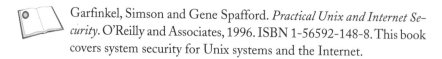 Garfinkel, Simson and Gene Spafford. *Practical Unix and Internet Security*. O'Reilly and Associates, 1996. ISBN 1-56592-148-8. This book covers system security for Unix systems and the Internet.

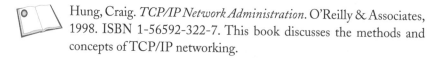 Hung, Craig. *TCP/IP Network Administration*. O'Reilly & Associates, 1998. ISBN 1-56592-322-7. This book discusses the methods and concepts of TCP/IP networking.

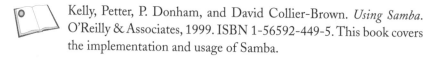 Kelly, Petter, P. Donham, and David Collier-Brown. *Using Samba*. O'Reilly & Associates, 1999. ISBN 1-56592-449-5. This book covers the implementation and usage of Samba.

 Schmidt, Friedhelm. *The SCSI Bus and IDE Interface*. Addison Wesley Longman, 1997. ISBN 0-20117-514-2. This book gives you all the details relating to the IDE interface and SCSI bus.

 Siever, Ellen. *Linux in a Nutshell*, O'Reilly & Assocates, 1997. ISBN 1-56592-167-4. This book gives you a look at the Linux operating system and its concepts.

http://www.linuxdoc.org/ is the Linux Documentation Project. This site links to many FAQs and HOWTOs related to Linux.

 http://www.samba.org contains documentation for Samba and information about the current development of Samba.

 http://www.sendmail.org contains documentation for sendmail and information about the current development of sendmail.

Installation

Terms you'll need to understand:

✓ Media

✓ Package

✓ Autodetect

✓ Bootloader

✓ X Window System

Techniques you'll need to master:

✓ Planning a successful installation

✓ Installing a Red Hat Linux system successfully

✓ Partitioning hard drives

✓ Understanding installation options and packages

✓ Configuring peripherals during installation

✓ Installing bootloader successfully

✓ Troubleshooting the installation

The underlying goal of becoming an RHCE is to certify your skills in the installation, configuration, and administration of a Red Hat Linux system. The first step to achieving your goals as an RHCE is to master the skills involved in installation. In this chapter, I'll discuss the steps to successfully install a Red Hat 6.2 system.

Getting Started

Before you begin your installation of Linux, you have to decide why you are installing Linux in the first place. What are your needs? What do you want to do? Linux has a vast variety of applications, system uses, and support options. Deciding what you're going to do in advance will help you decide what to install or set up.

Server vs. Workstation

You can use Linux in either a server or a workstation environment. In fact, if necessary, you can use it in both. If you are just a home user, or perhaps a work-at-home user, you're probably looking to set up a workstation. On your workstation, you can set up all your dial-up applications, as well as work on your home programming projects and more. However, if you are trying to set up a router, a file server, an Internet gateway, a mail server, a Dynamic Host Control Protocol (DHCP) server, or even a Quake server, you need to evaluate your requirements for setting up a server.

Hardware Requirements

If you're planning to set up an at-home or office workstation, your hardware requirements are minimal. Although it's doubtful you would be very happy surfing the Net—or compiling a new kernel—on a 486/33 with 16MB of RAM, it is possible. Linux can use most PC hardware. To see if your hardware is supported visit **www.redhat.com/hardware/**.

Note: Just-released hardware, if not released with a Linux driver, is typically supported within a few weeks of its release.

If you want to set up a router or a firewall, you can use any basic hardware setup. In fact, using a router or a firewall isn't CPU- or memory-intensive. You can therefore set up an adequate router on a 486 with 16MB of memory and a 250MB hard disk. Depending on your setup, you might also need to include networking hardware, such as network interface cards (NICs), modems, ISDN adapters, or even frame relay cards.

If you want to set up a network file server, your hardware requirements will be different from those when you are setting up a simple workstation or a router. NFS servers are not CPU bound, so a slower system such as a 486 is adequate. However, you should evaluate your speed and size requirements. If you will be serving a large number of files, or large files, you must keep ample hard disk space. If your machine will be serving a large number of users, or will be kept under high load, you should consider hard disk speed as well. You may opt to use SCSI disks, which have faster access times than IDE disks. Using SCSI disks, however, requires that you use a SCSI adapter. Memory is used on an NFS server for cache. Larger amounts of memory provide faster writing and accessibility on commonly used files.

If you are planning to set up a database server, you should evaluate all your input/output (I/O) needs. Database servers are very CPU-intensive, so you need a CPU that can handle the number of users using the system. As when implementing an NFS server, you need ample amounts of disk space and memory. The speed of your hardware (hard disk and memory) may also be a large factor when you choose hardware.

Pre-Installation

To make your Red Hat 6.2 installation go smoothly, you should plan as much of the installation as possible before beginning. Make sure you have several documentation and information resources available for quick reference during the installation or for troubleshooting afterward. An excellent resource for this is the *Red Hat 6.2 Installation Guide*. This guide is included with the retail version of Red Hat, which you can purchase directly from Red Hat (**http://www.redhat.com/**) or from a reseller. A hard copy of the manual is also available from Red Hat. You can find an electronic version of this manual on your Red Hat 6.2 CD in the /doc/install-guide/ directory. In addition, you can download the manual for free from Red Hat's Web site at **http://www.redhat.com/support/manuals/**. In addition, other great documents can be found on Red Hat's Web site at **http://www.redhat.com/docs/**.

Preparing Your Installation Media

After you have gathered the necessary installation materials, it's very important to make sure you have all the necessary media—such as your installation CD and boot disks—prepared. With Red Hat 6.2, different media can be used—or in some cases, are required—depending on the method you decide to use to boot the installation program.

You should also have access to any peripherals you want to set up during the installation, as well as all the technical information for any hardware connected to, or installed inside, the machine. If you are planning to install over a network, you should ensure that you are properly connected to your network and that you have located a stable server to install from.

Using a CD-ROM

If you have a bootable CD-ROM, you can start your installation by booting from the Red Hat 6.2 distribution CD. Make sure your BIOS is set to boot from the CD-ROM first. If you are planning to set up a dual-boot system (discussed in Chapter 7) and already have a DOS partition on the drive, you can choose to use the autoboot feature, located under the directory /dosutils on the Red Hat 6.2 CD. However, if you don't have a bootable DOS partition or a bootable CD-ROM, you must use a boot floppy.

Using a Boot Floppy

If the boot floppy is not included with your installation media, you can create it by using either rawrite (on DOS) or dd (on a Unix machine). Using either of these utilities writes the boot image to a floppy disk. You can run rawrite directly from the Red Hat 6.2 CD by following these steps:

1. Load the CD and change into the \dosutils directory.

2. Run **rawrite**. You are asked to supply the path to the boot directory that you want to load. For instance, for boot.img, enter **\images\boot.img**. You are then asked to provide your target. You are using a floppy disk, so choose **A:**.

3. You are next prompted to insert a floppy disk and press Enter. The process takes a few minutes, but when it's finished, you have a working boot disk.

To use the dd utility on a Unix system to create a boot disk from the CD, first mount the CD-ROM. Next, type the command **dd if=/***mnt/cdrom***/images/ boot.img of=/dev/fd0**, replacing */mnt/cdrom* with the mount directory of your CD-ROM. You might also need to replace **/dev/fd0** with the appropriate mount point of your floppy disk. The boot image, named boot.img, is on the Red Hat 6.2 CD under the /images directory. You can also download the boot.img file from one of Red Hat's FTP mirrors. A list of mirrors can be found at **http:// www.redhat.com/mirrors.html**.

Special boot floppies are required in these situations:

➤ If you're planning to install Red Hat Linux by using a PCMCIA network card or CD-ROM drive

➤ If you're planning to install Red Hat Linux via Network File System (NFS) or FTP

When you need one of the special boot disks just listed, you can create it by using the same method for creating a regular boot disk, as discussed earlier in this section. As we discussed for creating a regular boot disk, you can use rawrite (DOS) or dd (Unix) to write the special boot image to a floppy disk. The image

required to use PCMCIA devices during the installation is called pcmcia.img.
The image required to install via NFS or FTP is called bootnet.img.

Planning Your Configuration

During the installation, you are prompted for several configuration, setting, and installation options (including network settings, host and domain information, root password, and hardware specifications). Before beginning your installation, you should have all this information prepared so that you don't have to find it—or figure it out—during the installation process.

One of the most important configuration issues involves the physical hard drive installation. You should know exactly which drive and which partition you plan to install on. Knowing this information is especially important if you have multiple drives or if you have existing partitions from a previous Linux installation or other operating system. Specifying the wrong drive or partition during the installation will destroy any information on the drive, and you will not be able to recover it.

You should also plan your partition layout. If you're installing on a small drive, or setting up a long-term dedicated service machine, you may opt simply to install all the packages and directories in one partition (in addition to your swap partition). For installations on machines with multiple operating systems, existing partitions, or very large drives, it's best to create multiple partitions. The most common dedicated partitions are set up for the following filesystems:

➤ /

➤ /home

➤ /var

➤ /tmp

➤ /boot

➤ /usr

➤ swap

Setting up separate filesystems is helpful when you are managing large filesystems. Splitting filesystems among separate partitions saves rebuild time if one filesystem becomes corrupted; it also sets up better security when other users attempt to access the system. In addition, setting up these separate filesystems makes system upgrades easier. For example, creating a separate filesystem for users' home directories allows you to upgrade the entire system without damaging user data.

In addition to planning your physical installation, you should have the information prepared for configuration settings and installation options when prompted. Some of this information will include network settings, host and domain information, root password, and hardware specifications.

Installation Process

The installation method for Red Hat has changed significantly with each release. The release of Red Hat 6.1 was the first to introduce a graphical interface for the installation. However, for machines that wouldn't support X or for users (like me) who were accustomed to the text interface, both options were available.

Beginning Your Installation

As I mentioned earlier in this chapter, you begin your installation in different ways depending on your method of installation. The most standard installation type uses a boot floppy and the Red Hat 6.2 CD-ROM. Some options don't require a boot floppy at all. Others don't require the CD but require special boot floppies. The most common types of installations include DOS autoboot, boot floppy/CD combination, NFS, FTP, and hard drive installations.

DOS Autoboot Install

To begin your installation without using a boot floppy, you should have a bootable DOS partition on your machine. Boot to the DOS partition. Next, insert your Red Hat CD and change into the /dosutils directory. Under the /dosutils directory is a tool named autoboot.exe, which automatically boots from a DOS machine into the Linux installation. At the first welcome screen, press Enter at the "boot:" prompt to choose to Install Or Upgrade a Red Hat machine. If you want to do this in text mode, type **text** at the "boot:" prompt.

 The commercial Red Hat 6.2 CD is bootable. Therefore, for a system whose BIOS can support booting from CD-ROM, simply enable this option in your BIOS and boot directly from the CD-ROM.

Boot Floppy Install

To begin your installation using the standard boot floppy and the CD-ROM, simply turn on the machine with the boot floppy in the floppy drive. At the welcome screen, press Enter at the "boot:" prompt if you want to either install or upgrade your Red Hat machine via the graphical interface. If you want to use the text interface, type **text** at the "boot:" prompt and press Enter. If you are using a PCMCIA CD-ROM or network card for the installation, you must use the special

PCMCIA boot floppy that contains the pcmcia.img boot image. When prompted, choose to install with the CD media.

Installation Method

After you've booted with your selected boot floppy, you'll be prompted to choose which type of installation you want to use. Currently, there are five types of installations. See Table 5.1.

Installing Red Hat: The First Stage

The first step of the installation is to configure the installation process itself. It asks for your language, your keyboard style, and your mouse style (graphical interface only).

The installation process opens with a welcome screen that asks you to select the language that you want to use to install Red Hat. Red Hat 6.2 supports most European languages, including English, German, and Icelandic (see Figures 5.1 and 5.2).

Next, you are prompted for your keyboard configuration. Depending on the interface you're using (graphical or text), you have different options at this stage. With the graphical interface, you are prompted for the keyboard model you're using, the type of layout you'd like, and whether or not to use dead keys. You're even given the option to test your keyboard selection. See Figure 5.3. If you're using the text interface, you're prompted for the model of keyboard you're using. See Figure 5.4.

If you're using the graphical interface, you'll then be prompted for your mouse configuration. The text interface prompts you for your mouse configuration during the third phase of installation (when you configure the rest of your peripherals). The two interfaces differ slightly; with the graphical interface, you can specify the port and device of your mouse, but with the text interface, you specify only the model of your mouse. See Figures 5.5 and 5.6.

Table 5.1 Installation methods.	
Method Type	**Description**
CD-ROM	Installs from either an internal CD-ROM or a PCMCIA CD-ROM. Requires the regular or PCMCIA boot disk.
FTP	Installs from an FTP server. Requires the network or PCMCIA boot disk.
Hard Drive	Used if Red Hat Linux files were downloaded or copied to a local hard drive. Requires the regular or PCMCIA boot disk.
HTTP	Installs from a Web server. Requires the network or PCMCIA boot disk.
NFS Image	Installs from an NFS server hosting a Red Hat Linux CD-ROM or a mirror of Red Hat Linux. Requires the network or PCMCIA boot disk.

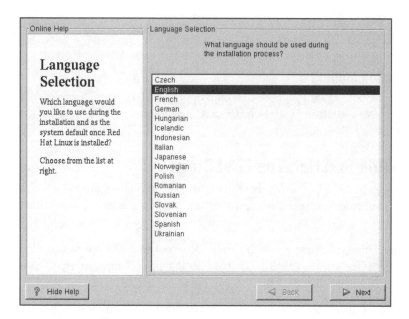

Figure 5.1 Language Selection (graphical interface).

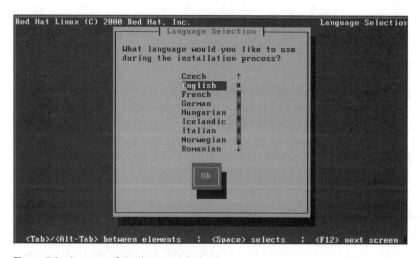

Figure 5.2 Language Selection (text interface).

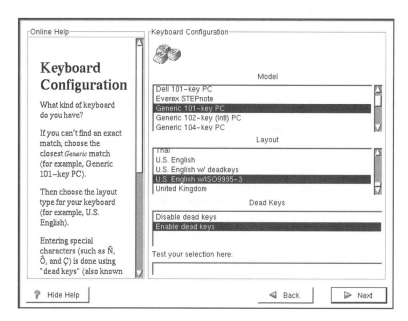

Figure 5.3   Keyboard Configuration (graphical interface).

Figure 5.4   Keyboard Selection (text interface).

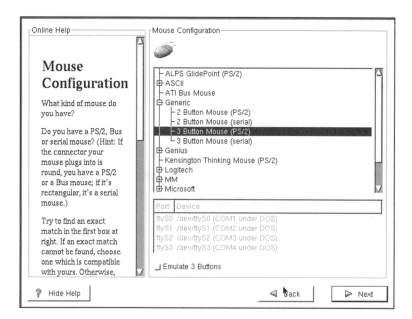

Figure 5.5 Mouse Configuration (graphical interface).

Figure 5.6 Mouse Selection (text interface).

Installing Red Hat: The Second Stage

The first steps during the second stage of your installation determine the overall plan for your installation. In this stage, you choose whether to do a regular installation or upgrade an existing Linux installation. If you choose to do a regular installation, you have to choose either a preconfigured option—such as GNOME

Workstation, KDE Workstation, or Server—or a Custom installation. Figures 5.7 and 5.8 show the windows that prompt you to choose one of these options. Unlike previous versions of Red Hat's graphical installer, you are now given the opportunity to use fdisk instead of Disk Druid.

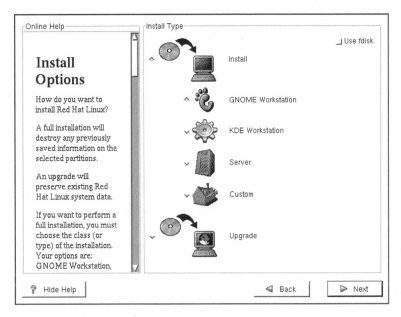

Figure 5.7   Install Type (graphical interface).

Figure 5.8   Installation Type (text interface).

GNOME and KDE Workstation Configurations

Choosing either Workstation configuration (GNOME or KDE) automatically installs the most common packages used on a personal workstation. In addition to the base Red Hat installation, some of the workstation features include many of the development packages. Both options install more X components than does the Server alternative. Packages such as graphics tools and multimedia are installed. The difference between the two Workstation options is the desktop environment. Choosing the GNOME option installs GNOME as your default environment and installs all of the GNOME tools and packages. Choosing KDE, obviously, installs KDE as the desktop environment and installs all of the KDE tools and packages. The differences between KDE and GNOME will be discussed in Chapter 9.

The Server Configuration

Choosing the Server configuration automatically installs many of the most common packages used on a networked server. Unlike the Workstation configuration, the Server configuration chooses the majority of the most stable packages. With the development packages and extra X Window tools eliminated, fewer packages are installed. Some of the features installed with these packages include:

➤ Anonymous FTP

➤ Caching name server

➤ BIND

➤ Advanced Perl

➤ PostgreSQL

➤ Samba

You should not choose a preconfigured type of installation if you are dual booting or have any other existing Linux partitions on any hard drive in your system. The Workstation installation will overwrite NT's bootloader in the MBR and will erase all other Linux partitions in your system. The Server installation will erase all partitions (including non-Linux partitions) from all of your hard drives.

The Custom Configuration

Choosing the Custom configuration allows you to set up any particular configuration you want. You are given two ways to select your packages: You can select either a feature that automatically selects the necessary packages or one that selects individual packages manually. You are even given the option to install everything, which is simple for new users.

Examining Hard Disk Options

After specifying your installation type, you'll specify exactly where you want the Linux installation to be physically placed. You do this by partitioning and formatting the disk and setting up mount points. If you are using the text interface, you are asked to select a disk-editing tool: either Disk Druid or fdisk. If you are using the graphical interface, you already chose a tool by selecting Use fdisk in the last prompt, or not selecting it. If you didn't select Use fdisk (see Figure 5.7), you'll automatically use Disk Druid. Next you are asked to specify the disks you want to partition. Red Hat will detect the drives on your system and, in both interfaces, will present you with a list of detected drives to choose from.

Disk Druid is Red Hat's install-time disk management utility. It can create and delete disk partitions according to user-supplied requirements as well as manage mount points for each partition. The traditional Linux disk-partitioning tool is fdisk, introduced in Chapter 3. The fdisk program is a bit more flexible than Disk Druid, but fdisk requires you to have some experience with disk partitioning and to be accustomed to using a text interface.

Disk Druid

Selecting Disk Druid presents you with a graphical user interface to help you partition the drive and select mount points on the drive. Disk Druid is available only when you're installing Red Hat Linux. The first screen is the Current Disk Partitions screen. This screen shows all currently established partitions and disk drive summaries. See Figures 5.9 and 5.10.

The differences between the two interfaces are minimal, with the graphical interface allowing you to reset the entire table or set up software RAID devices from the main menu. Each line in the Current Disk Partitions section represents a disk partition. Each line has five fields:

➤ *Mount Point*—Indicates where the partition will be mounted when Red Hat is installed.

➤ *Device*—Displays the partition's device name.

➤ *Requested*—Specifies the minimum size requested when the partition was created.

➤ *Actual*—Shows the space that is currently assigned to the partition.

➤ *Type*—Shows the partition's type, such as Linux Native, Linux Swap, or other type.

Figure 5.9 Disk Druid (graphical interface).

Figure 5.10 Disk Druid (text interface).

Each line in the Drive Summaries section represents a hard disk on your system. Each line has six fields:

➤ *Drive*—Shows the hard disk's device name.

➤ *Geom [C/H/S]*—Shows the hard disk's geometry, which consists of three numbers that represent the number of cylinders, heads, and sectors. The hard disk geometry is reported by the hard disk itself.

➤ *Total*—Shows the total space available on the hard disk.

➤ *Used*—Shows how much of the hard disk space is currently assigned to partitions.

➤ *Free*—Shows how much of the hard disk space is still available.

➤ *Used*—Shows a bar graph that represents the space currently used on the hard disk.

The buttons located at the bottom of the screen are what makes Disk Druid a popular tool. With the Add button, you can add partitions to a drive. With Edit, you can modify attributes of the partition selected under the Current Disk Partitions section. With Delete, you can delete current partitions. With Reset (graphical interface only), you can reset the entire partition table. The OK and Back buttons allow you to navigate backward and forward as well as through the installation, depending on whether you are finished or need to return to the first step.

 If you're setting up different partitions for separate filesystems, you must mount each partition to the particular filesystem. For instance, if you're setting up a partition for /var, set the mount point to /var (as opposed to /).

fdisk

The traditional Linux partitioning tool is fdisk. It's available both during and after installation. After installation, you can use fdisk when repartitioning drives, adding drives, and so on. It is a text-based tool and is not considered very user-friendly.

Note: You should be familiar with disk partitioning before using fdisk.

If you selected Use fdisk with the graphical interface, you'll execute fdisk in a window exactly as you would with the text interface or after installation. See Figure 5.11. When you select fdisk to edit partitions, you see the Partition Disks dialog box (text interface method shown in Figure 5.12), which lists every disk on your computer.

To edit a specific disk, highlight the disk you'd like to partition and then select Edit. Next, you enter fdisk and can partition the disk you selected. (You can repeat this process for each disk you want to partition.) When you're finished, select Done.

After selecting a drive, you are dropped into a command-line program to edit the selected drive. At the "Command (m for help):" prompt, type **m** and press Enter. Doing so gives you a list of all available commands (as discussed in Chapter 3).

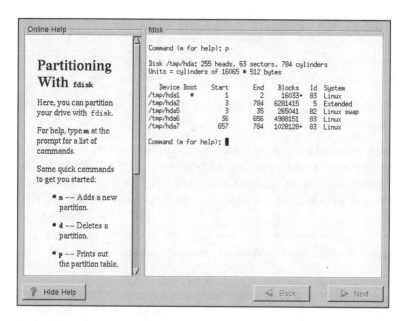

Figure 5.11 fdisk (graphical interface).

Figure 5.12 fdisk (text interface).

First, enter **p** to print the current partition table. You can then add and delete partitions as needed, change their type, and more.

After setting up all the appropriate partitions, enter **w** to write to the table and exit. You are then returned to Disk Druid, where you are asked to specify your mount points. See the previous section on Disk Druid for details.

Partition Schemes

In addition to setting partitions for filesystems or operating systems, you must dedicate a partition to Linux Swap. The Linux Swap partition is used as virtual random access memory (RAM). The size of the swap partition is typically determined by the amount of installed RAM in the system and the size of your hard drive; however, the size is limited to 2GB. After you select the partitions for your drive and set them to be the proper partition types, the Red Hat installation formats the swap space and the separate partitions. The following is an example of a recommended partitioning scheme for a Red Hat Linux server:

➤ 300MB / (root; this size may vary)

➤ 16MB /boot

➤ 300 through 700MB /usr

➤ 512MB /home (minimum)

➤ Swap partition with a maximum of 2GB

➤ The sizes of /tmp and /var vary, depending on the number of users and the size of your system

A typical Red Hat Linux installation uses the DOS-style partition table, which recognizes only four primary partitions. To resolve this problem, create extended partitions that hold logical partitions. An extended partition can hold up to 12 partitions, allowing for a maximum of 16 partitions on one drive. Regardless of the number of primary partitions, the first logical partition always has a device number of 5. For example, the first logical partition on the first IDE hard drive would be named hda5.

Formatting

After completing your partitions with either Disk Druid or fdisk, you are prompted to format your drives. At this point, there are no significant differences between the graphical and text installations except for appearance. In both interfaces you can select or deselect the partitions you want to format. You can also select the option to check for bad blocks during your format.

Installing Red Hat: The Third Stage

During this phase of the installation, the graphical and text interfaces present items in different orders. We'll introduce things in the order in which Red Hat's graphical interface method introduces them.

Installing LILO

LILO (Linux Loader) is the Linux bootloader. During the initial configuration, you're prompted for where you want to install the bootloader: either in the master boot record (MBR) or in the first sector of the boot partition. Typical Linux systems use LILO as their chosen bootloader and install the bootloader in the MBR. Installing it here is especially important if you want the bootloader to manage multiple operating systems installed on the same system. However, if you plan to use another bootloader, such as the NT bootloader or OS/2 bootloader, you should install the Linux bootloader on the first sector of the boot partition and point your existing bootloader to the boot partition. See Figures 5.13 and 5.14.

The graphical interface and the text interface handle LILO configuration differently. The graphical interface (shown in Figure 5.13) allows you to set options for

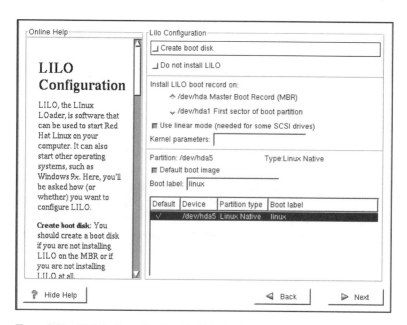

Figure 5.13   LILO Configuration (graphical interface).

Figure 5.14   LILO Configuration (text interface).

boot disks and to choose whether or not to install LILO, where to install LILO, and—with dual-booting or multi-booting systems—which operating system to load as the default. The graphical interface also gives you a few other options to customize your LILO configuration, such as boot label. The text-interface configuration handles boot disks, LILO installation location, and other operating systems in multiple windows. (LILO configuration is shown in Figure 5.14. Boot disk and installation location windows are not shown.) Other customization isn't allowed with this installation method.

If you've configured LILO properly, when you boot your freshly installed Linux system, you should be able to press the Tab key at the "LILO:" prompt and get a list of choices. For instance, if you set up LILO to dual-boot either Linux or Windows (if these are your boot image labels), pressing the Tab key should print

```
linux      windows
```

You can then either enter one of your options or let LILO time out. If it times out, the default operating system will automatically boot.

Network Configuration

If you selected and installed networking support, you're automatically prompted to enter your local networking information. (During installation, you're not prompted to set up dial-up information—you must configure dial-up after you have installed Red Hat Linux.) To set up networking, you can use Static IP addresses or DHCP. See Figures 5.15 and 5.16.

As with LILO configuration, with network configuration, the graphical interface handles everything in a single window, but the text interface uses multiple window prompts. In addition to the network configuration window shown in Figure 5.16, the text interface has a separate window for host-name information (see Figure 5.17).

When you set up a system for use with a static IP address, you're asked to provide standard local network information. You must enter a unique local IP address for your machine. This number should be assigned by your network administrator or Internet Service Provider. If you do not have an assigned address, do not simply pick a random address. You should use IANA-assigned space for private, non-routable addresses such as 192.168.x.x or 10.x.x.x. You are then asked to provide your netmask, gateway, and primary name server settings for the system. Next, you are prompted for your DNS information, such as domain name, host name, and backup name server locations.

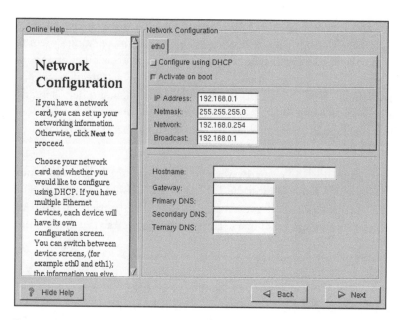

Figure 5.15 Network Configuration (graphical interface).

Figure 5.16 Network Configuration (text interface).

You should specify a host name for your machine even if you are not on a network. If you do not specify a host name, your machine will be called "localhost."

Figure 5.17   Hostname Configuration (text interface).

Time Configuration

Unlike some operating systems, Linux- and Unix-based systems are affected if the system time is not set properly. One of the core Linux applications affected is cron. Scheduled jobs will not run at the correct time of day if the time isn't set properly. During the time configuration stage of the installation, you're prompted for your time zone and asked whether or not you want to set your hardware clock to GMT (Greenwich Mean Time). A special feature of the graphical interface is that you can click on a map to indicate your location rather than scrolling through a long worldwide location list. See Figures 5.18 and 5.19.

Note: You should always check the Hardware Clock Set To GMT box unless you are dual-booting your system with Windows. Otherwise, Daylight Savings Time can upset your system.

Account Configuration

A new feature added since Red Hat 6.0 is the ability to create not only the root user during installation but at least one additional (optional) user as well. As I've mentioned previously, the graphical interface configures both of these options in one screen, whereas the text interface takes two screens.

One of the features of the graphical interface is that the system checks to see that your root password is valid before you commit it. If the password is too short, the system will automatically tell you. If the password is too easily guessed, the system will tell you that, too. When your password is valid, the system will report that the root password is accepted. See Figure 5.20.

Figure 5.18 Time Zone Selection (graphical interface).

Figure 5.19 Time Zone Selection (text interface).

Figure 5.20   Account Configuration (graphical interface).

Authentication Configuration

Red Hat Linux has two features that make passwords more secure: the implementation of MD5 passwords and shadow passwords. If you're going to be doing administration over a network with NIS, you can enable the use of NIS during this phase as well. It is always recommended that you enable both MD5 and shadow passwords unless you are using NIS.

Enabling MD5 passwords allows you to use a long password (up to 256 characters) as opposed to the standard 8 characters. Enabling shadow passwords helps to protect your password files by storing them in a file, /etc/shadow, that is readable only as root.

The graphical and text interfaces have the same options for authentication configuration. With both, you have three options: enable MD5 passwords, enable shadow passwords, and enable NIS.

Package Group Selection

During the Custom configuration installation, you are first given the option to select package groups to install. You can choose from among 26 groups, listed and described in Table 5.2, in addition to simply installing everything. The difference between the graphical and text interfaces at this stage is limited only to appearance, as shown in Figures 5.21 and 5.22.

Table 5.2 Installation package groups.	
Package Group	**Description**
Printer Support	Installs printer support to a local or network printer
X Window System	Installs support for a graphical user interface
GNOME	Installs tools within the X Window System
KDE	Installs the X Window environment KDE
Mail/WWW/News Tools	Enables your machine to manage and use mail and Internet services
DOS/Windows Connectivity	Allows connections to and from DOS and Windows clients
Graphics Manipulation	Installs packages to read, create, and alter graphics files
Games	Installs games for entertainment
Multimedia Support	Installs packages that allow multimedia use
Networked Workstation	Enables the machine to communicate with other machines on a network
Dial-Up Workstation	Enables the machine to communicate with other machines via a modem
News Server	Sets up the machine to be used as a news server
NFS Server	Allows the machine to serve as a network file server
SMB (Samba) Connectivity	Enables the machine to communicate with Windows clients
IPX/NetWare Connectivity	Installs the capability to communicate with or as NetWare clients
Anonymous FTP Server	Installs the packages necessary to allow anonymous file transfer service
Web Server	Installs packages necessary to provide HTTP and Web service
DNS Name Server	Sets up the machine to serve as a domain name server
Postgres (SQL) Server	Enables the machine to host a SQL database server
Network Management	Allows the machine to manage network workstations remotely
Authoring Publishing	Enables the capability to edit documents with publishing capability
Emacs	Installs the popular text editing tool
Development	Allows the machine to be used to program
Kernel Development	Installs packages necessary for programming kernel code
Clustering	Enables the system to host or participate in cluster projects
Utilities	Installs multiple system utilities
Everything	Installs everything

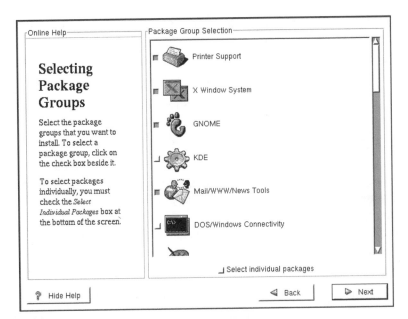

Figure 5.21 Package Group Selection (graphical interface).

Figure 5.22 Package Group Selection (text interface).

Selecting Individual Packages

Choosing the option Select Individual Packages at the bottom of either screen allows you to select or deselect all the packages manually. Unlike some early distributions, in this distribution, these packages are now sorted into a directory tree, arranged within 6 categories divided into 28 subcategories. The text interface for this stage is similar to the design of the Package Group Selection screen, as shown in Figure 5.22. The graphical interface, however, is quite different, presenting the category tree in a window on the left and the package icons on the right. To select a package, click on the icon; a large red checkmark will appear. To deselect the package, click on the icon again. See Figure 5.23.

The first category is Amusements. Within this category, you can find two subcategories: games and graphics. Games include programs such as fortune and xbill. Graphics include items such as xmorph and xscreensaver.

The second category (and the largest in package quantity) is Applications. The 13 subcategories list all the applications available for initial installation. The applications are divided into application-type groups, including archiving, communications, cryptography, databases, editors, engineering, file, Internet, multimedia, productivity, publishing, system, and text. Manually selecting these packages is helpful when you're budgeting disk space or when you don't want a lot of programs that you'll never use.

Some of the most used applications on Linux can be found in these groups:

➤ *Applications/Communications*—Includes programs such as mgetty, sendfax, minicom, and dip for use with fax, modem, and serial console connectivity.

➤ *Applications/Editors*—Includes the Emacs, jed, and vim text editors.

Figure 5.23   Individual Package Selection (graphical interface).

➤ *Applications/Internet*—Includes mail readers, news readers, Web browsers, chat clients, and compression tools.

➤ *Applications/Multimedia*—Includes tools such as GIMP (for graphic manipulation) and programs such as rhsound and mpg123 (for use with audio and other multimedia projects).

➤ *Applications/Publishing*—Includes text-manipulation tools, such as ghostscript, groff, and pdf.

➤ *Applications/System*—Includes many of the system-specific tools. Some of the most used packages in this group are the mtools and the netcfg, pciutils, screen, and rdate tools.

The next category is Development. The five subcategories contain all the development packages. You can use development packages for debugging programs, programming and compiling, and including the latest features of a specific program. The five Development subcategories and their most commonly used packages are:

➤ *Development/Debugging*—Includes program-debugging tools, such as gdb and lsof.

➤ *Development/Languages*—Includes the most commonly used language compilers, such as ecgs, **Perl,** python, **Tcl,** and tk.

➤ *Development Libraries*—Includes libraries such as Mesa, XFree86, GNOME, and qt.

➤ *Development/System*—Includes the packages needed to install kernel headers and kernel source.

➤ *Development/Tools*—Includes packages to install cvs, make, and patch.

The largest group of packages (in installation size) is the Documentation group. Within this group you can:

➤ Select individual documentation packages for specific programs, such as sendmail, XFree86, or GIMP.

➤ Select the Linux man-pages and FAQs (frequently asked questions).

➤ Install Linux HOWTOs in multiple languages, ranging from Chinese to English to Polish.

The next category is for System Environment. The five subcategories include packages to set up and configure your system. The very heart of the Linux installation is found within these groups. They are:

➤ *System Environment/Base*—Contains such popular packages as ipchains, mkkickstart, and yp-tools.

➤ *System Environment/Daemons*—Contains such packages as apache, BIND, dhcp, inetd, and Squid.

➤ *System Environment/Kernel*—Contains important packages such as kernel-BOOT and kernel-smp.

➤ *System Environment/Libraries*—Contains library packages such as gtk, libjpeg, qt, and svgalib.

➤ *System Environment/Shells*—Contains packages for shells, such as bash2, mc, and tcsh.

The final category is for User Interface packages. Within this group are three categories from which you can select individual packages. These packages are used, and in some cases required, for setting up your X Window graphical user interface. The groups are:

➤ *User Interface/Desktops*—Choose from among the multiple desktop environments that you can use with Linux. Some of these include AfterStep, FVWM, KDE, and WindowMaker.

➤ *User Interface/X*—Here you can find X tools and fonts, as well as gdm and xinitrc.

➤ *User Interface/X Hardware Support*—Here you can find configuration tools, video hardware drivers, and support, as well as XF86Setup and Xconfigurator.

After selecting all the packages you plan to install on the system, you will be notified if there are any package dependency requirements that need to be met. This means that if you select one package that requires another package to run appropriately and you didn't select the required package, you are prompted to install the required package.

X Configuration

If X was one of the packages you chose to install, you'll be prompted to configure your X options. You'll be prompted to configure your video, monitor, and X Window System options.

You are first asked to set up your monitor. Many popular monitor types are already listed and configured with standard vertical and horizontal refresh rates and frequencies. If your monitor isn't listed, choose the Custom option, and find the horizontal and vertical frequency and refresh rates in your owner's manual. If you can't locate your owner's manual, try looking for information on the manufacturer's Web site. See Figures 5.24 and 5.25.

Note: Setting a frequency or refresh rate higher than what your monitor can support might damage your monitor.

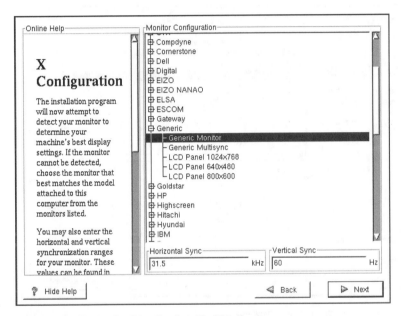

Figure 5.24   Monitor Configuration (graphical interface).

Figure 5.25   Monitor Configuration (text interface).

Next, Red Hat Linux looks for your video card; if the card isn't detected, you're prompted to select your video card from a list. If your video card isn't listed, select the Unlisted Card option. Red Hat then installs the appropriate X server for your video card. At this stage, there are a few differences between the graphical and text interfaces. The graphical interface makes it easier to customize, test, or even just skip X configuration. See Figures 5.26 and 5.27.

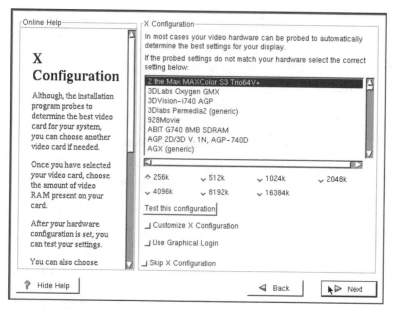

Figure 5.26   X Configuration (graphical interface).

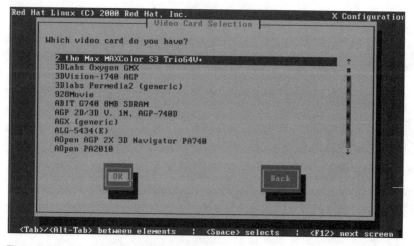

Figure 5.27   X Configuration: Video Card Selection (text interface).

After you select your monitor, X runs an automatic test. Your screen might flash, and you are then prompted to confirm whether your screen appears to be running properly and at your selected resolution. To complete the setup of the X Window System under Red Hat 6.2, you can select a new feature to automatically start X at boot-time.

Installing Red Hat: The Final Stage

After all the dependency requirements are met, Red Hat begins the physical installation process. It creates the physical filesystem on the drive to which you're installing, checks to see that you have adequate disk space, and finally begins installing the chosen packages. In addition, Red Hat 6.2 automatically detects the type of CPU you have installed and optimizes the installed kernel. The autodetected types of CPUs include Pentium Pro, PII/PIII, and AMD's K5 and K6. All other CPUs are set up with the default 386 settings.

 During the installation process, you can view installation messages and other information on the first five virtual consoles. Pressing Alt+F1 displays the installer. Pressing Alt+F2 presents a bash shell. Pressing Alt+F3 displays an Installer message log. Pressing Alt+F4 shows all of your kernel messages. Pressing Alt+F5 displays the standard output of mke2fs.

Verifying Your New Installation

After you complete your installation, the first thing you'll do is restart your machine. When your machine successfully boots, log in as "root" with the root password you selected during the installation. Before trying to use programs or services on the newly installed Linux machine, view your dmesg log file by entering **cat /var/log/dmesg** at the prompt. The output of dmesg is a log of the messages that you see during boot-time. Within the dmesg log, you can look for the messages stating that the kernel has initialized your partitions, your ethernet card, and more. Listing 5.1 shows a sample section of dmesg output.

Listing 5.1   Snippet from /var/log/dmesg.

```
................................ done.
PCI: PCI BIOS revision 2.10 entry at 0xfb5a0
PCI: Using configuration type 1
PCI: Probing PCI hardware
Linux NET4.0 for Linux 2.2
Swansea University Computer Society NET3.039
NET4: Unix domain sockets 1.0 for Linux NET4.0.
NET4: Linux TCP/IP 1.0 for NET4.0
```

```
IP Protocols: ICMP, UDP, TCP, IGMP
Starting kswapd v 1.5
Detected PS/2 Mouse Port
pty: 256 Unix98 ptys configured
Real Time Clock Driver v1.09
PIIX3: IDE controller on PCI bus 00 dev 39
PIIX3: not 100% native mode: will probe irqs later
    ide0: BM-DMA at 0xf000-0xf007, BIOS settings: hda:pio, hdb:pio
    ide1: BM-DMA at 0xf008-0xf00f, BIOS settings: hdc:pio, hdd:pio
hda: IBM-DHEA-36480, ATA DISK drive
ide0 at 0x1f0-0x1f7,0x3f6 on irq 14
hda: IBM-DHEA-36480, 6197MB w/476kB Cache, CHS=790/255/63, (U)DMA
eth0: 3Com 3c905 100baseTx at 0x6100, 00:10:4b:63:05:94, IRQ 17
```

After viewing the dmesg file, check to see that things are working properly. Take a look at your /var/log/messages file to see if any processes have any errors. In addition, examine your installation process in /tmp/install.log.

Troubleshooting Your Installation

After viewing the dmesg logs, you might notice that specific pieces of hardware aren't loading properly. If you think a piece of hardware has a compatibility issue—or perhaps the driver for your hardware was not available during installation—check out the "Hardware Compatibility HOWTO" from the Linux Documentation Project at **http://linuxdoc.org/HOWTO/Hardware-HOWTO.html**.

Another troubleshooting source is Red Hat, which offers a hardware guide for the Red Hat distribution. Red Hat also offers version-specific lists for older versions of Red Hat. These lists can be found at **http://www.redhat.com/hardware/**. Although both Red Hat and the Linux Documentation Project list much of the same information, the Red Hat list is most often more accurate and current because Red Hat follows the support for each individual version.

One of the most common installation problems other than hardware support relates to LILO. Occasionally, a disk sector is bad and LILO doesn't install to it properly. Other times, LILO doesn't work because it was configured incorrectly. One of the best ways to troubleshoot your LILO problems is to watch the output of LILO itself.

Watch for your LILO prompt. If you don't get any part of the LILO prompt, LILO didn't load. If you get an L, the first-stage bootloader is loaded and started. If you get LI, the second-stage bootloader is loaded. If you get LIL, the second-stage bootloader is started. If you get LIL?, the second-stage bootloader was loaded at an incorrect address. If you get LIL-, the descriptor table is corrupt. If you get LILO, all of LILO has been loaded correctly.

When you're comfortable with your current Linux installation, you must check for errata. Errata lists contain updates, bug fixes, and more for your fresh Linux installation. For Red Hat's errata list, visit **www.redhat.com/support/errata/**. You should download and install all necessary update packages. These packages can be downloaded from **ftp.updates.redat.com** or a mirror site.

Practice Questions

Question 1

> What command(s) can you use to create a Linux installation boot floppy?
>
> ○ a. **bb** and **rawwrite**
>
> ○ b. **dd** and **rawrite**
>
> ○ c. **vi** and **pico**
>
> ○ d. **mkboot disk**

Answer b is correct. The dd and rawrite tools are the Unix and DOS tools used to create an installation boot disk. The **mkbootdisk** command (answer d) is used to create after-installation boot disks, such as those used in Rescue boot-disk sets. Answers a and c are incorrect because **bb** is not a valid command, and both vi and pico are text-editing tools, not commands for writing to a boot floppy.

Question 2

> What types of installations require a special boot disk? [Check all correct answers]
>
> ❑ a. PCMCIA
>
> ❑ b. FTP
>
> ❑ c. NFS
>
> ❑ d. HTTP
>
> ❑ e. Samba

Answers a, b, c, and d are correct. An installation that requires a PCMCIA device (answer a)—such as a CD-ROM or a network card—during installation needs a boot disk made with the pcmcia.img image. FTP (answer b), NFS (answer c), and HTTP (answer d) all require a boot disk made with the bootnet.img. Answer e is incorrect because Samba is no longer supported as of Red Hat 6.2.

Question 3

How can you troubleshoot LILO problems after installation?

You can troubleshoot LILO problems by examining how LILO responds when you boot the computer. If you don't get the LILO prompt and don't boot, you should use the boot disk to see that LILO was installed and to check that it will be loaded. If you receive a part of the LILO command, such as L or LIL?, you can tell what happened (not all of the bootloader was loaded or started, or the address or descriptor table is corrupt, for example).

Question 4

Where can you find out about hardware compatibility issues?

Several online resources are available to help you learn about current hardware compatibility and other hardware issues. You can find the Red Hat-specific site at **http://www.redhat.com/hardware/**. The Linux Documentation Project, a general Linux hardware compatibility resource, is located at **http://linuxdoc.org/ HOWTO/Hardware-HOWTO.html**.

Question 5

What logs should you view after an installation to ensure proper installation as well as to troubleshoot installation problems? [Check all correct answers]

❏ a. /var/log/messages

❏ b. /var/log/maillog

❏ c. /tmp/install.log

❏ d. /bin/dmesg

Answers a and c are correct. You should read /var/log/messages and /tmp/install.log after installation. Answer b is incorrect because /var/log/maillog is used to log mail transactions sent by sendmail. Answer d is incorrect because /bin/dmesg isn't a log itself; however, the output of the command does provide helpful debugging information.

Question 6

> What is a bootloader?

A bootloader is a program used to manage the boot process of an operating system. Many bootloaders, such as LILO, can manage the boot processes of multiple operating systems, allowing you to boot more than one operating system from separate partitions on the same machine. At this time, however, you cannot boot multiple operating systems simultaneously.

Question 7

> What network setting options are you given during the installation process?
>
> ○ a. Static, DHCP
>
> ○ b. Dynamic, static, DHCP
>
> ○ c. DHCP, NIS, dial-up
>
> ○ d. Kickstart, routable, assigned

Answer a is correct. Although you can choose to install PPP support, you aren't given the option to configure it during installation. Also the dynamic, routable, and assigned options listed in answers b and d are incorrect because they are not valid options for a Red Hat Linux installation.

Question 8

> You can no longer use either fdisk or Disk Druid during the text or the graphical installation methods.
>
> ○ a. True
>
> ○ b. False

Answer b (false) is correct. In Red Hat 6.1, if you chose either the graphical or the text installation interface, you were limited to using Disk Druid to partition your hard drive. However, 6.2 added fdisk into the graphical interface so you can use whichever you choose for either installation method.

Question 9

Why do you use the "Emulate Three Buttons" option during mouse configuration?

You use this option when you are installing a two-button mouse. The third button is used in some applications for special purposes. It is most commonly used to aid in the Copy and Paste feature of X. (Highlight the appropriate text with the left mouse button to copy it, and then click on the appropriate place with the middle mouse button to paste the text.) You then have this functionality by clicking on both buttons simultaneously.

Question 10

What services can't be configured during installation? [Check all correct answers]

❑ a. PPP

❑ b. Sound

❑ c. Video

❑ d. Scanner

❑ e. Apache

❑ f. Trackball

Answers a, b, d, and e are correct. Although you can install Apache during installation, you can't configure it. Answer c is incorrect because video is configured during the X Window System installation. Answer f is incorrect because the trackball is configured during mouse installation.

Task 1

Practice installing the Red Hat Linux 6.2 distribution on the Intel platform. Try the different Workstation, Server, and Custom installations and see how they are different. Read and install different packages to learn how they interrelate. Use the different types of installation media, and try the installation via NFS, HTTP, FTP, and more. Become comfortable with maneuvering through the different installation prompts, options, and programs.

Need to Know More?

Red Hat Software, Inc. *Red Hat Linux 6.2: Operating System Installation Guide.* ISBN 1-58569-076-7. Chapters 3 through 6 discuss the installation steps of Red Hat 6.2 in depth. You can also find this online

at **http://www.redhat.com/support/manuals/**.

http://www.redhat.com/knowledgebase/rhlinuxdocs.html/—Within the documentation portion of **http://www.redhat.com**, Red Hat's Web site, you can find links to PostScript versions of the previously mentioned *Red Hat 6.2 Installation Guide* that you can download and print, as well as HTML versions that you can search online.

Basic Configuration and Administration

. . . .

Terms you'll need to understand:

✓ Peripheral

✓ User

✓ Package

✓ Interface

✓ Mount

✓ Mount point

✓ User environment

Techniques you'll need to master:

✓ Administering users

✓ Configuring peripherals

✓ Mounting filesystems

✓ Using Red Hat Package Manager (RPM)

✓ Using kudzu

✓ Configuring networking

✓ Using virtual consoles

The development of Red Hat 6.2 saw a large increase in the number of services and programs you could install and configure automatically during the installation process. With Linux, as with most operating systems, you still have some configuration to do after your installation. To be a successful RHCE, you must know how to configure packages, programs, and peripherals that aren't installed during installation, and you must be able to perform system administration tasks.

System Configuration Tools

One of the most common myths about using Linux is that it's hard to configure and customize a system after the initial installation. Although this statement was true in the early years of Linux, you no longer have to configure, install, or upgrade system components by hand. Today, Red Hat includes several tools that make the configuration of your Linux system much simpler. Two of these tools are linuxconf and Red Hat's control-panel. In addition to these configuration management tools, you can run many configuration programs manually, such as authconfig, kbdconfig, mouseconfig, setup, and timeconfig. Red Hat 6.1 also introduced a tool called kudzu to help detect and configure new hardware added to the system after the initial installation.

Using linuxconf

This popular tool allows you to configure and control many parts of your system. In addition, linuxconf can manage a wide range of programs and tasks, such as adding new users (described here) and getting connected to a network (discussed later in this chapter).

To run linuxconf, you must be the *superuser*, also known as *root*, on your system. At the root prompt, type **linuxconf** to invoke the program linuxconf, which is located in the /bin directory.

The linuxconf program offers you four types of interfaces. You can use the *command-line mode* to configure your system by using scripts. You can use the *character-cell mode*, which, like the Red Hat installation program, allows you to use an easy-to-follow graphical user interface without the use of X. You can also use an *X-Window-based mode*, which uses a point-and-click tree interface. The last interface is a *Web interface*, which uses all the advantages of the Web for remote administration tasks. It even works well with text-based browsers, such as lynx. By default, linuxconf runs in either character-cell or X Window mode.

Administering Users

To add users when you're in X Window mode, follow these steps:

1. Invoke the linuxconf program by typing **linuxconf** at the root prompt.

2. To open the Users Accounts tab, shown in Figure 6.1, select Config, then Users Accounts, then Normal, then User Accounts.

3. If you have more than 15 accounts on the system, linuxconf provides you with a filter screen, where you can select a smaller range of accounts. To get the full list, select Accept without changing any of the parameters.

4. The Add button will open the User Account Creation dialog box, in which you enter all the information for a new account. You are then presented with seven fields in which to supply information for the account:

   ➤ *Login Name* —This is the only required field.

   ➤ *Full Name* —This is for the user's full name.

   ➤ *Group* —This allows you to specify any specific group that should be assigned to the account. By default, linuxconf assigns a group that is equivalent to the login name.

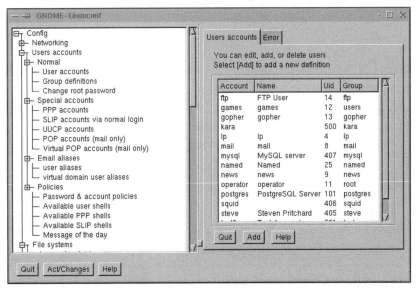

Figure 6.1   The Users Accounts tab of the linuxconf program.

➤ *Supplementary Groups* —This is where you can add the user to supplementary groups, in addition to a single group. To specify more than one group, simply leave a space between each group name.

➤ *Home* —This gives you the option of specifying a specific home directory. The default is /home/*$user*, where *$user* is the user's login name.

➤ *Shells* —This allows you to specify the location of the shells. This field has a drop-down box that displays the default shell.

➤ *User ID* —This is the number associated with individual user accounts. The system automatically sets this number when the account is created.

5. When all the appropriate fields are filled, click on the Accept button. You are then prompted to enter the user's password and confirm it. Passwords must have at least six characters.

6. When finished, click the Accept button.

After creating a user account, you can change the user's information or password by returning to the User Accounts window in linuxconf. To do so, open the Config branch of the tree, and select Users Accounts, then Normal, then User Accounts. In the window, choose the user you want to change, and then modify the user's entries as needed. You can edit all user accounts this way with the exception of root. To change root's password, use the menu to go to Config; then select Users Accounts.

Red Hat's control-panel

Red Hat's control-panel, shown in Figure 6.2, is an X application that serves as a launching pad for several configuration tools. To start Red Hat's control-panel, start up an xterm as root while in X, and then type **control-panel**. Next, select the button for whichever tool you want to run.

Note: When running control-panel, you should not edit any configuration files that it might use.

Some control-panel tools are Users and Groups, printer configuration (printtool), and network setup (netcfg). You can also configure extras by using the kbdconfig, timeconfig, mouseconfig, and sndconfig tools, discussed later in this chapter.

User and Group Configuration

The Users and Groups configuration tool allows you to add, delete, and edit user and group settings. To list current system users, click the Users button. Use the Add, View/Edit, and Remove buttons to add, edit, or delete user files. When you add or edit user files, you can set up the username, the password, the user and

Figure 6.2   Red Hat's control-panel.

group ID, the user's full name, the home directory, and the shell. You can also set up a user's private information, such as office address, office phone number, and home phone number.

To list all current groups listed on the server, click the Groups button. You are then given the option of adding, editing, and removing groups with buttons listed at the bottom of the screen. When adding or editing group files, you can enter information, including the group name, the group password, the group ID, and the list of users who belong in the group.

Printer Configuration

The printer configuration tool is called printtool. It edits the /etc/printcap file, which is used to configure your printers. Running printtool will open a screen that displays any current printer queues that are listed in /etc/printcap. The buttons along the bottom of the screen allow you to edit, add, or delete printer queues. In addition, you can reload your printers, reload the lpd print daemon, or print test pages to your selected printers in the Tests menu. Adding a printer is simple. You are asked for your printer name, the spool directory, and the printer device. You can then select your printer type from a list and select some options, if necessary, such as page size.

Network Configuration

Choosing the network configuration tool runs the netcfg program. The first screen lists your machine host name and domain and allows you to search for host names under additional domains. Here, you also list your current name servers. If you make any changes in the list, you must save your information and reactivate your network device.

By choosing the Hosts button, you can add, edit, and delete different hosts to which your machine can connect, and you can add, edit, and delete aliases for these hosts. Adding or editing your hosts requires the IP address for the host machine, the full name of the host, and a nickname for it. When you edit these hosts, you are actually editing your /etc/hosts file.

Choosing the Interfaces button lists all current interfaces installed on your machine. Some typical interfaces include lo (for local host), eth0 (for Ethernet), and ppp0 (for PPP) connections. From this screen, you can add, edit, copy, alias, delete, and turn on and off different interfaces. When you add an interface, you're given the option of PPP (Point-to-Point Protocol), SLIP (Serial Line Internet Protocol), PLIP (Parallel Line Internet Protocol), Ethernet, ARCnet, Token Ring, or pocket ATP. Depending on the type, you're asked to provide options such as authentication type, addresses, and protocols.

If you choose the Routing button, you see a list of any special routing rules you have set up. You can also set up your network gateway here. From this window, you can add, edit, and delete routing options. To edit a static route, click the Add button. Here you can enter a device, the network, the netmask, and gateway options.

To configure network information without X, use netconfig. The netconfig tool runs the same interface as the network configuration stage of the Red Hat text installation.

Configuring Extras with Linux Administration Tools

Many system administrators enjoy being able to configure, reconfigure, or simply fix their extra settings and peripherals, including keyboards, the clock, a mouse, and sound cards. There are several administration tools available on Linux to do these tasks. Some of the most commonly used ones include kbdconfig, timeconfig, mouseconfig, sndconfig, setup, and authconfig. Each of these configuration programs is run in console menu mode (this mode is also used during the installation process). In fact, authconfig, kbdconfig, timeconfig, and mouseconfig are actually used in the installation process.

If you get a new type of keyboard, or are experimenting with keyboards in other languages, you might want to use the kbdconfig tool. To invoke the kbdconfig tool, type **kbdconfig** at the root prompt. You are then prompted with a blue, red, and yellow screen that asks you to select the type of keyboard you have. When you have selected your keyboard, use the Tab key to select the OK button and then press Enter. It's that simple.

You can just as easily adjust your time settings. To do so, use the timeconfig tool by typing **timeconfig** at the root prompt. You can then select your time zone and use Tab to select OK. This utility is a favorite for administrators who travel among several time zones.

To install a new mouse or trackball, use the mouseconfig tool. To do so, type **mouseconfig** at the root prompt. Choose your appropriate mouse from the list, and then use the Tab key to select OK.

A little more involved, albeit not much, is the sound configuration tool. To set up sound on your system, use the sndconfig tool by typing **sndconfig** at the root prompt. The screen first prompts you to autoprobe for plug-and-play sound cards that can be configured automatically. If no card was found, you're prompted to select your sound card from a list. After you have the appropriate sound device selected or detected, your system runs a few test sounds to verify that your card is working. If you hear the appropriate sounds, use the Tab key to select OK, and you'll be finished.

Unlike some of the other configuration tools, the sndconfig tool adds entries into your /etc/conf.modules file. The sndconfig tool sets the driver, IRQ, and IO settings — as well as any aliases that might be needed — in this file.

Note: Depending on your X Window environment (see Chapter 9), there are special daemons that can be used. Enlightenment uses a sound daemon called esd, and KDE uses a sound daemon called kaudioserver.

If you want to change your current password and authentication settings, you can use the authconfig tool. The authconfig tool allows you to configure shadow passwords, MD5 passwords, and even NIS authentication. The interface of authconfig is duplicated from the original installation.

For a menu of configuration options, you can use the setup tool. The setup tool allows you to reconfigure multiple items by using the tools just described — such as kbdconfig, timeconfig, and authconfig — while also allowing you to set system boot services with ntsysv and to change your network or X configuration. See Figure 6.3.

Figure 6.3   The setup tool's interface.

Hardware Configuration

Older versions of Linux made hardware configuration much more difficult compared to other operating systems, such as Microsoft Windows, especially with newly released hardware. Many new hardware devices simply weren't supported, and you were required to either write your own drivers or wait for someone else to. Today's versions of Linux make installing new hardware very simple. You can now use both PCI and ISA plug-and-play devices. Advanced block device support is now enabled. You can even have Red Hat Linux automatically detect newly added hardware during the boot process.

Plug and Play

When installing various device cards, you'll find two types of cards and different methods to configure each of them. The oldest of the two cards is the ISA card. ISA cards are connected to your computer via ISA slots on your motherboard. Some ISA cards are configured manually by setting jumpers located directly on the card. Newer ISA cards are Plug-and-Play (PnP) compatible, which means they can be configured with system tools. A newer type of device card is the PCI card, which is connected to your computer via the PCI interface on your motherboard. All PCI devices are PnP compatible.

Note: The 2.4 series of kernels will have built-in support for ISA PnP, so the manual tools (discussed next) won't be required. The tools will still work but not the same way they do with the 2.2 kernel series.

ISA PnP devices are configured with isapnp tools. The main tool, isapnp, uses a configuration file, isapnp.conf, to configure the ISA PnP device. An additional ISA PnP tool is pnpdump. The pnpdump tool is used to scan your ISA PnP cards and to dump the resource data from your cards to stdout (standard output). Some of this data includes IO ports, interrupts, and DMA channels. A third tool is pnpprobe. The pnpprobe tool is used to scan your ISA bus for PnP sound cards. The pnpprobe tool uses pnpdump to retrieve the sound card information.

To install a jumperless ISA card, follow these steps:

1. Run the following command: **pnpdump > /etc/isapnp.conf**.

2. Edit the /etc/isapnp.conf file and make changes as needed.

3. Run the following command: **isapnp /etc/isapnp.conf**.

Hard Drive Controllers

Support and tools to interface with your hard drive controllers have greatly improved in the last few versions of Red Hat Linux. A tool used to set low-level parameters for your hard drive controllers is hdparm. The hdparm tool can allow you to enable or disable various parameters on your hard drive, such as 32-bit I/O support for an EIDE controller.

One popular feature, especially among server installations of Red Hat Linux, is the support for RAID (Redundant Array of Independent [or Inexpensive] Disks). A new feature of Red Hat 6.2 is the ability to configure RAID during the installation process. RAID configuration is prompted during the installation phase when you configure your hard disk partitions with Disk Druid (see Chapter 5 for details).

Use RAID when you want to use multiple hard disk drives as one logical drive. There are multiple types of RAID, which are indicated by the level number. All RAID levels use methods of mirroring and striping data. *Mirroring data* refers to having identical copies of data in separate locations (disks). *Striping data* refers to distributing data across multiple disks, not simply copying it. RAID level 5 (referred to as RAID 5) is the most common form of RAID. RAID 5 uses striping with parity across your RAID array. RAID 1 is used to mirror identical copies of data between disk pairs. RAID 0 is used for simply striping data across the disks in your array.

Some tools used when you're implementing RAID are mkraid, raidstart, and raidstop. The mkraid tool is used to initialize your RAID device array. The default configuration file used by mkraid is /etc/raidtab. The raidstart and raidstop tools are fairly self-explanatory. The first tool, raidstart, is used to start your RAID array configuration. The second tool, raidstop, is used to stop your RAID array configuration.

Detecting New Hardware

New to Red Hat in version 6.1 was kudzu. The kudzu tool probes for new hardware during a Red Hat system boot. With this new feature, you're immediately given the choice to configure the device now or later.

During the boot sequence, kudzu queries known control devices for newly attached devices or peripherals. Next, it queries the interrupts directly for device response. If a new device is detected, you're prompted to configure your new device. A database, located in /etc/sysconfig/hwconf, contains your hardware configuration information to be used by kudzu.

Note: Serial devices aren't detected by kudzu during boot. Serial devices are probed only during the initial installation process.

Filesystem and Mount Configuration

In order to read, write, or otherwise use additional filesystems and devices, you must be able to mount them. To do so, you must use the **mount** command and supply information such as the device, the filesystem type, and the mount point. Some filesystem types that are available include:

➤ *vfat* —Used to mount Windows partitions and filesystems

➤ *msdos* —Used to mount MS-DOS filesystems and devices

➤ *ext2* —Used for Linux filesystems

➤ *iso9660* —Used for CD-ROM devices

The syntax for using the **mount** command for a device is:

```
mount -t type /dev/device /mnt/mountpoint
```

Replace *type* with the filesystem type, *device* with the device or partition to be mounted, and *mountpoint* with the mount directory you want to use. For example, to mount an iso9660 filesystem of a CD-ROM to /mnt/cdrom, first make sure that the /mnt/cdrom mount point is created, and then issue this command:

```
mount -t iso9660 /dev/cdrom /mnt/cdrom
```

Many times, you can eliminate the filesystem type and mount point, allowing for easier mount procedures. For instance, rather than issuing the command, you can simply enter **mount /dev/cdrom**. You can do this because of the entries in the /etc/fstab file, discussed in Chapter 3. Entries in the /etc/fstab file set up default settings for mount options. Each entry sets default settings such as the mount point, the type of filesystem, how it should be mounted, if it's to be dumped, and in what order the filesystems should be checked. Here is an example of an /etc/fstab file:

```
/dev/hda3       /               ext2    defaults        1  1
/dev/hda1       /boot           ext2    defaults        1  2
/dev/hda4       swap            swap    defaults        0  0
/dev/fd0        /mnt/floppy     ext2    noauto          0  0
/dev/cdrom      /mnt/cdrom      iso9660 noauto,ro,user  0  0
```

The first entry specifies that **/dev/hda3** should be mounted to / (root) as an **ext2** filesystem with default mount options. It should be dumped and checked first. The second line specifies that **/dev/hda1** be mounted as /boot as an **ext2** filesystem. It should be mounted with the default mount options, should be dumped, and should be checked second. The third line specifies that **/dev/hda4** be mounted as **swap** as a swap filesystem with default mount options, but not be dumped or checked in any order. The fourth line specifies that **/dev/fd0** be mounted as **/mnt/ floppy** with an **ext2** filesystem but not mounted automatically at boot, and so on.

Note: When you read the /etc/fstab file, note the different device-naming conventions. For instance, /dev/hda1 is the first master hard drive. The h specifies that it's an IDE drive, and the 1 specifies that it's the first partition on the drive. However, /dev/sdb3 indicates that it's the second (slave) SCSI drive. The 3 indicates that it's the third partition on that drive.

Adding entries to /etc/fstab (or changing them if necessary) doesn't require you to restart any services to make the changes go into effect. In fact, after changing the /etc/fstab file, you can mount the devices in several manners, such as

```
mount /mnt/mountpoint
```

or

```
mount /dev/device
```

The unsupplied information, such as *type, mountpoint,* or *device* (as needed) are automatically assigned. You can use this convention unless you decide to read from a device with other filesystems, and so on, that are specified in the file. For instance, if your floppy has an msdos filesystem, specify **–t msdos** for the type options. To unmount any filesystem or device, use the **umount** command as you would use the **mount** command, as in

```
umount /mnt/cdrom
```

Managing Packages with RPM

RPM, which you use to manage packages, is open source. It can be used on several other Linux distributions and even commercial Unix systems other than Red Hat. RPM can run in many modes. Some of these include the ability to install, query, verify, check signatures, uninstall, and build RPM packages in addition to rebuilding the RPM databases; fix file permissions; and set owner and group settings. RPM files are usually named with the .rpm extension, but this naming convention is for practice only. The .rpm extension doesn't give special technical meaning to a file. Unlike DOS files, where renaming TEXT.EXE to TEXT.TXT would cause the executable to stop functioning, test.rpm could be renamed as test_tst or even just as test, and RPM would still recognize the package file.

Getting to Know RPM

Much like Linux, RPM didn't just magically appear and work. It was developed over time, based on several other package-management projects. The first development of today's RPM was found in RPP. RPP was used in the first Red Hat Linux distributions. In fact, its first features are still the foundation for the purpose and features of RPM today. RPP is credited with being the initial source for the simple one-line commands used to install and uninstall packages. RPP also introduced the scripts that are run before and after packages are installed and uninstalled. The initial query and verify features were also introduced with RPP. Unfortunately, the features available with RPP just were not enough.

The need for more features led the Red Hat software developers to peer in on the projects for package management that the developers of the BOGUS distribution were developing. The BOGUS developers, led by Rik Faith, were working on a package-management project called PMS (Package Management System). The feature that RPP was lacking that PMS had mastered was the concept of *pristine sources*. Pristine sources allowed the packager to release versions of software and to track the changes made to the previous version.

Three more steps were taken before we had the RPM we all know and love today. Interestingly enough, Red Hat software itself supported and/or developed all three steps. In the first step, Faith and Doug Hoffman had a contract with Red Hat Software to produce PM, the new updated Package Manager that incorporated the features of RPP with the pristine-source feature of PMS. Although PM's functionality was close to that of the RPM we have today, it still lacked good database design and had no multiple architecture support. PM was never used in a commercially available product.

Red Hat developers Marc Ewing and Erik Troan completed the last two steps for developing RPM. The first of these two steps introduced the first version of the official RPM, which was developed in Perl. The last step rewrote RPM in the C development language to increase the program's speed. Long after the C rewrite, new developments such as package dependencies were added.

Installing, Uninstalling, and Upgrading with RPM

The fundamental job of RPM is to add and remove components from your system. An RPM file is actually a type of compressed archive. Using the **rpm** command, you can install, delete, and upgrade these RPM-archived packages.

To install an RPM file, use the command-line option **-i** (for install). For example, to install an RPM file for sendmail (such as sendmail-8.9.3-20.i386.rpm), enter

```
rpm -i sendmail-8.9.3-20.i386.rpm
```

To uninstall a package, use the command-line option **-e** (for erase). To uninstall the sendmail-8.9.1-2.i386.rpm sendmail package, enter

```
rpm -e sendmail-8.9.3-20.i386.rpm
```

Another task that you can perform with RPM is to upgrade individual components or packages on your system without having to completely reinstall them. Unlike the configuration files of tar files or gzip packages, the configuration files of RPM packages are preserved when you upgrade. Therefore, you won't lose your configuration. To upgrade a package, use the -U option (for upgrade). To upgrade to the sendmail-8.9.3-20.i386.rpm sendmail package, enter

```
rpm -U sendmail-8.9.3-20.i386.rpm
```

> When you are installing or upgrading a package, it's helpful to use the **-v** and **-h** options. The **-v** option (for verbose) prints the name of the file within the package it's installing. The **-h** option (for hash mark, #) prints hash marks to show how far the installation has progressed. An example of using both of these options is:
>
> ```
> rpm -ivh sendmail-8.9.1-2.i386.rpm
> ```

Another helpful RPM installation option is **–F** (for freshen). Freshen allows you to automatically compare a list of RPM files against the RPM files already installed on your system. If an RPM within the list of RPMs is newer than the one on your system, it's automatically upgraded. If an RPM file within the list isn't newer than the one on your system (or isn't even installed on your system), it's ignored. To use the **–F** option, run

```
rpm -F *.rpm
```

from the directory that contains the list of RPM files you want to compare. Note that *.rpm refers to every RPM file in that directory. You can also use other wildcards, file names, or combinations thereof to get whatever result you are looking for.

Note: Several commands can be issued to RPM at the end of the string following two dashes (- -). To force a package to install, use - -force. To ignore package dependencies and install, use - -nodeps. To identify uninstalled packages that Red Hat requires, use - -redhatprovides (this option requires the rpmdb-redhat package to be installed).

Querying with RPM

RPM was designed to have querying capabilities. The RPM archives have custom binary headers that contain data about the package and its contents, allowing you to query individual packages very easily. You can search through your system database for packages and files, find out to which package a file belongs, and so on.

To query for a specific package, use the -q option (for query). Using the **rpm –q** option requires an argument that specifies the package name, such as libc. However, passing an –a option (for all) to the –q option, such as

```
rpm -qa
```

queries and prints all installed RPM files on your system. Here's a sample output of querying specifically for all the libc packages you have installed on a system:

```
# rpm -q libc
    libc-5.3.12-31
```

This output shows that this particular system has two libc packages installed: **libc-5.3.12-31** and **libc-5.3.12-28**. To get information about those specific packages, you can use the –i option with the query. The format for this is

```
rpm -qi packagename
```

The output of this command gives you information such as the name of the package, any relocations (if applicable), the version, the vendor that distributed it, the release number, the build date, the installation date, and the source RPM. In addition, it gives you a summary of the package and a detailed description of the package and its use.

Additional options used with the **rpm query** function are the –l (for list) and the –f (for file) options. The –l option queries for the contents of an RPM file. The –f function queries files of an RPM. The **rpm –ql** command is used against an existing RPM file. It lists all the files and directories that are contained within the RPM. For instance,

```
rpm -ql libc
```

lists all the files and directories of the **libc** package. The **rpm –qf** command is used against an existing file; using this command on a file queries for the package that owns the specific file. For instance, doing an

```
rpm -qf xbill
```

while you're in the /usr/lib directory yields

```
xbill-2.0-6
```

which means that the xbill-2.0-6 RPM file installed the /usr/lib/xbill file.

 You aren't always expected to use the package name. If you are using Linux's tab completion feature, the **–p** option is especially useful. This option specifies that you are using the full package file name, not just the package name. For instance, using **rpm –qi libc** gets the same results as using **rpm –qip libc-5.3.12-31.src.rpm**.

Verifying with RPM

In addition to using RPM to query for specific files you've already installed on your system, you can verify packages that you've installed against the original package stored in an RPM database or the package's origin. You verify a package when you want to check for problems, such as corrupted or missing files, within it. After verifying a package, you can reinstall the package because any current configurations you have set for the package are preserved.

To verify a package, you use the -V option (for verify). The output of the -V option is a string of eight characters, possibly followed by a **c** (indicating that it's a configuration file) and then followed by the path and file name. The most important information in the output is the eight-character string, in which each character displays the result of the comparison between one attribute of the file compared to the value of the same attribute recorded in the RPM database. A single period (.) for a specific character means that the attribute matched. Table 6.1 lists the eight characters and their attributes.

To give you an idea of what verifying a package looks like, here is an example of verifying the sendmail package:

```
$rpm -V sendmail
     G.    /etc/aliases.db
S.5   .T   /var/log/sendmail.st
```

The output shows two files with differences: aliases.db and sendmail.st. The aliases.db file has different Group attributes; the sendmail.st file has different file sizes, MD5 sums, and Mtimes.

Verifying RPM Origin

Another item worth verifying from your RPM is the origin of your RPM. To verify the origin, RPM can check the GPG (GNU Privacy Guard) signature of the package. You can check the GPG signature in one of two ways: either with the -K option or with the -checksig option.

Other RPM Utilities

Since RPM 3.0.4, you've been able to install, upgrade, and freshen RPM packages over a network through either an FTP or an HTTP connection. An FTP connection allows *globbing*, or specifying more than one file at a time, whereas an HTTP connection allows you to specify only one file. Here's an example of updating all of your RPM packages:

```
rpm -Fvh ftp://updates.redhat.com/6.2/i386/*.rpm
```

Another useful utility is rpmfind. The rpmfind utility allows you to locate the packages you need to install via Internet servers and mirror sites. When using

Table 6.1	Output of the RPM Verify option.
Character	**Attribute**
5	MD5 sum
S	File size
L	Symlink
T	Mtime
D	Device
U	User
G	Group
M	Mode (includes permissions and file type)

rpmfind, you're actually working with a database found at **http://rpmfind.net/ linux/RPM/index.html**. If the package you're searching for can be found in this database, rpmfind will automatically give you the option to download the package and its dependencies.

Using Graphical RPM Tools

RPM offers two graphical administration tools: Gnome-RPM (also called GnoRPM), which is a GUI tool that replaces glint as the package-management tool; and Kpackage, which is similar to GnoRPM but uses the QT/KDE toolkit.

To invoke either GnoRPM or Kpackage, type **gnorpm** or **kpackage**, respectively, from the root prompt. When GnoRPM is running, you're presented with a browser-style window (shown in Figure 6.4). In the left window is a directory tree available for packages. The packages are split among several directories, such as Amusements, Applications, and Development. The right window lists the files in that directory. Some of the buttons along the top are Install, Upgrade, Uninstall, and Query, and they are all options available with the manual RPM tools. When Kpackage is running, you're presented with nearly the same layout and the same functionality. See Figure 6.5.

Building RPMs

RPM would not be nearly as effective if you could not build your own RPM packages. Using the -b option (for build) with **rpm** allows you to build your own package. In addition to the -b option, you can use the -t option (for tar files) to look inside tar files for the spec file to use.

Figure 6.4 The GnoRPM tool.

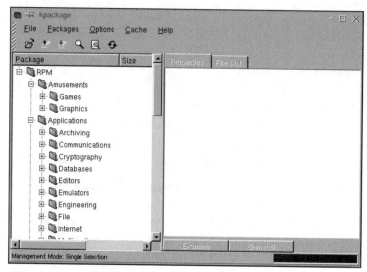

Figure 6.5 The Kpackage tool.

After specifying the first argument, you must specify the stage of building and packaging that is to be done. Here are some options and what they do:

➤ **-bp** —Executes the "%prep" stage from the spec file. This stage typically unpacks the source and applies any needed patches.

➤ **-bl** —Tells RPM to do a list check. The "%files" section from the spec file is macro expanded, and RPM checks to make sure the files exist.

➤ **-bc** —Tells RPM to do the "%build" stage from the spec file, following the prep stage. Essentially, it's the equivalent of a "make install."

➤ **-bb** —Has RPM build a binary package. This build is done after the prep, build, and install stages.

➤ **-ba** —Builds both binary and source packages. This option is also used after the prep, build, and install stages.

After changing RPM files, including patches and updates, you may opt to rebuild the RPM file to include the new changes. There are two ways to use RPM in this manner: you can use the --**recompile** option or the --**rebuild** option. When you run RPM with either option, RPM installs the named source package and then automatically does a prep, compile, and install. In addition, the --**rebuild** option builds a new binary package. After the build has been completed, the build directory is automatically removed (by using --**clean**), and the source and spec files for the package are removed.

Basic Networking

The favorite features of Linux are centered around its networking capabilities. Red Hat Linux supports a number of network interfaces and protocols, ranging from modem to network interface card and from TCP/IP to IPX.

Exploring /etc/sysconfig

The files found under the /etc/sysconfig/ directory are files that scripts use to execute during boot-time. These files are named by the devices that they configure, such as clock, mouse, and network.

Beneath the /etc/sysconfig/ directory is a directory that contains network script files. These are located under /etc/sysconfig/network-scripts/. The network-scripts directory contains scripts such as ifcfg-eth0, ifup, ifdown, and ifup-ppp. The "if" in these scripts stands for interface. The rest of the naming convention is self-explanatory. The ifcfg script configures the named device, and ifcfg-ppp configures the PPP interface. The most common networking tools and scripts that you'll use are netcfg, ifconfig, ifup, ifdown, and netstat. Multiple user interfaces for these tools are available, including usernet, rp3, and usernetctl.

Using the netcfg Tool

The network configurator tool is a graphical tool that you use to add, delete, and configure network interfaces, devices, and more. To start the netcfg tool, type **netcfg** at the root prompt. Figure 6.6 shows the interface of netcfg.

Figure 6.6 The netcfg tool.

With network configurator, you can configure name services, network hosts, network interfaces, and even routing. Several buttons allow you to perform various tasks:

➤ *Names* —Here you can set up your system host name and domain. In addition, you can set up host names that are searchable as well as your preferred name servers.

➤ *Hosts* —Here you can directly edit the /etc/hosts file. You can also add, edit, or remove hosts entries, such as machine alias settings.

➤ *Interfaces* —This is a little more interesting. Here you can add, edit, clone, alias, remove, activate, and deactivate your network interfaces. Some interfaces that you can see here are your loopback, Ethernet, and PPP interfaces. You can assign IP addresses to each interface and set their protocol configuration type (such as DHCP or none). You can also specify to activate the interface at boot-time as well as change the state that the interface is currently in (active or inactive).

➤ *Routing* —This allows you to set up routing options. The basic routing options you can set up here include your default gateway and default gateway device. If you have more than one interface for which you want to set routing rules, you can also add them here.

Using the ifconfig Tool

You use the ifconfig tool to print your current network setup. The output includes settings for your loopback, Ethernet, PPP, and other interfaces if they are active. Listing 6.1 shows sample output of ifconfig on a system with an Ethernet connection to a network. The active interfaces are identified by **eth0** and **lo** on the left. Within each section, you see the hardware address, inet address, broadcast address, netmask address, I/O settings, and more.

Listing 6.1   Sample output of ifconfig.

```
eth0     Link encap:Ethernet  HWaddr 00:80:C8:42:73:E3
         inet addr:192.168.0.15 Bcast:192.168.0.255
         Mask:255.255.255.0
         UP BROADCAST RUNNING  MTU:1500  Metric:1
         RX packets:104 errors:0 dropped:0 overruns:0 frame:0
         TX packets:97 errors:0 dropped:0 overruns:0 carrier:0
         collisions:0 txqueuelen:100
         Interrupt:3 Base address:0x300
```

```
lo      Link encap:Local Loopback
        inet addr:127.0.0.1  Mask:255.0.0.0
        UP LOOPBACK RUNNING  MTU:3924  Metric:1
        RX packets:48 errors:0 dropped:0 overruns:0 frame:0
        TX packets:48 errors:0 dropped:0 overruns:0 carrier:0
        collisions:0 txqueuelen:0
```

Using the ifup, ifdown, and netstat Commands

The **ifup** and **ifdown** commands are used to administer the network connections manually. You can **ifup** *(interface)* to activate the interface and **ifdown** *(interface)* to deactivate an interface. For example, to bring up the eth0 interface, type **ifup eth0**.

 Using the **ifup** command doesn't bring the interface up after you reboot!

After you have a routing table established, or a network connection, you can monitor your routing table by using the **netstat** command. In addition to printing your routing table, it displays your network connections, interface statistics, masquerade connection, netlink messages, and more.

To view the different information, you pass the specific options to **netstat**. To view the routing table, enter **netstat –r**. To view the interface information, enter **netstat –i**. To view any of your masqueraded connections, enter **netstat –M**.

User Interface Tools

There are two graphical interfaces and one command-line interface commonly used to allow non-privileged users to start and stop network interfaces. These tools are often used to allow non-root users to activate the PPP (dial-up) connection for the system.

The two graphical interfaces include usernet and rp3. The usernet tool gives you a window displaying the different network interfaces available to your system. Clicking on an interface window displays a window prompting you whether to activate or deactivate an interface. See Figure 6.7. The second graphical interface is rp3. The rp3 tool gives you a list of interfaces available on your system. Selecting the appropriate interface gives you a single screen, similar to usernet, that

Figure 6.7 The usernet interface.   **Figure 6.8** The rp3 interface.

monitors the traffic on the interface. After clicking the interface monitor, you're given the option to start and stop the interface. See Figure 6.8.

A command-line tool that allows non-root users to access network settings is usernetctl. The usernetctl tool is used by invoking the tool, specifying the interface, and telling it what to do to the interface. See the following for usage:

```
usernetctl <interface-config> <up|down|report>
```

User Administration

For most Linux administrators, the most time-consuming and important job is user administration. User administration can involve such things as adding and deleting user accounts, modifying user information, setting up basic user shell settings, and setting up user window managers.

Adding User Accounts

There are several ways to add new user accounts to your system. You used to have to add users manually, but you can now also use command-line tools—such as useradd, passwd, and mkpasswd—as well as graphical tools—such as linuxconf and userconf—to set up user accounts, passwords, home directories, shells, and more.

Adding user accounts manually can be a very tedious task. You first have to edit the user and groups files to add the user information in /etc/passwd and /etc/group, respectively. Next, you must create the user's home directory and copy the default files and user directories from /etc/skel. Finally, you have to change the ownership of the new home directory so that the directory is owned by the new user.

The most popular Linux (and Unix) user addition tool is useradd, which is the same as adduser. To add a new user by using the useradd tool as root, enter **adduser** *newuser* where *newuser* is the new user's username. Next, if you want to set the user's password, enter **passwd** *newuser*. You are prompted to enter the user's password and then confirm it. Or, if you want to generate a random password, enter **mkpasswd** *newuser* instead of using **passwd**. The **adduser** (or **useradd**) command automatically sets up the user's home directory by copying the files located in /etc/skel.

As mentioned earlier in this chapter, linuxconf is a graphical-user-interface tool used to set up many things, including new users, in Linux. To invoke linuxconf, enter **linuxconf** at the root prompt. Then move through the directory tree in the left screen to go through Config, then Normal, then User Accounts. Next, click the Add button. You are next prompted for information such as the login name, the user's full name, his group (optional), any additional groups, and special permissions. After choosing the Accept button, you are asked to enter a user password and confirm it.

You can use another graphical-user-interface tool, userconf, to add users. The userconf tool, which is a little more user-friendly than linuxconf, has buttons and self-explanatory tabs (rather than the directory tree). To invoke userconf, enter **userconf** at the root prompt. To add a user, click User Accounts and then on the Add button. You can then add the user information exactly as you do when you use linuxconf.

Deleting User Accounts

A good system administrator keeps a good audit on the users on her machine. The main thing to keep track of is which users are active and which aren't. You should disable accounts that are no longer being used, such as those for employees no longer working there. Leaving old accounts active on your system is a security risk. When you disable the account, make sure to remove all the files the user had on the system. By keeping the old accounts on the system (disabled), you prevent the possibility of reusing UIDs (user IDs), thus maintaining a higher level of security.

You can remove users from your system in several ways: You can remove them manually, remove them within a group (with groupdel), or use the friendly interfaced tools such as userdel or linuxconf. Each tool differs, and which one you use is simply a preference.

If you don't like to trust automatic programs, or if for some reason your tool isn't functioning or isn't available, you can remove the user account manually. First, edit your password file and remove the line assigned to the user. Next, remove the user's entry in the /etc/group file. Finally, rename, move, or delete the user's home directory, including the .login and .profile files within that directory.

System administrators who are accustomed to administering a large group of users, or users for a large corporation, might want to set up their users by group. For instance, you might have set up all users in the Sales department in the group named Sales. You might also have set up temporary contractor users in the group named Contractor. Using the **groupdel** *contractor* command removes all system entries referring to that group. Keep in mind, however, that you must manually search your filesystems for remaining files. Another problem with using groupdel is that you can't remove a primary group for an existing user.

The most popular Unix user-deletion tool is userdel. To delete a user with it, enter the **userdel** *username* command from the root prompt. The userdel tool automatically removes the user's entries in both the /etc/passwd and /etc/group files. Using the userdel tool without any options removes these two entries but not the user's home directory and files. To remove these, pass **userdel** the **–r** option. For example, the command

```
userdel -r username
```

removes *username*'s entries in the /etc/passwd and /etc/group files as well as *username*'s home directory.

As you've seen, linuxconf is a very useful tool, and you can use it to delete your user accounts. To do so, you are given a few options that are unavailable when you use other deletion methods. After starting linuxconf from the root prompt, you're presented with the directory tree in the left window of the screen. In the directory tree, select Config, then Users Accounts, then Normal, and then User Accounts. To select the user you want to delete, double-click the username. Then click the Delete button. You're then prompted to choose to archive the account's data, delete the account's data, or leave it alone. After you've chosen an option, choose Quit and then Activate Changes.

Modifying User Information

A time will come when you need to modify a user's information. Perhaps your user gets married and has a new last name. Maybe you just need to change the user's password or permissions. Whatever the reason, there are ways you can modify the user's account without having to re-create it.

To change a user's password, you can manually edit the user's /etc/passwd entry, run the **passwd** command, use linuxconf, or even assign a random password by using the **mkpasswd** command. In addition, some **useradd** command options allow you to specify such information when you create the user account. For a complete list of options available, use the **man useradd** command.

Running the **passwd** command from the root prompt prompts you to change the root password. To change a user's password by using **passwd**, run

```
passwd username
```

You are then prompted to change and verify the *username*'s new password. This command is also made available to users for their own passwords. However, only root can use the **passwd** command to change other users' passwords.

If you want to change a user's login name, groups, shell, or home directory, you can use a command-line utility called usermod. You can use usermod only when a user isn't logged in or otherwise active on the system. To learn more about how to use usermod, run the **man usermod** command at the shell prompt.

Understanding the Basic User Environment

Any time a user account is created, either manually or with a user administration tool, a certain number of default files and directories are created in the user's home directory (located at /home/*username*). By default, the files that are copied into the user's home directory include .Xdefaults, .bash_logout, .bash_profile, and .bashrc, which I'll discuss more fully in the next section.

These default files are copied from the /etc/skel directory, which contains "skeleton" files that are used by default when a new user account is created. Anything found in this directory is automatically copied to a user's directory when the directory is created. For instance, when KDE is installed, two files are copied automatically to the /etc/skel directory. The two files are .kde and .kderc, which are configuration files for the KDE Window Manager. You should put anything else you would like to have copied into a user's home directory in /etc/skel as well.

 Adding files to /etc/skel affects only new users created on the system. You must manually copy any additional files you want existing users to have.

The /etc/skel Files

The .Xdefaults file is the basic X Window System resources file. Users use this file when they start up their X sessions. The .Xdefaults file is used by every type of Window Manager, including KDE, Window Maker, Enlightenment, AfterStep, and fvwm. You'll find the following within the .Xdefaults file:

➤ Settings for basic X Window applications. For instance, the .Xdefaults file contains the defaults (such as color, size, and font options) for the emacs and XEmacs editors.

➤ Settings (such as color, highlight options, and scrolling) for Xterm.

➤ Other system options for X, such as scrolling and the visual bell.

The .bash_logout file is a bash-shell logout script. A default Red Hat 6.2 .bash_logout script is very simple, as you can see in the following example:

```
# ~/.bash_logout

clear
```

The default .bash_logout script simply tells the shell to clear the screen after logout. In the .bash_logout file, you can set bash to do a number of other things. For instance, you can have the shell execute the fortune program, sleep for five seconds, and then clear. To do so, add the path and executable for the fortune program and then add a **sleep 5** line within the script.

A bit more complex, the .bash_profile script is used to run the bash shell, briefly discussed in Chapter 3. Some options that are set in .bash_profile include alias settings, path settings, and startup programs. In fact, the alias settings aren't supplied within the .bash_profile file itself. Instead, it calls the .bashrc file and executes the alias settings there. Listing 6.2 shows a sample .bash_profile file.

Listing 6.2   Sample .bash_profile script.

```
# .bash_profile
# Get the aliases and functions
if [ -f ~/.bashrc ]; then
    .~/.bashrc
fi

# User specific environment and startup programs

PATH=$PATH:$HOME/bin
BASH_ENV=$HOME/.bashrc
USERNAME=""

export USERNAME BASH_ENV PATH
```

The .bashrc file is executed when called by the .bash_profile script. The .bashrc file contains any alias and function settings. Therefore (customizable for each individual user), you can set aliases for commands, such as alias **ls –l** to **ls** so that each time you run **ls**, you get **ls –l**. Here's a sample .bashrc file (keep in mind that .bashrc isn't required to run bash):

```
# .bashrc

# User specific aliases and functions

alias rm='rm -i'
alias cp='cp -i'
alias mv='mv -i'

# Source global definitions
if [ -f /etc/bashrc ]' then
      ./etc/bashrc
fi
```

Note: If you ever have to create a user manually, be sure to copy all the files from the /etc/skel directory!

Virtual Consoles

The virtual console is a feature of Linux that is most coveted by people using other operating systems. Virtual consoles allow you to have multiple text-based logins on separate virtual screens on your system.

To access separate virtual consoles on your system from a console screen, use a combination of the Alt key and one of the function keys; Alt+F1, Alt+F2, and so on. (Note: The + doesn't mean press the plus sign key. It means to press and hold the Alt key then press the Function key.) To navigate between an X session and a virtual console, press Ctrl+Alt+F1 to leave your X session and return to the first console; then press Alt+F7 to return to your X session.

By default, six virtual consoles are available after installation, Alt+F1 through Alt+F6. In your /etc/inittab file, however, you can change your console settings and the number of consoles available on your system. Listing 6.3 is a sample excerpt of the /etc/inittab file where you specify virtual console settings.

Listing 6.3   Snippet of the /etc/inittab file.

```
#
# inittab   This file describes how the INIT process should set up
#           the system in a certain run-level.
#
```

```
# Author:    Miquel van Smoorenburg,
<miquels@drinkel.nl.mugnet.org>
#            Modified for RHS Linux by Marc Ewing and Donnie Barnes

# Run gettys in standard runlevels
1:2345:respawn:/sbin/mingetty tty1
2:2345:respawn:/sbin/mingetty tty2
3:2345:respawn:/sbin/mingetty tty3
4:2345:respawn:/sbin/mingetty tty4
5:2345:respawn:/sbin/mingetty tty5
6:2345:respawn:/sbin/mingetty tty6
```

Adding additional lines to the section of the /etc/inittab file shown in Listing 6.3, such as

```
7:2345:respawn:/sbin/mingetty tty7
```

enables your seventh virtual console.

Note: You aren't limited to 12 consoles. In fact, you can have up to 24. To access tty13–tty24, press (and hold) the left Alt key, the left Shift key, and a function key. F1 represents tty13, and F12 represents tty24.

You can also set console settings in your /etc/security/console.perms file. This file controls the options (such as privileges that are set during login) for your console user group. Permissions for the console user group typically include shutdown, halt, and reboot.

To keep a log such as /var/log/messages scrolling on an unused virtual terminal (such as 12), as root you can run **tail –f /var/log/messages > /dev/tty12**.

Practice Questions

Question1

> Where can you enable or disable virtual consoles?
>
> ○ a. /etc/inittab
>
> ○ b. /etc/consoles.conf
>
> ○ c. /etc/virtual.consoles
>
> ○ d. /etc/X11/consoles.conf

Answer a is correct. In the /etc/inittab file, there's a section that allows you to specify virtual console settings. They are in a format similar to **1:2345:respawn:/sbin/mingetty tty1**. To add an additional virtual console, simply replicate the line in numerical order at the end of the list, where the numerical order represents the **1:** and the **tty1** is equal to your virtual console number (,**8:** and **tty8**, for example). To disable a virtual console, simply delete the corresponding line.

Question 2

> How can you navigate around virtual consoles (*x* means console number)?
>
> ○ a. Ctrl+w*x*
>
> ○ b. Alt+w*x*
>
> ○ c. Alt+F*x*
>
> ○ d. Alt+a+*x*

Answer c is correct. Alt+Fx, where Fx is a function key, is used to navigate between virtual consoles. Answers a, b, and d are incorrect because Ctrl, a, and w aren't valid virtual console options.

Question 3

> How could you unmount a device? [Check all correct answers]
>
> ❑ a. **unmount /dev/device**
>
> ❑ b. **umount /mnt/device**
>
> ❑ c. **umount /device**
>
> ❑ d. **umount /root**

Answers b, c, and d are correct. This is true when the device's mount point is equal to either **/mnt/device** (as listed in answer b) or simply **/device** (as listed in answer c). Answer d unmounts the /root filesystem. This option is valid if /root is mounted on a separate hdax device. Answer a is incorrect because **unmount** isn't a valid command; it would be possible only if **unmount** were aliased to the **umount** command.

Question 4

> Where are default user files kept?
>
> ○ a. /etc/user.defaults
>
> ○ b. /usr/user.defaults
>
> ○ c. /usr/skel
>
> ○ d. /etc/skel

Answer d is correct. The /etc/skel directory contains all "skeleton" directories and files that are automatically installed into a user's home directory when they are created with tools such as useradd, userconf, and linuxconf.

Question 5

> How can you add Mary, a new user, to your system?
>
> ○ a. Add Mary to the /etc/passwd file and the /etc/group file, and create her home directory in /home (copying files from /etc/skel).
>
> ○ b. Use useradd.
>
> ○ c. Use adduser.
>
> ○ d. Use linuxconf.
>
> ○ e. All of the above.

Answer e is correct. You can add an account for Mary manually (answer a) if you want or need to. The tools in answers b, c, and d are also available.

Question 6

Which of the following can you use for multiple administration and configuration tasks? [Check all correct answers]

❑ a. linuxconf

❑ b. control-panel

❑ c. Xconfigurator

❑ d. XF86Setup

Answers a and b are correct. Both of these tools can perform, or are linked to, multiple configuration tasks. Although answers c and d are also configuration tools, they are limited to X setup and don't configure administration or other tasks.

Question 7

How can you print your active network interfaces?

○ a. **netstat –r**

○ b. **ifconfig**

○ c. **netcfg**

○ d. **cat /net.status**

Answer b is correct. Answer a is incorrect because it's used to print your current routing table, not network interfaces. Answer c is incorrect because, although it's used to configure your network, it doesn't simply report the active interfaces. Answer d is incorrect because there's no such thing as **cat /net.status**.

Question 8

> What commands can you use to rebuild a source RPM file? [Check all correct answers]
>
> ❑ a. **--rebuild**
>
> ❑ b. **--rbld**
>
> ❑ c. **--recompile**
>
> ❑ d. **--rb**

Answers a and c are correct because those options are used by RPM to rebuild an RPM source file. Answers b and d aren't valid options.

Question 9

> What is RPM?
>
> _____

RPM is the Red Hat Package Manager. It's used to install, uninstall, and manage packages that are installed on a Red Hat Linux system.

Question 10

> What command can you use to find RPMs you need on the Internet?
>
> ○ a. **findrpm**
>
> ○ b. **- -redhatprovides**
>
> ○ c. **rpmfind**
>
> ○ d. **rpm -F**

Answer c is correct. Answer a is incorrect because it's invalid. Answer b is incorrect because it only tells you what uninstalled package a file might belong to. Answer d is incorrect because **rpm –F** is a command to freshen a package, not find one on the Internet.

Task 1

After installing your fresh Red Hat Linux system, go back through and configure your peripherals again. Change your mouse settings. What does that do?

Task 2

If a network is available, configure your machine for one. Set up your machine for a static IP address. Change it to use a DHCP server (if available).

Task 3

Browse your Red Hat CD (or installation download) or the Internet for RPM files that aren't already installed on your system. Perhaps install an additional Window Manager. Try upgrading to a new version of RPM (if available). How do you go about doing that? Switch to virtual console 10. What do you mean, it doesn't work? Fix that!

Need to Know More?

 Baily, Edward C. *Maximum RPM*. Sams Publishing, Indianapolis, IN, 1997. ISBN 0-672-31105-4. The first section of this book, including Chapters 1 through 8, covers all aspects of using RPM to manage RPM packages.

 Frisch, Æleen. *Essential System Administration*. O'Reilly & Associates, Sebastopol, CA, 1995. ISBN 1-56592-127-5. Chapters 2, 5, 9, and 12 cover Unix essentials for filesystems, user accounts, disks, and printing. Linux methods were modeled after these.

 Heckman, Jessica Perry. *Linux in a Nutshell*. O'Reilly & Associates, Sebastopol, CA, 1997. ISBN 1-56592-167-4. Chapters 4, 13, and 14 are an excellent reference for the Linux Bourne Shell (see Chapter 4) and Linux system and network administration commands (Chapters 13 and 14).

 http://linuxdoc.org/—The Linux Documentation Project contains a section with various Linux HOWTOs, including installation, networking, RPM, and other items discussed in this chapter.

 http://www.rpm.org/—Under the Documentation portion of the RPM Web site, you can get HOWTOs and other information references about RPM. In addition, development information can be located in the Resources section of the site.

 http://www.solucorp.qc.ca/linuxconf/—For the latest downloads, patches, and HOWTOs for using linuxconf, be sure to visit the Linuxconf Home Page, found at this address.

Advanced Installation

Terms you'll need to understand:

✓ Dual-boot

✓ Boot manager

✓ Clone

✓ Prototype

Techniques you'll need to master:

✓ Installing a multi-boot system

✓ Implementing an automatic installation system

✓ Installing a PCMCIA (laptop) system

In addition to the standard Red Hat Linux installation, several other installation methods and options are available. These options allow you to boot multiple operating systems or even automate the installation. You might even need to install a system that is to be run *headless*, meaning without a monitor and keyboard. Special hardware, such as a PCMCIA system (laptop), also requires special installation and configuration methods. Your typical Red Hat Linux user probably does not even know that most of these options exist. However, becoming an RHCE means that you do know about them and you can set up and configure them properly.

Dual-Booting Linux

Administrators often like to dual-boot their systems. This means that the administrator installs more than one operating system and then chooses which one to run.

Note: Currently, running more than one operating system simultaneously is possible only by using software packages such as VMware.

You can set up your machine to prompt you to choose which OS you want to run at boot-time. In this section, we'll discuss setting up your machine with the option to boot either Linux or Microsoft Windows.

Partitioning Disks

To dual-boot your machine with Linux and Windows, you must create separate partitions on your hard drive for each operating system. It's typically best to create at least four partitions for this—or more if you decide to create separate partitions for /home, /var, and other directories on your Linux filesystem.

The four primary partitions are for Linux /boot, for Windows, for Linux Native, and for Linux Swap. Creating the first partition (50MB or smaller) for Linux /boot allows the system to more easily boot properly. This setup is especially useful on large disks with more than 1024 cylinders and on disks that require LBA mode. The following is an example of a partition table on a system with four partitions:

```
Disk /dev/hda: 240 heads, 63 sectors, 839 cylinders
Units = cylinders of 15120 * 512 bytes

    Device Boot    Start       End    Blocks   Id  System
/dev/hda1              1         7     52888+  83  Linux
/dev/hda2    *         8        75    514080    b  Win95 FAT32
/dev/hda3             76       813   5579280   83  Linux
/dev/hda4            814       839    196560   82  Linux swap
```

The first partition is a boot partition for Linux. It's a Linux Native partition and is mounted to /boot. The second is a DOS partition, which is used for an installation of Windows 98. The third and fourth partitions are also for Linux. The third is the root partition, which is a Linux Native partition and mounted to /. The fourth is a Linux Swap partition and is not mounted to any filesystem.

Sometimes you might want to dual-boot a system after you already have an initial operating system, such as Windows, installed. To dual-boot the Windows system with Linux, you must resize or shrink your current Windows partition. In the dosutils directory of your Red Hat Linux 6.2 CD-ROM is a DOS tool called fips, which you can use to resize your current DOS or Windows partitions. A commercial program that allows you to do the same thing is PartitionMagic by PowerQuest Corporation. PartitionMagic is a DOS program that can resize many types of partitions safely without destroying data. Since version 4, PartitionMagic also resizes existing Linux partitions.

Installing Both Operating Systems

A dual-boot system set up from scratch is much easier to configure properly and will most likely have fewer errors. By default, you should always install your alternate (not Linux) operating system first. Doing so allows you to configure the bootloader during your Linux installation so you can boot multiple operating systems. . In addition, some other operating systems format the entire disk during their default installations. By installing the non-Linux operating system first, you eliminate the risk of the other operating system deleting your Linux installation.

If you use the other operating system to partition your disk, simply leave the unpartitioned space available for Linux. Red Hat Linux can format and partition the unallocated space during installation. Some administrators find it helpful to partially begin the Red Hat Linux installation before installing the guest operating system. By this I mean you can start the Red Hat Linux installation and proceed to the point where you format the drive; then you stop the Red Hat Linux installation to install the guest operating system. You can then use Disk Druid (discussed in Chapter 5) or fdisk (discussed in Chapters 3 and 5) during the Red Hat Linux installation to set up all your partitions. Make sure you create your DOS or guest operating-system partition and set it to the appropriate type (for Windows, this is type b). You can then write the partition table. When the Linux installation moves to the next stage, you can reboot the system and begin installing your guest operating system.

Boot Managers

Several boot managers can boot Linux as well as manage other operating systems booting on the same system. Some of the popular ones include:

➤ *LILO*—Discussed in Chapters 3 and 5, and short for Linux Loader, this is the default bootloader used with Linux. Red Hat, as well as most Linux vendors, recommends that you use it as your default boot manager.

➤ *System Commander*—This is a commercial product that you can purchase from a local software vendor.

➤ *SysLinux*—This executes the Linux boot-up from a DOS filesystem.

Even if you decide not to use LILO as your boot manager, you still need LILO to manage your Linux boot-up. You decide where to install LILO based on the default boot manager you decide to use. If you are using LILO, then choose to install LILO in the master boot record (MBR) on your system. If you choose to use another boot manager, such as System Commander, install LILO to the superblock of the /boot partition.

The LILO Boot Manager

If you are using LILO as your default boot manager, you can select the operating system to boot during the installation process. After your system performs its default BIOS checks and detection, you see the "LILO:" prompt. If you leave this prompt alone, whatever operating system is chosen as the default simply boots.

To interrupt the automatic process and specify which operating system to boot, press the Shift key as soon as you see the "LILO:" prompt. To see which boot options are available, press the Tab key. You can then specify which operating system to boot, as well as any options that you might require. These options —as well as the default boot operating system, the delay of the "LILO:" prompt, and more —are specified in the /etc/lilo.conf file. The following is an example of an /etc/lilo.conf file on a system that is dual-booted with Red Hat Linux 6.2 and Windows 98:

```
boot=/dev/hda
map=/boot/map
install=/boot/boot.b
prompt
delay=10
timeout=50
default=linux

image=/boot/vmlinuz-2.2.14-5.0
    label=linux
```

```
read-only
root=/dev/hda3

other=/dev/hda2
    label=dos
```

The first line (**boot=/dev/hda**) specifies the boot device and specifies where LILO is to be installed. In this case, it specifies to install LILO to the MBR of /dev/ hda. If the first line had been

```
boot=/dev/hda1
```

it would have specified to install LILO to the first partition of the /dev/hda1 superblock. Likewise,

```
boot=/dev/sda
```

would have specified to install LILO to the MBR of the SCSI device.

The second line (**map=/boot/map**) specifies the path to the system map file. The /boot/map file contains the names and locations of the kernel or kernels to boot. The third line (**install=/boot/boot.b**) indicates the location of the boot sector.

The rest of the /etc/lilo.conf file specifies settings and arguments that go into effect at the "LILO:" prompt. The **delay** option sets the amount of time you have to press the Shift key at the "LILO:" prompt (to interrupt the default boot process and specify any other options or boot operating systems). The **timeout** option is used to specify the amount of time that the system continues to boot by default if a key has been pressed but nothing was manually executed at the "LILO:" prompt.

The next two lines are related to the root (/) directory. The **root=/dev/hda3** specifies to mount /dev/hda3 as the root filesystem. The **read-only** option specifies to mount the root filesystem as read only, allowing you to check the root filesystem with fsck. Default Red Hat Linux 6.2 systems specify the **read-only** option after each image entry in /etc/lilo.conf. You can specify **read-only** or **root=** before the **image** entries, making it a global setting, which does not require you to set it for each entry.

The last section following the **image** sections mimics the Linux **image=** lines, but it has different boot images and label names. This section is labeled as an **other** entry. The **other** entry tells LILO that there is a bootable system on another partition—for example, the entry other=/dev/hda2 tells LILO that a bootable system resides on the second partition of the first hard drive (hda2). The remaining options under the **other=** entry specify options used to boot the system. In this case, the **other=** entry specifies booting the DOS partition, which happens to be Windows 98.

Note: After changing the /etc/lilo.conf file, always be sure to rerun LILO to activate your changes. To do this, type /sbin/lilo at the root prompt.

Configuring Network Installations

Red Hat Certified Engineers often work in large environments where manual installations from CD-ROM media are not only tedious but also slow compared to installing over a network. Therefore RHCE candidates should be comfortable setting up the network installation servers and creating ways to automate the installations.

Configuring Network Installation Servers

As I discussed in Chapter 5, there are three methods of network installations that a Red Hat client can install with: FTP, HTTP, and NFS.

FTP Installation Server

Setting up an FTP installation server allows clients accessible on your network to install Red Hat from a publicly accessible FTP directory. If your public directory was /home/ftp/install/RedHat, you would need to copy all of the CD-ROM's contents from the RedHat directory into /home/ftp/install/RedHat.

HTTP Installation Server

An HTTP installation server requires your server to support HTTP connections. Setting up HTTP access is quite similar to setting up FTP access. Instead of copying the contents of the RedHat directory into a public FTP folder, you need to place the contents into your HTTP accessible folder, such as /home/httpd/html/install/RedHat. If you decide to support both FTP and HTTP installations, rather than wasting disk space with two copies of the contents of RedHat, simply create a symbolic link (**ln −s**) between the two directories.

NFS Installation Server

An NFS installation server requires a little more work to set up than do the previously mentioned FTP and HTTP servers. For an NFS server, you must properly have nfsd running on the machine. For the installation information, you must create an entry in the /etc/exports file for NFS to create the export. If you had the information located in the FTP directory, /home/ftp/install/RedHat/, you would add an entry to /etc/exports, like this:

```
/home/ftp/pub/RedHat        (ro)
```

Once you have your export entry, you must either restart your NFS server or use the **exportfs /home/ftp/pub/RedHat** command.

Managing Your RPM Installation

After you have set up the network installation server of your choice, you can opt to change the RPMs available for installation by either adding or removing RPMs from the RPMS directory of the install location. You can add or remove RPMs by using the tool called genhdlist. The genhdlist tool can be found under /misc/ src/anaconda/utils. After you've added or removed the RPMs, simply run **genhdlist**, specifying the directory where your RPMs are located:

```
genhdlist /home/ftp/install/RedHat/i386/
```

Installing Automatically Using kickstart

Many large companies and hardware resellers often need to configure Red Hat Linux on many machines. If all the machines have the exact same hardware configuration and need the exact same software configuration, you can automate the installation by using a program called kickstart.

The kickstart program automates your installation by automatically answering the questions that the installation program asks. The kickstart utility works with an ASCII-based instruction file that can be supplied from a boot floppy installation disk or even from an NFS server.

The kickstart program automatically installs Red Hat Linux using several methods. The two main supported methods are CD-ROM-based and NFS-based installations. FTP and HTTP installations, though not commonly advertised, are supported as well.

The kickstart program uses a kickstart configuration file called ks.cfg. The ks.cfg file contains all the configuration answers to all the questions that are asked during an installation. If an answer is not provided in the ks.cfg file, the installation pauses and prompts you to answer the question. After you answer the question, the automatic installation resumes. A sample ks.cfg file follows:

```
lang en_US
network --bootproto dhcp
cdrom
device ethernet
keyboard "us"
zerombr yes
clearpart --linux
part /boot --size 16
part / --size 250
```

```
part swap --size 128
part /usr -size 1000 -grow -maxsize 2000
install
mouse ps/2 --emulthree
timezone --utc US/Central
xconfig --monitor "lcd panel 1024x768"
rootpw redhat
auth --useshadow --enablemd5
#lilo --append 'anything-needed'
%packages
@ KDE Workstation
%post
```

This example shows a very simple and very basic ks.cfg file. The first line specifies that English is the selected language. The second line specifies your network configuration, which in this case is DHCP. The third line specifies the installation medium. This line contains either **cdrom** or **nfs -server** *name.of.server* **-dir /** *pathtoimage/imagefile* and so on. The next two lines configure any devices such as Ethernet and keyboard.

The next five lines in this file relate to the hard disk and its partitioning. The first option, **zerombr**, instructs Red Hat Linux to clear the current partition information. The **clearpart** option specifies to clear all the Linux partitions on the disk. The three **part** options specify the partitions to be created on the disk, including partition type, mount point, and size. I'll discuss changes to the ks.cfg file in more detail later in the chapter (see "Using Diskette-Based kickstart").

The next option, **install,** is a required parameter stating that you will do a fresh installation of Red Hat Linux. The next three options in this sample ks.cfg file are additional configuration settings. The **mouse** option allows you to set the mouse type in addition to any options you need, such as emulating three buttons. The **timezone** option specifies the time zone to set on your machine. The **xconfig** line specifies which X server to install and which type of monitor you are using.

The final options set system information and installation information. The **rootpw** line allows you to specify the root password. If you have the encrypted version of your root password, you can use the following option line:

```
rootpw -iscrypted $whatever%the?scheme*is
```

The **auth** line allows you to permit the use of shadow passwords and MD5. In addition, if your systems are going to use LILO, you can install and configure LILO by using the **lilo** option. You can also append any information that LILO needs by using the **-append** option.

The next section specifies the packages that you want to install. Under the **%packages** line, you can specify individual names of packages to be installed. This line is used if the system will use a custom configuration or if you're going to install additional packages. In addition, you can specify to install the default configuration (such as workstation or server). To do so, use the kickstart file options **@ KDE Workstation, @ GNOME Workstation,** or **@ Server** as needed. Make sure that if you use one of these options, you place a space between the @ sign and the setting.

The final option is called **%post**. This section runs any special commands after the system has been installed. For example, you might want to run a command in the **%post** section that sets up your name server. To do so, type

```
echo "nameserver 192.168.0.254">>/etc/resolv.conf
```

where *192.168.0.254* is your specified name server.

Using Diskette-Based kickstart
The most common type of kickstart installation uses a kickstart boot floppy and a CD-ROM. The required boot floppy uses a ks.cfg configuration file. The ks.cfg file is created based on the installation information on your prototype machine. This means that in order to have a successful ks.cfg boot disk, you must manually set up one machine with the specific settings that you need on the system. After installing the system with everything you want, you can create the ks.cfg file. To do this, run the **mkkickstart** command and redirect the output to the ks.cfg file. For example,

```
mkkickstart >ks.cfg
```

can be run only as root. The mkkickstart utility then probes your prototype system for its configuration. When it's finished, view the ks.cfg file to ensure that everything was detected properly.

After you have created the ks.cfg file, copy it to your boot disk. The appropriate boot disk for this system uses the standard boot.img boot image. Copy the ks.cfg file to the boot diskette's top-level or root directory.

To start your kickstart installation, boot your system with the boot floppy, and have the Red Hat Linux CD-ROM in the CD-ROM drive. At the boot prompt, enter **linux ks=floppy**. Your installation should run automatically from that point.

Using Network-Based kickstart

To use the network-based kickstart utility, you must have an NFS server available on your network to service the installations. In addition, you have to use the StaticIP, bootp, or DHCP scheme for your system. To use a DHCP server, you should have the configuration information for the newly installed system, the location of the kickstart file to be used, and the location of the NFS server available on the DHCP server. The NFS server is used to supply the installation files; however, the DHCP server is set to supply the network information as well as individual ks.cfg files for the installed machines, if necessary.

To start a network-based kickstart installation, you simply need a Red Hat Linux boot disk created with the bootnet.img boot image. At the "boot:" prompt, type **linux ks**. This command looks for the NFS and DHCP servers automatically and obtains all the necessary information.

Setting up network-based kickstart network installations is a bit complex and differs from network setup to network setup. Therefore, documentation for this process is limited. Although knowing network kickstart procedures will be helpful to your career if you work in a large company, extensive knowledge of this process is unnecessary for your RHCE certification. However, you should have a good working knowledge of the process.

Practice Questions

Question 1

What type of boot image is required to use kickstart when you use a CD-ROM?

○ a. bootnet.img

○ b. boot.img

○ c. ks.cfg

○ d. ks.img

Answer b is correct. Answer a is incorrect because the bootnet.img image file is used for doing network installations. Answer c is incorrect because ks.cfg is a configuration file used with kickstart, not a boot image. Answer d is incorrect because ks.img isn't a valid option.

Question 2

You must have a DHCP server in order to use kickstart.

○ a. True

○ b. False

Answer b is correct. A DHCP server is not required with either type of kickstart installation. The CD-ROM doesn't require the DHCP server during installation, even if you're planning to use DHCP for the systems. In addition, with network installations, DHCP servers are required only if you need the DHCP server to assign individual ks.cfg files for each machine (to assign individual static IP addresses and so on).

Question 3

How do you create a kickstart boot floppy?

To create a kickstart boot floppy, you first need to create the boot floppy with the appropriate boot image. When you use a CD-ROM, you create the boot image with the boot.img file. For network installations, you use the bootnet.img files. To create the boot disk, use the **dd** command on Linux (as described in Chapter 5). Next, you must create your kickstart configuration file, named ks.cfg, by running **mkkickstart** on the machine prototype that you want to clone. Write the output of **mkkickstart** to the file ks.cfg by typing **mkkickstart >ks.cfg**. Make any changes you want to the configuration file, and then copy the ks.cfg file to your boot floppy.

Question 4

What are the **%post** entries in the ks.cfg file used for?

○ a. Logging entries

○ b. Scripts run during installation

○ c. Configuration options

○ d. None of the above

Answer d is correct. The **%post** entries are scripts or commands that are run after the installation. Although these scripts might indicate some logging, or configuration options, they can be set up only with the scripts that are run there.

Question 5

How do you force kickstart to prompt you for information during an installation? Why would you want to do this?

To force kickstart to prompt you for an answer or setting during installation, simply do not provide the setting in the ks.cfg file. Doing this is helpful if you want to specify IP addresses without using a DHCP server or if peripherals such as video or mouse differ on various machines.

Question 6

Why do you need to run LILO after editing lilo.conf?

- ○ a. To rerun configuration settings and apply them to the appropriate LILO files, such as /boot/map
- ○ b. To add new operating systems or kernels installed on the system to the LILO boot manager
- ○ c. To save changes you've made in lilo.conf to the MBR or super-block
- ○ d. To check for errors made when editing lilo.conf
- ○ e. All of the above

Answer e is correct. Running LILO after editing the lilo.conf file allows LILO to update its files, such as /boot/boot.b, to add new volumes and so on (answer a). Adding new boot partitions, kernel images, and so on (answer b) also requires running LILO so that they will be recognized as options during boot-time. Answer c is questionable as correct because anything written to the /etc/lilo.conf file is saved when writing the physical file, but running LILO would save the changes to your boot configuration. Answer d is true as well; running LILO finds settings within the file that are duplicated labels or invalid boot images.

Question 7

Why is the root filesystem mounted read-only during the LILO execution but then remounted read/write later during the boot process?

- ○ a. So that crackers cannot get root information with boot sniffers during the boot process
- ○ b. So that if system tasks fail during boot-up, you can run **fsck** on the filesystem without risking damage
- ○ c. So that you cannot write to the root filesystem without root's password
- ○ d. So that other operating systems, such as Windows, can't overwrite your root partition

Answer b is correct. If your boot fails when checking filesystems or other LILO boot options, the filesystem can be dropped to a shell and you can manually check the filesystem without risking damage to the filesystem. Answers a and d are incorrect because those options are impossible to do and therefore invalid.

Question 8

> How can you interrupt the boot process to boot a different operating system if one is already installed?
>
> ○ a. Press Ctrl+Alt+Delete after the "Loading MS Windows" prompt
>
> ○ b. Press Shift after the "boot:" prompt
>
> ○ c. Press Tab after the "LILO:" prompt
>
> ○ d. Press Enter after the "LILO:" prompt

Answer c is correct. You can also press the Shift key at the "LILO:" prompt. Answer a is incorrect because pressing Ctrl+Alt+Delete while loading Windows or Linux reboots the system. Answer b is incorrect because if you are getting a "boot:" prompt, you are booting with an installation disk. In addition, the Shift key won't help you with that option. Answer d is incorrect because pressing Enter at the "LILO:" prompt automatically boots the default operating system or kernel image.

Question 9

> If you are installing Windows on a dual-boot system with Linux, why should you install Windows first?
>
> _____

You aren't required to install Windows first on a dual-boot system, but if you plan to use LILO as your default boot manager, doing so is recommended. By installing Windows first, you avoid the risk of overwriting your master boot record where LILO is installed or of destroying your Linux partitions altogether.

Question 10

> Linux allows you to run Windows and Linux at the same time.
>
> ○ a. True
>
> ○ b. False

Answer b is correct. At the current time, Linux does not allow you to boot multiple operating systems simultaneously. Commercial products, such as VMware, are available that enable you to run other operating systems on virtual machines on Linux but not coexisting on a machine.

Task 1

One of the most repeated special installation options you will use is Linux's ability to multi-boot systems for free. Partition a system with the recommended partition methods and layouts (or even better for partition-crazy zealots), and install Windows or another available operating system in one partition.

Task 2

For those needing a little more challenge, figure out how to dual-boot different Linux distributions. Successfully configure a machine to boot Linux by default, but give yourself the option of booting one or more operating systems.

Task 3

Pretend you have 500 machines just like yours on which to install Red Hat Linux. Use kickstart and develop a boot disk that sets up all 500 machines just like yours. What if 250 of them have larger hard drives? Change the ks.cfg file to reflect this change for the other boot disks. Set them up to prompt you when it's time to set up your X configuration.

Need to Know More?

 Red Hat Linux 6.2: Operating System Installation Guide. Red Hat Software, Inc. Appendix F covers the kickstart installation processes.

 Negus, Chris. *Red Hat Linux Bible.* IDG Books Worldwide, 1999. ISBN 0-764-54574-4. Chapters 1 and 2 cover Red Hat installation.

 McCarty, Bill. *Learning Red Hat Linux.* O'Reilly & Associates: Sebastopol, CA, 1999. ISBN 1-565-92627-7. Chapters 2 and 3 address Red Hat installation issues.

 http://linuxdoc.org/ —The Linux Documentation Project contains links to HOWTOs available for Linux-based operations. Follow the HOWTO links to the Kickstart HOWTO (**http://linuxdoc.org/ HOWTO/KickStart-HOWTO.html**).

 http://www.redhat.com/support/manuals/RHL-6.2-Manual/ref-guide/ch-dualboot.html/ —Appendix D covers dual booting with Red Hat Linus and other operating systems.

Advanced Configuration

Terms you'll need to understand:

✓ Quota

✓ Runlevel

✓ Initialization script

✓ Kernel module

✓ **make** process

✓ cron

Techniques you'll need to master:

✓ Setting up user quotas

✓ Understanding runlevels

✓ Understanding system initialization scripts

✓ Mastering /proc

✓ Understanding the Linux kernel

✓ Compiling a Linux kernel

✓ Configuring a Linux kernel

✓ Setting up cron jobs

✓ Configuring bash

The objective of the RHCE program is to promote advanced skills among its participants. Although one of the goals of Red Hat software is to package a product that an average skilled Linux user can use easily, the goals for an RHCE are set higher. An RHCE should be skilled not only in installation methods but also in configuration methods. An RHCE should also be able to customize all parts of the system—from the kernel to the bash shell. This chapter will discuss many types of advanced configuration methods.

Understanding Quotas

Quotas are essential to system administrators who are administering the data, Web servers, and so on of many users. The quota system is much like setting up a budget for how much disk space a user or group can use on a system.

For you to use system quotas, your Red Hat Linux kernel must be configured to use quotas. By default, the installed Red Hat Linux kernel already has quota support compiled in; however, if you're using a custom or recompiled kernel, you must ensure that quota support is compiled.

After kernel quota support is compiled, you need to see if the quota RPM is installed. To do so, enter **rpm −q quota**. If quota is installed from a Red Hat Linux 6.2 system and the quota RPM is installed, then

```
quota-2.00pre3-2
```

is returned to you. If you do not have the quota RPM installed, you can either obtain the RPM files from your favorite Red Hat FTP site or install them from CD-ROM. To install the quota RPM, simply run

```
rpm -Uvh quota*
```

from the directory that contains your quota RPM files.

The necessary quota files are started in the startup script, located in /etc/rc.d/ rc.sysinit. When executed, the script looks to see if the appropriate scripts are available and then runs **/sbin/quotaon** to turn on quotas. Here are a few snippets of code from the rc.sysinit script that is required to run quotas. This code should automatically be placed in your rc.sysinit file when you install the RPM:

```
# Update quotas if fsck was run on /.
if [ X"$_RUN_QUOTACHECK" = X1 -a -x /sbin/quotacheck ]; then
    action "Checking root filesystem quotas"
        /sbin/quotacheck -v /
fi
```

```
if [ -x /sbin/quotaon ]; then
    action "Turning on user and group quotas for root filesystem"
    /sbin/quotaon -a
fi
```

In addition to the script being started in the rc.sysinit file, you must have the quota options set in the /etc/fstab files. Editing the /etc/fstab files allows you to enforce the quota system on specific filesystems. The following example shows how **usrquota** and **grpquota** must be added to the /etc/fstab files to enable quotas on two filesystems:

```
/dev/hda2    /            ext2    defaults                      1 1
/dev/hda7    /home        ext2    defaults,usrquota,grpquota    1 2
/dev/hda5    /var         ext2    defaults,grpquota             1 2
/dev/hda6    /var/spool   ext2    defaults                      1 2
```

In this example, you notice that the /home filesystem is **usrquota**- and **grpquota**-enabled, but the /var filesystem has only **grpquota** enabled.

To set the quotas for specific users and groups, you would use edquota, the quota editor. The edquota tool allows you to set up disk limits per user, using the quota.user file.

 You can use a prototype to help set up user and group quotas by invoking the **–p** option with **edquota**.

Red Hat Linux also offers a few utilities to help you manage your quota system:

➤ */sbin/quotaon* —Running this utility as root turns on the quota system.

➤ */sbin/quotaoff* —Running this utility disables the quota system.

➤ */sbin/quotastats, /sbin/quotacheck, /usr/sbin/repquota* —Running these utilities generates some reports for quota systems.

Understanding the /etc/inittab File

The /etc/inittab file describes which processes are started at boot-time and during normal operation. In addition, this file contains the settings for the virtual consoles and such. The /etc/inittab file is documented very well, explaining what each section of the file is for.

The first section is for information only. It states the use and author of the file. The second section discusses the seven *runlevels*, which are the different states in which the system is running. Runlevel 0 is the halt state. Runlevel 1 indicates that the system is running in single-user mode. Runlevel 1 allows you to administer your system without multi-user support.

Did you forget your root password? You can boot into runlevel 1 (single-user mode) and change the password.

Runlevel 2 is multi-user mode, but it has no networking support. Runlevel 3 is full multi-user mode and does offer full networking support. Runlevel 4 isn't used. Runlevel 5 on Red Hat Linux is full multi-user mode, and it boots into an X-based login screen. Runlevel 6 is for rebooting. Following the runlevel descriptions is a line that starts with **id:**. This line specifies the default runlevel to boot into. After your system is booted into a particular runlevel, you can access other runlevels by using the **init** or **telinit** commands. By issuing an **init 6** command at the root prompt, you can command the system to reboot. However, issuing an **init 1** command tells the system to boot into single-user mode. These commands can be issued only by root. Here is an example of an /etc/inittab file:

```
#
# inittab    This file describes how the INIT process should set up
#            the system in a certain run-level.
#
# Author:    Miquel van Smoorenburg, <miquels@drinkel.nl.mugnet.org>
#            Modified for RHS Linux by Marc Ewing and Donnie Barnes
#
# Default runlevel. The runlevels used by RHS are:
#   0 - halt (Do NOT set initdefault to this)
#   1 - Single user mode
#   2 - Multiuser, without NFS (The same as 3, with no networking)
#   3 - Full multiuser mode
#   4 - unused
#   5 - X11
#   6 - reboot (Do NOT set initdefault to this)
#
id:3:initdefault:
```

The third section of the /etc/inittab file details the boot sequence. It starts the system initialization with the rc.sysinit script (see "Understanding System Initialization

Scripts," later in this chapter). This section then calls the rc files shown in the following code.

```
# System initialization.
si::sysinit:/etc/rc.d/rc.sysinit

l0:0:wait:/etc/rc.d/rc 0
l1:1:wait:/etc/rc.d/rc 1
l2:2:wait:/etc/rc.d/rc 2
l3:3:wait:/etc/rc.d/rc 3
l4:4:wait:/etc/rc.d/rc 4
l5:5:wait:/etc/rc.d/rc 5
l6:6:wait:/etc/rc.d/rc 6

# Things to run in every runlevel.
ud::once:/sbin/update
```

The fourth section sets specific commands and options. In particular, it maps the Ctrl+Alt+Delete key sequence, which automatically reboots the system. You can disable or change that option here.

```
# Trap CTRL-ALT-DELETE
ca::ctrlaltdel:/sbin/shutdown -t3 -r now
```

The fifth section of the /etc/inittab file sets up your virtual consoles (also discussed in Chapter 6). This specific setup is the default and allows up to six virtual consoles. To add additional virtual consoles, duplicate the lines and then change the first field and the **tty** field to represent the appropriate number of your virtual console. Here is a snippet of the /etc/inittab file that sets your virtual consoles:

```
# Run gettys in standard runlevels
1:2345:respawn:/sbin/mingetty tty1
2:2345:respawn:/sbin/mingetty tty2
3:2345:respawn:/sbin/mingetty tty3
4:2345:respawn:/sbin/mingetty tty4
5:2345:respawn:/sbin/mingetty tty5
6:2345:respawn:/sbin/mingetty tty6

# Run xdm in runlevel 5
# xdm is now a separate service
x:5:respawn:/etc/X11/prefdm -nodaemon
```

As set in the /etc/inittab file, root can use **init** and **telinit** to access other runlevels during regular operation. You can also use these two commands to shut down or reboot a system. You don't have to memorize these **init** commands; Red Hat Linux offers the **shutdown** command, which allows you to safely shut down your system. With **shutdown**, you can specify to halt with the **–h** option and reboot with the **–r** option. Passing a **–t** option in addition to either the **–r** or **–h** option allows you to specify the time. For instance, **shutdown –r** specifies a reboot right now, whereas **shutdown –ht 300** specifies a shutdown in 300 seconds.

Understanding System Initialization Scripts

System initialization scripts, all of which are found under the /etc/rc.d directory, are used to boot the system. Some of the most popular system initialization scripts are /etc/rc.d/rc.sysinit, /etc/rc.d/rc.serial, etc/rc.d/rc.local, and /etc/rc.d/rc0.d through /etc/rc.d/rc6.d (runlevel directories).

rc.sysinit

The /etc/rc.d/rc.sysinit script is the main startup script. Its main purpose is to check all the local filesystems. If there is a problem with performing the filesystem check, the rc.sysinit script is instructed to drop out of the existing shell, send the administrator an error message, and reboot the system. In addition, the rc.sysinit script instructs a filesystem to use quotas. Listing 8.1 includes some excerpts of the rc.sysinit script. This script is quite lengthy, so I have removed some of the extensive sections. For a complete look, take a glance at your /etc/rc.d/rc.sysinit file. The excerpts include the information related to filesystem checking and quotas.

Listing 8.1   Excerpts of the rc.sysinit script.

```
# Start up swapping.
action "Activating swap partitions" swapon -a

# This sets up some filesystem check options
if [ -f /fsckoptions ]; then
      fsckoptions='cat /fsckoptions'
   else
      fsckoptions=
fi

if [ -f /forcefsck ]; then
      fsckoptions="-f $fsckoptions"
fi

_RUN_QUOTACHECK=0
if [ ! -f /fastboot ]; then
       STRING="Checking root filesystem"
```

```
        echo $STRING
        initlog -c "fsck  -T -a $fsckoptions /"
        rc=$?

        if [ "$rc" = "0" ]; then
              success "$STRING"
            echo
        elif [ "$rc" = "1" ]; then
              passed "$STRING"
            echo
          fi

        # A return of 2 or higher means there were serious
        # problems.
        if [ $rc -gt 1 ]; then
            failure "$STRING"
            echo
            echo
            echo "*** An error occurred during the file
                    system check."
            echo "*** Dropping you to a shell; the system
                    will reboot"
            echo "*** when you leave the shell."

            PS1="(Repair filesystem) \#"; export PS1
            sulogin

            echo "Unmounting file systems"
            umount -a
            mount -n -o remount,ro /
            echo "Automatic reboot in progress."
            reboot
        elif [ "$rc" = "1" ]; then
            _RUN_QUOTACHECK=1
          fi
fi

# Remount the root filesystem read-write.
action "Remounting root filesystem in read-write mode"
mount -n -o remount,rw /

# Update quotas if fsck was run on /.
if [ X"$_RUN_QUOTACHECK" = X1 -a -x /sbin/quotacheck ]; then
    action "Checking root filesystem quotas"
    /sbin/quotacheck -v /
fi
```

```
# XXX Disabled to avoid complaints on root later with quotaon -a
#if [ -x /sbin/quotaon ]; then
#    action "Turning on user and group quotas for root filesystem"
     /sbin/quotaon /
#fi

# Check filesystems
if [ ! -f /fastboot ]; then
    STRING="Checking filesystems"
        echo $STRING
        initlog -c "fsck  -T -R -A -a $fsckoptions"
        rc=$?
         if [ "$rc" = "0" ]; then
                success "$STRING"
                echo
        elif [ "$rc" = "1" ]; then
                passed "$STRING"
                echo
        fi

        # A return of 2 or higher means serious problems.
        if [ $rc -gt 1 ]; then
                failure "$STRING"
                echo
                echo
                echo "*** An error occurred during the file system
                     check."
                echo "*** Dropping you to a shell; the system will
                     reboot"
                echo "*** when you leave the shell."

                PS1="(Repair filesystem) \#"; export PS1
                sulogin

                echo "Unmounting file systems"
                umount -a
                mount -n -o remount,ro /
                echo "Automatic reboot in progress."
                reboot
        elif [ "$rc" = "1" -a -x /sbin/quotacheck ]; then
          action "Checking quotas" /sbin/quotacheck -v -R -a
        fi
fi

# Mount all other filesystems (except for NFS and /proc, which is
# already mounted). Contrary to standard usage,
```

```
# filesystems are NOT unmounted in single user mode.
action "Mounting local filesystems"
    mount -a -t nonfs,smbfs,ncpfs,proc

if [ -x /sbin/quotaon ]; then
    action "Turning on user and group quotas for local
filesystems"
    /sbin/quotaon -a
fi

# Now we have all of our basic modules loaded and the kernel
going,
# let's dump the syslog ring somewhere so we can find it later
dmesg > /var/log/dmesg
```

rc.serial and rc.local

The /etc/rc.d/rc.serial file was used in older versions of Linux. It is rarely used on any current systems, and when it is, it is only for backward compatibility. Most of the functionality of the old rc.serial file can now be found in the rc.local file.

The /etc/rc.d/rc.local file is used to configure local computers. All the commands and scripts that run with this file are executed after the computer boots but before anyone logs into the system. The rc.local file is also executed after a system runlevel is changed. One of rc.local's jobs is to create the login banner that by default displays your kernel version and machine type. To change this, you can edit this file. A sample /etc/rc.d/rc.local file follows:

```
#!/bin/sh

# This script will be executed *after* all the other init scripts.
# You can put your own initialization stuff in here if you don't
# want to do the full Sys V style init stuff.

if [ -f /etc/redhat-release ]; then
    R=$(cat /etc/redhat-release)

    arch=$(uname -m)
    a="a"
    case "_$arch" in
        _a*) a="an";;
        _i*) a="an";;
    esac

# This will overwrite /etc/issue at every boot.  So, make any
# changes you want to make to /etc/issue here or you will lose
```

```
# them when you reboot.
   echo "" > /etc/issue
   echo "$R" >> /etc/issue
   echo "Kernel $(uname -r) on $a $(uname -m)" >> /etc/issue

   cp -f /etc/issue /etc/issue.net
   echo >> /etc/issue
fi
```

The actual prompt is displayed by /etc/issue and /etc/issue.net. The file, however, is overwritten by /etc/rc.d/rc.local. Therefore, any manual changes you make in the /etc/issue and /etc/issue.net files must also be reproduced in the rc.local file.

Runlevel Directories

The system runlevel directories are /etc/rc.d/rc0.d through /etc/rc.d/rc6.d. These directories don't actually contain real files or scripts. Instead, they contain links to scripts that are located in the /etc/rc.d/init.d directory.

The links in the rcX.d directories are run through when the system accesses the rc.sysinit system initialization script. Each directory contains symlinks to real scripts. Here is an excerpt of the files in /etc/rc.d/rc0.d:

```
lrwxrwxrwx 1 root root 13 Jun 15 1999 K10xfs -> ../init.d/xfs
lrwxrwxrwx 1 root root 13 Jun 15 1999 K15gpm -> ../init.d/gpm
lrwxrwxrwx 1 root root 13 May 9 19:54 K20nfs -> ../init.d/nfs
```

Each symlink in each of the rcX.d files is noted with an S or a K at the beginning of the symlink file name. S indicates that the script is to be started; K indicates that it should be stopped. Following the S or K is a two-digit number that indicates the order in which the scripts are to be run. For example, 10 gets run before 15.

Following is a list of the scripts that are started or stopped between the seven runlevels. Each time another runlevel is accessed, such as with **init 1**, all the services in the associated rcX.d directory are performed.

➤ *rc0.d*—K00linuxconf, K05keytable, K08autofs, K10xfs, K10xntpd, K15gpm, K15httpd, K15sound, K20isdn, K20nfs, K20rstatd, K20rusersd, K20rwhod, K25squid, K30sendmail, K35dhcpd, K35smb, K45named, K45sshd, K50inet, K55routed, K60atd, K60crond, K60lpd, K61ldap, K65identd, K70nfslock, K75netfs, K80random, K83ypbind, K89portmap, K90mysql, K90network, K92apmd, K92ipchains, K95kudzu, K96pcmcia, K99syslog, S00killall, S01qhalt

➤ *rc1.d*—K00linuxconf, K05keytable, K08autofs, K10xfs, K10xntpd, K15gpm, K15httpd, K15sound, K20isdn, K20nfs, K20rstatd, K20rusersd, K20rwhod, K25squid, K30sendmail, K35dhcpd, K35smb, K45named, K45sshd, K50inet,

K55routed, K60atd, K60crond, K60lpd, K61ldap, K65identd, K70nfslock, K75netfs, K83ypbind, K89portmap, K90mysql, K90network, K92apmd, K92ipchains, K95kudzu, K96pcmcia, K99syslog, S00single, S20random

➤ *rc2.d* —K08autofs, K10xntpd, K15httpd, K15sound, K20isdn, K20nfs, K20rstatd, K20rusersd, K20rwhod, K25squid, K35dhcpd, K35smb, K45named, K45sshd, K50inet, K55routed, K60atd, K61ldap, K65identd, K70nfslock, K75netfs, K83ypbind, K89portmap, K92ipchains, K95kudzu, S05apmd, S10network, S20random, S30syslog, S40crond, S45pcmcia, S60lpd, S75keytable, S80sendmail, S85gpm, S90mysql, S90xfs, S99linuxconf, S99local

➤ *rc3.d* —K01kdcrotate, K10xntpd, K15httpd, K15postgresql, K15sound, K20isdn, K20nfs, K20rstatd, K20rusersd, K20rwhod, K25squid, K35dhcpd, K35smb, K45arpwatch, K45named, K55routed, K61ldap, K82autofs, K83ypbind, K90mysql, K92anacron, K92ipchains, K96irda, S05kudzu, S10network, S11portmap, S14nfslock, S16apmd, S20random, S25netfs, S30syslog, S35identd, S40atd, S40crond, S45pcmcia, S50inet, S55sshd, S60lpd, S75keytable, S80sendmail, S85gpm, S86oss, S90vmware, S90xfs, S99linuxconf, S99local

➤ *rc5.d* —K08autofs, K10xntpd, K15postgresql, K20isdn, K20nfs, K20rstatd, K20rusersd, K20rwhod, K25squid, K35dhcpd, K35smb, K45arpwatch, K45named, K55routed, K61ldap, K83ypbind, K92ipchains, S05apmd, S05kudzu, S10network, S11portmap, S14nfslock, S20random, S25netfs, S30syslog, S35identd, S40atd, S40crond, S45pcmcia, S50inet, S55sshd, S60lpd, S75keytable, S80sendmail, S85gpm, S85httpd, S85sound, S85mysql, S90xfs, S99linuxconf, S99local

➤ *rc6.d* —K00linuxconf, K05keytable, K08autofs, K08vmware, K10xfs, K10xntpd, K15gpm, K15httpd, K15sound, K20isdn, K20nfs, K20rstatd, K20rusersd, K20rwhod, K25squid, K30sendmail, K45sshd, K50inet, K55routed, K60atd, K60crond, K60lpd, K61ldap, K65identd, K70nfslock, K75netfs, K80random, K83ypbind, K89portmap, K90mysql, K90network, K92apmd, K92ipchains, K95kudzu, K96pcmcia, K99syslog, S00killall, S01reboot

Understanding the Linux Kernel

The Linux kernel is the foundation on which Linux is based. The Linux kernel, in fact, is where Linux gets its name. As discussed in Chapter 3, the Linux kernel was developed as a hobby by a student named Linus Torvalds in Helsinki, Finland. The Linux kernel, combined with many applications and GNU tools, is what makes up Red Hat Linux today. In this section, I'll discuss technicalities of the kernel, good housekeeping practices, kernel modules, kernel configuration, kernel compiling, and more.

Kernel Basics

There are two types of Linux kernels: *monolithic* and *modular*. Monolithic kernels are much like old-style Unix kernels. All the system support is compiled directly in the kernel. Therefore, if SCSI support is required, all the SCSI drivers and so on are compiled directly in the kernel. This creates a much larger kernel, but it runs a little faster at boot-time. In addition, monolithic kernels use a constant amount of RAM.

On the other hand, the only drivers that modular kernels need compiled are those required at boot-time. Remaining drivers and support are installed as modules and are loaded only when needed. The modular kernel method is less secure than the monolithic kernel method; however, the modular kernel method is more memory-efficient and allows the kernel to be much smaller.

Some systems require the use of ramdisks. Initial ramdisks are required when support—such as SCSI support during boot-up—is needed. The ramdisk is noted in your /etc/lilo.conf file as an **initrd=** comment. I'll discuss creating this file later in this chapter.

Kernel Housekeeping

Good kernel housekeepers know how to keep their kernels clean and their systems functioning. It's a good habit to never delete an existing kernel when you compile a new one or when you install a new one with an RPM. Rather than overwriting your existing kernel, rename it. You can then set up LILO, the Linux boot loader, to boot your existing kernel as a choice, just in case your new kernel is unbootable.

If your new kernel is unbootable, do not fret. You kept your existing kernel to boot from, didn't you? Chances are you might have misconfigured your system, maybe even set the wrong options during your configuration, or possibly have a missing or corrupt kernel source. If one of these situations happens, try debugging your kernel problems by noting the errors you receive when compiling or booting. If you can't solve the problem, try and try again. Just remember that wherever you visit, clean up after yourself. Leaving behind old configurations from previous trials might make future attempts less successful.

Kernel Modules

Kernel modules are used in modular kernels. Kernel modules are loaded as needed when support for a specific device or protocol is required. Modules that the kernel uses are located in the /lib/modules/ directory. The files located under /lib/modules/ are separated by kernel versions. For instance, on my system, I have installed kernel 2.2.12-20 and 2.2.14-5.0. Therefore, I have a directory under /lib/modules/ for each kernel.

When a request is made for a service from a module that either hasn't been loaded or isn't compiled directly into the kernel, the kernel (using kmod) tries to load the needed module. To find the needed module, kmod runs modprobe, which looks into /lib/modules/, then into the appropriate kernel directory, and then into the appropriate device directory, if needed.

Red Hat Linux provides a number of tools that make controlling modules simpler. These tools include lsmod, insmod, rmmod, and modprobe. The lsmod tool tells you which modules are running. A sample output of lsmod follows.

```
Module             Size   Used by
parport_pc         7304   0  [vmppuser]
parport            7452   0  [vmppuser parport_pc]
lockd              30344  1  (autoclean)
sunrpc             52132  1  (autoclean) [lockd]
ds                 6696   2
i82365             29800  2
pcmcia_core        44480  0  [ds i82365]
ppp                19500  0  (autoclean) (unused)
slhc               4312   0  (autoclean) [ppp]
```

The insmod tool loads a specific module manually. The rmmod tool removes any idle modules that aren't being used. The modprobe tool automatically loads all base modules that are needed for a specific service.

Module Configuration

Module loading used to be handled in Red Hat Linux by **kerneld**. As of the 2.2 Linux kernel, **kerneld** became obsolete. The Red Hat Linux kernel now uses **kmod,** a kernel process, to handle the loading of kernel modules.

One configuration file used with modularized kernels is /etc/conf.modules. The /etc/conf.modules file specifies commands, options, paths, and so on for modules. In addition, this file sets up any module aliases and parameters that might be required.

Red Hat Linux also has a kernel configuration tool (kernelcfg) that is used in X to help configure kernel modules. To run this tool, enter **kernelcfg** at the root prompt. The window shown in Figure 8.1 appears.

The Kernel Configurator lists the installed modules on your system. You can then add or delete modules with the Add and Remove buttons located at the

Figure 8.1 The Kernel Configurator.

bottom of the window. In addition, you can edit current modules to add any arguments you may require. The fourth button, Restart kerneld, allows you to restart kerneld on older Red Hat Linux systems. With **kmod**, this button is deprecated.

Kernel Configuration

The files you need to boot a kernel are located in the /boot directory. These files include System.map, boot.b, boot.0300, initrd, and kernel boot images (typically named with the vmlinuz prefix). The System.map file is a file that you use to debug the kernel. The boot.b file is the file that LILO creates; it's used in the second stage of LILO and is pointed from LILO in the master boot record. The boot.0300 file is a backup of your master boot record that is created when you install LILO. The initial ramdisk used to boot a system that uses SCSI during the boot process is called initrd. The vmlinuz files are the kernel boot images that are created during the kernel's **make** process.

Kernel source and documentation are located under the /usr/src/linux directory. Under this directory you'll find a number of files and resources that you might find helpful when compiling or even debugging your kernel. Some of these files include the CREDITS file, which gives credit to many of the contributors to the Linux kernel, as well as the Documentation directory, which contains many text files with details about hardware, kernel files, and more. The Documentation directory also contains files that are required for compiling a kernel, such as Makefile and System.map. By default, any work you do with the Linux kernel will take place under this directory.

Kernel Configuration Tools

The first step in compiling (or recompiling) a kernel involves the make tool, which allows you to select and deselect exactly which options you want to include and modularize for the new kernel. These configuration settings are stored in a file in /usr/src/linux/.config. There are three methods of using the make tool to help you configure your kernel: **make config, make menuconfig,** and **make xconfig.** Each of these methods creates a file with the .config extension that is used when you're making the zImage or bzImage of the kernel.

Note: To successfully use the make tool, be sure you have all the appropriate packages installed. All methods of make require the glibc-devel, egcs, make, kernel-headers, kernel-source, bin86, and cpp packages. If you opt to use the make menuconfig option, you must also have the ncurses and ncurses-devel packages installed. If you opt for the make xconfig option, you must have X Window support.

The first method, **make config,** is a text-based tool that you use to configure your kernel options. This tool is considered to have the most difficult interface for configuring a kernel. However, **make config** is a standard tool and is used in all Linux distributions. When you use **make config,** you are prompted line by line to include support for a specific item. Following each question, you are given up to four options: **y** for yes, **n** for no, **m** for modularize, and **?** for help. Choosing the **?** option gives you details about what the particular item is and what the default settings are. The default settings for a particular item are noted with the option being capitalized. For instance, the first question—"Prompt for development and/ or incomplete code/drivers (CONFIG_EXPERIMENTAL) [Y/n/?]"—has a default answer of "Y" or yes. To use the default answer, you can press Enter. The following displays the interface used in **make config:**

```
rm -f include/asm
( cd include ; ln -sf asm-i386 asm)
/bin/sh scripts/Configure arch/i386/config.in
#
# Using defaults found in .config
#
*
* Code maturity level options
*
Prompt for development and/or incomplete code/drivers
(CONFIG_EXPERIMENTAL) [Y/n/?]
*
* Processor type and features
*
Processor family
(386, 486/Cx486, 586/K5/5x86/6x86, Pentium/K6/TSC, PPro/6x86MX)
[PPro/6x86MX]
   defined CONFIG_M686
```

```
Math emulation (CONFIG_MATH_EMULATION) [N/y/?]
MTRR (Memory Type Range Register) support (CONFIG_MTRR) [Y/n/?]
Symmetric multi-processing support (CONFIG_SMP) [N/y/?]
```

The second type of **make** method is **make menuconfig**. This method is one of the most popular among Red Hat Linux users. It gives you a graphical window-based display without requiring you to use the X Window System. When you use **make menuconfig**, you are presented with a directory-tree menu system. Follow-ing each selection, you are presented with the available options. To include an option, press the **Y** key; to exclude it, press the **N** key; and to modularize it, use the **M** key. Letters that are highlighted are considered hotkeys; they allow you to quickly maneuver through the menu options. To exit a window, select the Exit option or press the Escape key twice. Figure 8.2 shows you the **make menuconfig** interface.

The third type of **make** method is **make xconfig**. This method is very popular among new Linux users and users who are accustomed to graphical interface tools. The **make xconfig** tool requires that full X Window System support be used. When starting **make xconfig**, you are presented with a window with buttons for each class of configuration. After choosing a configuration button, you are prompted, in a tree style, with the options available. You can then select, deselect, or modularize each option by choosing the corresponding button next to the item.

One of the benefits of using this **make** method over the standard **make config** method is the backward mobility of the configuration. This means that if you change your mind, or make a mistake, you can move back and change the option with **make xconfig**; you can't do this with **make config**. With the **make config**

Figure 8.2   Linux Kernel Configuration (**make menuconfig**).

method, you must restart your configuration process. Figure 8.3 shows the graphical user interface used with the **make xconfig** method.

Kernel Configuration Options

When configuring a kernel by using any of the make tools described earlier in this chapter, you are presented with at least 20 divisions of configuration options. These options range everywhere from configuration tool preferences to hardware support and even development tools. This section discusses the different categories of options available, the settings available, and the standard preferences and practices for each category.

Note: The options described in the following sections are not necessarily listed in the order in which your make option presents them. The order in which you configure your kernel does not affect the kernel in any way. These options and descriptions are based on the compilation of kernel 2.2. Options for other kernels, older or newer, might have fewer or additional options and categories because more hardware and other technologies are supported.

Code Maturity Level

One of the first categories concerns Code Maturity Level options. The Code Maturity Level option sets whether the kernel configuration tool prompts you for development or incomplete support options within the kernel. If you set this option to No, all development and incomplete support options are automatically disabled. It is recommended that you set this option to Yes. Many tools require development packages in order to work properly.

Linux Kernel Configuration		
Code maturity level options	Ethernet (1000 Mbit)	Ftape, the floppy tape device driver
Processor type and features	Appletalk devices	Filesystems
Loadable module support	Token ring devices	Network File Systems
General setup	Wan interfaces	Partition Types
Plug and Play support	Amateur Radio support	Native Language Support
Block devices	IrDA subsystem support	Console drivers
Networking options	Infrared-port device drivers	Sound
QoS and/or fair queueing	ISDN subsystem	Additional low level sound drivers
Telephony Support	Old CD-ROM drivers (not SCSI, not IDE)	Kernel hacking
SCSI support	Character devices	
SCSI low-level drivers	Mice	Save and Exit
Network device support	Joysticks	Quit Without Saving
ARCnet devices	Watchdog Cards	Load Configuration from File
Ethernet (10 or 100Mbit)	Video For Linux	Store Configuration to File

Figure 8.3 Linux Kernel Configuration (**make xconfig**).

Processor Type and Features

The first question, regarding Processor Family, sets certain assumptions for the kernel. When the Processor Family option is set to 386, the kernel you compile should run on *any* x86-compatible processor. Using any higher CPU family makes the kernel assume certain capabilities in the processor (which might have a large impact on performance on that type of CPU). Therefore, the resulting kernel probably won't run on anything lower than the family you specify.

The next three questions allow you to set Intel Pentium/PII/PIII options. Disabling the serial number at boot-up makes the kernel disable the CPU ID serial number that is embedded on the new PIII CPUs. Enabling PII/PIII Extended/Fast FPU (floating-point unit) save-and-restore support is required to make use of the new PIII 128-bit XMM registers. Enabling CPU-specific MMX/MMX2 optimization functions allows the use of the MMX registers and 128-bit MMX2 registers.

The Math Emulation option turns on the kernel software's floating-point emulation. This is safe to turn on even for CPUs with hardware floating-point units because the kernel detects the FPU at boot-up and disables emulation. Turning this option on increases the size of the kernel, however, so it's necessary only for 386, 486SX, and other CPUs without hardware floating-point units.

The MTRR Support option can have a huge impact on performance. This option allows you to turn on write-combining for certain cards, such as video cards on the PCI or AGP bus. This option is available only on Pentium II (and higher) and K6-2 (and higher) CPUs. It's safe to turn this option on for CPUs that don't support it because it adds just a small amount of additional code to the kernel.

The Symmetric Multiprocessing Support option turns on SMP support in the kernel. This is also safe for uniprocessor systems. However, turning on this option might slow such systems down slightly, and it adds a small amount of code to the kernel.

The setting for Maximum Physical Memory allows you to set the maximum RAM amount the kernel will recognize. By default the kernel sees a maximum of 1GB. The alternate option is 2GB.

Note: New 2.4 kernels have support for 4GB on x86 platforms.

Loadable Module Support

You are given the option to configure loadable module support—required for modular kernels—during kernel configuration. The three options available under this heading are to enable loadable module support, to set version information on all symbols for modules, and to enable the kernel module loader. For modular kernels, you must select Yes for Loadable Module Support and Kernel Module Loader. The Set Version Information choice is optional. The modular version setting is used to make modules usable after a kernel compilation without your having to recompile the module.

General Setup

The general setup section of the kernel configuration options has about 29 options. The first option is to enable BIGMEM support. This is required if you want to use more than 1GB of memory. Two of the main options in this section are for networking and PCI support. If you set the Networking Support option to No, the configuration tool automatically disables all networking-related configuration options. If you want any networking connectivity, you should set this option to Yes.

As with the Networking Support option, choosing No for the PCI Support option automatically disables all PCI-support-related configuration options. If your motherboard has any PCI slots or PCI support, choose Yes for this option. Most 586 (and higher) processors and motherboards have PCI onboard. If your motherboard does not have PCI onboard, choose No.

The remaining options in this section set system preferences. Other hardware support options and other system options are available here. Kernel support for specific types of binaries (such as a.out, java, and ELF binaries) is located here. In addition, specific hardware support, such as whether to support PC style or foreign hardware, is set here.

Your power management support is also located in this set of options. If your BIOS can support Advanced Power Management (APM), you should select Yes here. The remaining APM options allow you to specify how APM manages CPU calls, shutdown options, suspend options, and more.

Plug and Play

Most Intel computers use some sort of plug-and-play hardware. Therefore, under the Plug and Play Support category, you can decide whether to supply support for plug-and-play hardware in your kernel. Most administrators answer Yes to this option. Also found in this category is support for autoprobing for parallel devices on your system. If any parallel devices will be used on your system, enable this option. It's recommended to modularize this option so that the support is loaded only when needed.

Note: With 2.2.x (and newer) kernels, Plug and Play Support is used only for parallel devices.

Block Devices

The Block Devices section of kernel configuration is quite extensive and very specific. Within this section, you can specify floppy-disk, CD-ROM, tape, IDE, SCSI, and ATAPI device support. With the exception of IDE disk support, most of these options should be modularized to be loaded as needed.

In addition to these media devices, PCI and IDE chipset support options are available. Here, you enable whichever chipset you have on your system and disable the rest. Besides the chipset information, you can select device support, such as loopback, network block, multiple device driver, and ramdisk support. Loopback device support is typically modularized, whereas network block support and multiple-device-driver support are enabled only if needed. Ramdisk support is required by SCSI-booted systems that need to use initial ramdisks (initrd) to boot. If you use SCSI hard drives, you should enable this option.

The final options in this section include XT hard disk support and parallel-port IDE device support. If your system will access an XT hard disk, you should enable the support. If you think you might ever connect a parallel-port IDE device, such as a CD-ROM drive, tape drive, or other IDE device, it's recommended to modularize this support.

Networking Options

The Networking Options section contains all the configuration options for everything related to networking, including hardware, software, and protocols. The Packet Socket option turns on an interface that allows programs to communicate directly with network devices. Programs such as tcpdump, packet sniffers, and dhcpcd (a DHCP client) use the interface to send and receive packets without going through the kernel TCP stack.

The Kernel/User Netlink Socket option turns on support for communication between certain network-related parts of the kernel and user processes. This option is currently used by the kernel to publish routing messages (when **CONFIG_RTNETLINK** is on) and by **arpd** and the ethertap device.

The next two prompts are related to kernel firewalling options. The first prompts for support for network firewalls. Selecting Yes turns on support for IP firewalling, masquerading, and so on. The second prompts for support for socket filtering. Selecting Yes enables support for user-space socket filters.

The Unix Domain Socket option turns on support for Unix domain sockets, which are heavily used by many programs, such as syslogd and X, even when a system is not connected to a network. You should enable this option except in embedded applications where you know that no communication over Unix domain sockets will occur.

Enabling support for the TCP/IP networking option includes support for TCP/IP networking, which many normal programs use heavily. Again, turn this option on except in embedded applications where you know you won't use TCP/IP.

Several other TCP/IP-related configuration options appear in this section. The first option includes experimental support for the new IPv6 networking protocol, which will sometime soon replace the current TCP/IP protocol (IPv4) used on the Internet. If you want to test IPv6 on your network, turn on this driver.

Within this section, you're also prompted for support of other networking protocols, such as IPX and AppleTalk DDP. Enabling the IPX option turns on support for the IPX protocol, which older versions of Novell's NetWare NOS use. Enabling the AppleTalk DDP option turns on support for the AppleTalk protocol, which Apple MacOS networks use to share files and printers.

Three experimental options are available to enable support for networking over amateur radio links: CCITT X.25 Packet Layer, LAPB Data Link Driver, and 802.2 LLC. You can use X.25 over amateur radio, as well as over serial links and Ethernet. LAPB is a link-level protocol that is used with the X.25 protocol. The 802.2 LLC choice is another option for a link-level protocol (over Ethernet) for X.25.

The next options allow you to enable support for various network operations. The first option allows experimental support for bridging. Enabling this option allows the Linux kernel to act as an Ethernet bridge. The second option can enable support for wide area network (WAN) routing. This new option allows you to configure support for WAN adapter cards, such as Sangoma frame relay cards. A third, new network operation option is for fast switching. This new option allows support for direct NIC-to-NIC transfers. Be leery of this option, however, because it is not compatible with several other network options (such as kernel firewalling). Enable this option only if the system will act as a dedicated router.

A few options that manage network connectivity and flow are also available. One of the first options enables forwarding between high-speed interfaces. This option turns on support for hardware throttling when the network is congested. See the online help for this option if this sounds like something you need. Another option is new: support for CPUs that you suspect are too slow to handle the full bandwidth of the network they are attached to. Most often, you don't need to enable this option.

QoS and/or Fair Queuing

QoS (Quality of Service) is used to manage the distribution of packets over a network device. If you want to use the default scheduling algorithm, do not enable the option. If you consider yourself an expert and you'd like to experiment with other schedulers, enable this option.

Telephony Support

The options under Telephony Support enable or modularize functions used in telephony card equipment under Linux. The second option specifically enables support for Quicknet Technologies, Inc., cards.

SCSI Support

The first option for SCSI support is simply to enable SCSI support, which turns on support for SCSI devices. If you turn this option on, you are given the opportunity to configure various driver options and to configure support for various types of devices and interface cards. Unless you're booting off a SCSI device, it's safe to simply modularize this option in case you install a SCSI card or other SCSI device.

SCSI Low-Level Drivers

Beneath the SCSI Low-Level Drivers configuration option, there are 90 options to enable support and to customize settings for your SCSI support. Most of the options enable support for various SCSI chipsets, such as Adaptec AHA152X, Adaptec AIC7xxx, BusLogic SCSI, and NCR53c8xx. Other options allow you to configure bus reset delays, command queues, and more.

Network Device Support

There are several options available in the Network Device Support section. The first option, to enable support for network devices, allows you to configure support for various network devices. If you enable this option, you're prompted for specific network device support. If you select No for this option, the following network devices are automatically disabled.

Another network device option is for dummy net driver support. Enabling this option allows you to include support for a "dummy" network interface. Traffic sent to this interface is simply discarded. This option is useful for keeping a permanent IP address associated with a system, even though its only "real" network interface is PPP or SLIP.

A handy option located here is support for EQL (serial line load balancing). Enabling this option turns on support for load balancing over PPP or SLIP interfaces. You can use EQL to combine multiple lower-speed serial links into a single higher-speed network interface. Note that the other end of the link must also support this protocol.

Another device that you can enable is support for FDDI (Fiber Distributed Data Interface) drivers. Turning this option on allows you to configure support for

FDDI adapter cards. In addition to FDDI support, there is an option to enable frame relay DLCI support. Turning on this option allows you to configure support for frame relay adapter cards.

The next three options—PLIP, PPP, and SLIP support—allow you to enable these types of network connections. Enabling PLIP support enables parallel port connections. This option turns on support for the Parallel Line Internet Protocol, which works over specially modified parallel cables. Enabling PPP support enables point-to-point connections. This option turns on support for the PPP protocol, which is most commonly used for networking over serial links such as modems. Enabling SLIP support enables serial line connections. This option turns on support for SLIP, a protocol that predates PPP and that is used to network over serial links. PPP is a more robust protocol, so you generally won't need SLIP support. Turning the SLIP option on also allows you to configure various SLIP driver options.

New options found here include options for wireless networking. Some options include AT&T WaveLAN technology, Aironet Arlan, and wireless LANs that aren't ham radio.

ARCnet Devices

The configuration options under ARCnet Devices allow you to configure network cards with ARCnet chipsets. ARCnet is an old networking system that somewhat resembles Ethernet and that is used primarily on PCs.

Ethernet (10 or 100Mbit)

The most-needed option in this category is to enable Ethernet support. This option allows you to configure support for various Ethernet controllers. The most common varieties you'll find are 10Base-2 or Thinnet (10Mbps over coax cable), 10Base-T or twisted-pair (10Mbps over twisted-pair cable), 10Base-F (10Mbps over fiber-optic cable), 100Base-TX (100Mbps over two twisted-pair cables), 100Base-T4 (100Mbps over four standard voice twisted-pair cables), and 100Base-FX (100Mbps over fiber-optic cable). The 100Base Ethernets are also known as Fast Ethernet.

Ethernet (1000Mbit)

1000Mbit Ethernet is also known as Gigabit Ethernet. This is 1Gbps over fiber-optic cable or short copper links. The configuration options under Ethernet (1000Mbit) are to specifically support different varieties of Gigabit Ethernet cards.

AppleTalk Devices

AppleTalk is used when you need your Linux box to communicate in a Macintosh environment. The options within the AppleTalk Devices section configures support for various firmware and encapsulation options.

Token Ring Devices

Turning this option on allows you to include support for a few token-ring adapter cards in the kernel. Token ring is an old, slow, and expensive local-area-network system that IBM developed and heavily pushed several years ago. It's still commonly found in large IBM-centric organizations.

WAN Interfaces

This category contains options for enabling support for WAN devices, such as serial boards and I/O adapters. Vendor-specific devices such as Comtrol, MultiGate, and Sealevel Systems are found here.

Amateur Radio Support

One of the smaller categories includes options in your kernel configuration for amateur radio support. Turning on this option allows you to configure support for networking over amateur radio. You should enable this option only if you plan to work with radio networking.

Infrared Support

Another small category enables the new option of support for infrared devices. The main option in this category is to enable IrDA subsystems support. Enabling this option allows you to configure support for communication over certain infrared interfaces. This category includes an option for networking between infrared interfaces.

Infrared-port Device Drivers

This category contains a number of options for supporting various IrDA drivers, ports, and serial dongles. Specifically, you can select support for IrTTY using Linux serial drivers versus IrPORT using IrDA serial drivers. In addition, you can select various serial dongle types, such as ESI, ACTiSYS, Greenwich, or Parallax.

ISDN Support

You can select support for ISDN with the ISDN Support option. Enabling ISDN Support allows you to configure kernel support for ISDN adapter cards and for networking over ISDN.

Old CD-ROM Driver Support

Some systems use CD-ROM drives other than SCSI or current IDE CD-ROM drives. Enabling this option allows you to configure support for CD-ROM drives that use old proprietary interfaces, such as those commonly found on older sound cards. Typically, you don't need to enable this support.

Character Devices

Within the Character Devices category, there are approximately 12 configuration options. One of the first options is to enable support for virtual terminal devices. This is the standard way of supporting the keyboard/mouse/monitor combination of a system in Linux. You should consider this a required option on all systems other than embedded devices.

Another option allows the system console to be set to a virtual terminal. The system console is where kernel messages go and where logins are allowed in single-user mode. You should turn this option on unless you're sure you will always use another device, such as a serial port, for the system console.

Another Character Devices option is to enable support for standard, generic, dumb serial ports. Turning this option on allows you to set a serial port as the system console. To enable console support on the dumb terminal, you must enable support for the console on the serial port. Some additional serial-support options include Extended Dumb Serial Driver and Non-standard Serial Port Support. Enabling the Extended Dumb Serial Driver option allows you to turn on certain options for the standard serial driver, such as support for IRQ sharing. Enabling the Non-standard Serial Port Support option allows you to configure support for various intelligent serial boards.

The next option in this category is to enable support for Unix98 PTY. Turning this option on includes kernel support for the /dev/pts/*number* naming scheme for pseudo-terminal devices mandated by the UNIX98 specification. This system is supported in the GNU C library version 2.1 and higher. It is used by default in Red Hat 6.2 and higher.

If you plan to connect a parallel printer to the system, you must enable parallel printer support. In addition, there is an option to enable printer read-back. It turns on support for status read-back from printers. When this option is turned on, you get status information about the printer when you execute **cat** /**dev**/*lp0* (or whatever the printer device is).

Some older systems use an old-style QIC-02 tape drive. To enable support for this type of tape drive, you must turn on the QIC-02 Tape Support option.

Another option in this category is to enable watchdog timer support. Doing so allows you to configure support for the watchdog device, which is used to monitor system health by triggering a reboot if the device isn't written to in a certain period of time. The idea is that if a process's only job is to occasionally write to this device, and that process fails, something bad must have happened to the system. The watchdog device can be driven entirely by software that might not be reliable if the system has crashed. The watchdog device can also be tied to special hardware-monitoring cards. Most administrators don't use this software watchdog option.

To be able to read and write to a PC's CMOS, you must enable /dev/nvram support. This option turns on support for reading and writing a system's nonvolatile RAM (NVRAM) area. On PCs, this is usually called the CMOS. This can be used, for example, to store a small amount of information that will persist over reboots. Doing so can be very dangerous, though, because overwriting the NVRAM on a system will probably make it unbootable. Most administrators don't enable this option.

The last option in this category is for enhanced real-time clock support. This option turns on extended support for the real-time clock chip on most systems. This is generally handy to have available, and it is required for synchronization on SMP systems.

Mice

Special input devices, such as special mouse types, require different support within the kernel. In the Mice category, you can enable support for ATIXL bus mouse, Logitech bus mouse, Microsoft bus mouse, and even digitizer pads. Also, if you plan to use a PS/2 mouse instead of a serial mouse, you must enable the PS/2 mouse support here.

Joysticks

With gaming becoming more popular on the Linux platform, more specialized joysticks are being supported. Enabling joystick support allows you to select support for specific joysticks, such as those made by Gravis, Logitech, Microsoft, and Creative Labs.

Watchdog Cards

A popular monitoring system for Linux is Watchdog. Within the Watchdog Cards category, you can enable various features such as shutdown options, timer options, and WDT501 features.

Video for Linux

The category of Video for Linux is a bit misleading. This category is not for video display support, such as X support, but is for additional video option support. Enabling support for Video for Linux allows you to configure support options for various video-capture cards, TV tuner cards, and FM radio cards.

Ftape Support

Ftape is the floppy-tape device. Enabling the Ftape (QIC-80/Travan) Support option allows you to configure kernel support for various tape drives that use the standard PC floppy-disk interface.

Filesystem Support

The Filesystem Support category for kernel configuration currently contains options for about 14 filesystem types. One of the first options is Quota Support. Enabling this option turns on support for user and group quotas (usage limits) on filesystems.

Another option is for kernel automounter support. This option turns on kernel support for a daemon that can be used to automatically mount both local and remote filesystems. This option can be extremely convenient, especially on desktop systems.

One of the first options for types of filesystems is the experimental support option for the read-only ADFS filesystem. There are also options for supporting the Amiga FFS filesystem and the experimental Apple Macintosh filesystem. These options allow you to configure support for the native filesystems used by Acorn's RiscOS, AmigaOS, and MacOS, respectively.

To read DOS- and Windows-style FAT filesystems from Linux, you must have support for these filesystems. Enabling the DOS FAT fs support option allows you to configure support for DOS- and Windows-style FAT filesystems.

The standard filesystem used on CD-ROMs is the ISO9660 filesystem. To enable support for this system, you must select Yes for the ISO 9660 CD-ROM filesystem support option.

Some additional options for supporting foreign filesystems include support for the Minix fs, the read-only NTFS filesystem, and the read-only OS/2 HPFS filesystem. These options turn on support for the native filesystems of Minix (which was also once the native Linux filesystem), Windows NT, and OS/2, respectively.

The /proc filesystem support options turn on support for the /proc filesystem. An option that comes after this—/dev/pts filesystem for Unix98 PTYs—turns on support for the devpts virtual filesystem. This filesystem is used to create and remove pseudo-terminal device entries in /dev/pts as needed. If you have turned on support for Unix98 PTYs, turn this on.

The next option is QNX filesystem support. This support is experimental; when enabled, it provides support for the filesystem used by the QNX real-time OS. For read-only media, the ROM filesystem support option is used. This option turns on support for a lightweight filesystem designed for read-only media. This option is generally useful only for installation media and embedded systems.

A very important option is for the second extended filesystem, which is the standard filesystem on Linux. The second extended fs support option turns on support for this.

Two options that support other Unix filesystems include the System V and Coherent filesystem support option and the UFS filesystem support option. These two options allow you to turn on support for the filesystems used in many other Unix (or Unix-like) systems, especially some of the "genuine" Unix systems derived from AT&T or BSD code. The System V filesystem is used by some SysV-based systems such as SCO. UFS is used by many BSD-based systems.

Network File Systems

Multiple options are found beneath the Network File Systems category. The first option enables support for the Coda filesystem, an advanced filesystem that supports advanced features such as client caching of files.

The next few options deal with network filesystem (NFS) support. The first option enables direct support for the NFS filesystem and turns on support for the kernel client. This is the standard method of file sharing between Unix (and Unix-like) systems. Such support is generally good to have available. The second option enables support for the NFS server. This is new in the 2.2.x kernels. Using the new knfsd tools, the kernel does the work that was previously done with a user-space **nfsd** on earlier Linux systems. The knfsd tools are much more robust, and much cleaner, because the user-space nfsd could not easily access information such as inode numbers, which are passed between the NFS server and the client.

The next options set up support for Samba filesystems. The first enables SMB filesystem support. This option turns on support for the kernel SMB (Lan Manager/Samba/Windows NT) client. Mounted SMB shares appear as standard Unix-like filesystems. The second option enables the Samba Windows 95 bug workaround. The one case where you should turn this option on is for systems in which the only SMB shares that will be mounted are on Windows 95 systems.

The final option in this category is for NCP filesystem support. This is used to mount NetWare volumes. Enabling this option turns on support for NetWare client support in the kernel. Mounted NetWare volumes appear as standard Unix-like filesystems.

Partition Types

You can enable five major partition types in the kernel. These options turn on support for various partition-table formats that various operating systems use. The first option is for BSD disk-label support, which enables support for BSD-style partition tables. The second option is for Macintosh partition-map support. This is used on the Macintosh platform. The third option is for SMD disk-label support, which enables support for Sun partition tables. The fourth option is for support of the x86 Solaris partition table. The last option is the experimental support for Unixware slices. By default, Linux uses the DOS-style partition-table format.

Native Language Support

If you turn on FAT support, or support for the Microsoft Joliet extension to ISO9660, you are prompted for support for NLS, which is used to support the various character sets used around the world. These character sets are labeled by codepage and their appropriate number, such as codepage 437, which is the character set for the United States and Canada. Approximately 27 character sets, ranging from United States English to Turkish to Russian, are available.

Console Drivers

The four options in the Console Drivers category allow you to enable options for your Linux console. The first is the VGA text console support option. This option turns on support for the standard PC-style VGA text console. You should almost always turn this on for x86 systems.

The second is the video mode selection support option. It includes support in the kernel for switching VGA text modes by using the BIOS before the kernel boots into protected mode (and can no longer use the BIOS). To use this option, you must boot the kernel with the "**vga=**" option.

The third option is support for the dual-headed MDA text console. Enabling this new experimental option allows you to run with an old Hercules monochrome adapter and monitor on your system. This can be very handy for keeping something such as the system log displayed on a second monitor at all times.

The next option in this category is new: support for frame buffer devices. This option turns on support for frame buffer console devices, which are used primarily on non-x86 systems for graphical console support. On x86 systems, this can still be useful because there is an option for VESA frame buffer support, which lets you run with a graphical console at high resolution on any VESA 2.0-compatible video card.

Sound Support

For systems with sound cards, you should enable sound support. The prompt to enable sound support is simply Sound Card Support. Turning this option on allows you to configure support for sound cards and to configure various options for the Linux kernel sound driver.

Additional Low-Level Sound Drivers

If you are unable to find the support for your sound card within the Sound Support category, you might find it in the Additional Low-Level Sound Drivers category. Some of the options found here include AWE32 synth, Gallant Audio cards, and options for some sound-card joystick interfaces.

Kernel Hacking

A final category for configuring your kernel is Kernel Hacking. This category has only one option, which you use to configure support for the SysRq key. This option turns on support for various "magic" key sequences using Alt+SysRq (also PrintScreen) on the standard PC keyboard. These sequences can synchronize all mounted filesystems, kill all processes on the virtual console, reboot the system, and so on. This option can be very convenient, but you should not turn it on for systems where access to the system's console could be a security risk.

Compiling and Installing a Custom Kernel

When compiling and installing a kernel, you use various **make** options. There are as many as 11 options that you can use when compiling and installing your kernel from start to finish; I'll describe them in this section. Follow these steps to compile and install a new kernel:

1. You must first configure your kernel as discussed in the "Kernel Configuration Options" section earlier in this chapter. There are several options available to configure your kernel. First, to compile your kernel, you must be in the /usr/src/linux directory. Next, if you plan to configure your kernel completely from scratch, first use **make mrproper**. Doing so removes your current .config file and allows you to set up all new options for your kernel without knowing your current default configuration. If you want to see your

current default options, skip the **make mrproper** step. To finish configuring your kernel, use your choice of **make config**, **make menuconfig**, or **make xconfig**, as discussed earlier in this chapter.

2. Next, you must do some general kernel housekeeping. This means that you need to clean up any unneeded or temporary files from the kernel source tree. To clean up the source tree, run **make clean**.

3. Next, you must ensure that all dependencies are available and correctly placed. The two dependencies in particular are the kernel header files /usr/src/linux/ config.h and /usr/src/linux/proc_fs.h. To check for these dependencies, run **make dep**.

4. You must next create the kernel image. Your two options are **make zImage** and **make bzImage**. Both methods compile a kernel image, place it in the /arch/i386/boot directory, and then call the image either zImage or bzImage (depending on the method you use).

   The method you use depends on the size of your kernel. If your kernel image plus the compressed kernel image is smaller than 640K, you can use zImage. However, if your kernel is monolithic, or otherwise larger than 640K, you should use bzImage. Unless you're attempting to make the smallest possible kernel, it's always safe to use bzImage.

   After the image is created, copy the zImage or bzImage from the /usr/src/ linux/arch/i386/boot directory to the /boot directory. In the /boot directory, you might want to rename the image to something like vmlinuz-*the.kernel.version*, such as 2.2.18.

5. Next, you compile your modules. If you made a completely monolithic kernel, skip to Step 7. Otherwise, run **make modules** to compile all of your selected modules.

6. You must next install your compiled modules by running **make modules_install**. When you install the modules with this **make** option, **make** installs them to /lib/modules.

   Note: With the post-configuration make options—such as make clean, make dep, make bzImage, make modules, and make modules_install —you don't have to invoke each make command one at a time. You can string them together to run automatically without user intervention; to do this, run make clean dep bzImage modules modules_install . While letting this run, you can do whatever you want; you don't need to wait for any specific task until all make options are finished.

7. Next, create the ramdisk image (if required). The ramdisk image is used to preload block device modules (such as SCSI drivers to access SCSI hard drives) that are required during boot-time to access the root filesystem. To create this ramdisk image, use the **mkinitrd** command in the format **mkinitrd /boot/***newimage the.kernel.version* , where *newimage* is the name of the new ramdisk image and *the.kernel.version* is the kernel version.

8. Last, you set up LILO for your new kernel by editing the /etc/lilo.conf file. If you're installing your new kernel the recommended way (by adding it as an additional boot option to your existing kernel), you simply add another boot image section to /etc/lilo.conf. Otherwise, you change the current boot image section to reflect your new kernel image name and initrd image (if necessary). For instance, if you just compiled kernel 2.2.18, named the image /boot/vmlinuz-2.2.18, and created an initrd image to /boot/initrd-2.2.18, your new boot image section of /etc/lilo.conf should look like this:

```
boot=/dev/hda
map=/boot/map
install=/boot/boot.b
#prompt
delay=20
timeout=2400
root=/dev/hda3
read-only
image=/boot/vmlinuz-2.2.18
        label=2.2.18
        initrd=/boot/initrd-2.2.18
```

Note: After you have edited your /etc/lilo.conf file, make sure to install the new /etc/lilo.conf configuration by running /sbin/lilo.

The Vixie cron System

The Vixie cron system allows your machine to run specific commands at regularly specified intervals. You can set these commands to run hourly, daily, weekly, monthly, or even yearly. Both root and individual users can use the cron system.

The cron system uses configuration files named crontab. The system's crontab file is located in /etc/crontab. User-specific crontabs are in /var/spool/cron/ *username*. If a cron job specifies a standard **out** request, the output is emailed to the user who owns the job.

Looking at the /etc/crontab File

The system's crontab file is located in /etc/crontab. This file looks very simple. In fact, the /etc/crontab file, by default, is composed of only nine lines. Four of them are script settings, and one is a comment. A default /etc/crontab file follows:

```
SHELL=/bin/bash
PATH=/sbin:/bin:/usr/sbin:/usr/bin
MAILTO=root
HOME=/

# run-parts
01 * * * * root run-parts /etc/cron.hourly
02 4 * * * root run-parts /etc/cron.daily
22 4 * * 0 root run-parts /etc/cron.weekly
42 4 1 * * root run-parts /etc/cron.monthly
```

Note: The only difference between the system crontab file and a user's crontab file is the sixth field, which specifies which user the command should be run as.

The layout of root's /etc/crontab file was developed so that you can simply administer cron jobs and the crontab file itself. You don't have to specify line after line of cron jobs to be run; rather, when you set individual cron settings for each script or job, root's /etc/crontab file sets times for a script to execute all scripts within a specific directory. The script used to run the files within the specific directory is run-parts, located in /usr/bin/run-parts. Looking at the run-parts script, you can see that it opens the indicated directory, checks to see that it is in fact a directory, and runs all the scripts located within that directory. See the following script to understand how run-parts works:

```
#!/bin/bash

# run-parts - concept taken from Debian

# keep going when something fails
set +e

if [ $# -lt 1 ]; then
        echo "Usage: run-parts <dir>"
        exit 1
fi
```

```
if [ ! -d $1 ]; then
        echo "Not a directory: $1"
        exit 1
fi

for i in $1/* ; do
        [ -d $i ] && continue
        # Don't run [KS]??foo.{rpmsave,rpmorig,rpmnew} scripts
        [ "${i%.rpmsave}" != "${i}" ] && continue
        [ "${i%.rpmorig}" != "${i}" ] && continue
        [ "${i%.rpmnew}" != "${i}" ] && continue

        if [ -x $i ]; then
                $i
        fi
done

exit 0
```

The directories that run-parts is asked to run by default are divided and named by how often the job scripts within the directories are run. For instance, cron.weekly jobs run every week, and cron.daily jobs run daily. Some default jobs in cron.daily might be **logrotate** and **tmpwatch**. If specified, the logrotate script rotates all system logs, such as /var/log/messages and /var/log/maillog. The tmpwatch script searches the system and removes temporary files that haven't been accessed for a specified length of time.

Setting Up a User's crontab File

Setting up a crontab file for a user is a little more complex than setting up root's crontab. A user can create her own crontab file with the **crontab -e** command, which drops the user into edit mode. The user's crontab file is created in /tmp but is saved in /var/spool/cron/*username*. The user's crontab file is created with a layout similar to root's /etc/crontab file, but rather than the scripts being split off into directories, they are listed directly in the file, configuring individual time settings. In the crontab file, you can enter lines that look much like this:

```
#Description of Job to be run and when
* * * * * /path/to/script
```

Typically, it's good practice to add comments to each line for each job you run so that you can remember which job is running and when. You don't want to be manually looking up the script each time. The five asterisks (*) at the beginning of each script line are the five fields for setting when the script is to be run. If the field isn't set, the field has an asterisk. The first field indicates which minute of the hour the script should run. Valid settings for this field are 0 (or 00) through 59. If the five fields read 22 * * * *, the script runs on the twenty-second minute of every hour.

The second field specifies the hour of the day. Valid settings for this field are 0 through 23. If the five fields read 00 12 * * *, the script runs every twelfth hour at the zero minute of every day.

The third field indicates the day of month. Valid settings for this field are 0 through 31. If the five fields read 0 0 1 * *, the script runs the first day of every month at the zero hour and zero minute.

The fourth field specifies the month of the year. Valid settings for this field are 1 through 12. In addition, you can use names of the month (such as jan, feb, mar, and so on) here. If the five fields read 0 0 1 3 *, the job runs the first day of the third month of every year at the zero hour and zero minute.

The final script specifies the day of the week. Valid settings for this field are 0 through 7, where both 0 and 7 are Sunday. In addition, you can specify the day's name (such as sun, mon, tue, and so on). If the five fields read 0 12 * * 5, the job runs every Friday of every week of every month at the zero minute of the twelfth hour.

Each of the time fields also allows you to specify ranges and multiple run times. Using a dash (-) between two options in a field specifies that the script should run within the valid range. Using a comma to separate two options in a field specifies that the script should run at both times. For instance,

```
30 12 1,15 2,4,6,8,10,12 * /usr/sbin/rm -rf /home/user/tmp/*
```

removes all files under the tmp directory in the user home directory at 12:30 P.M. on the first and fifteenth days of every other month, starting in February and including April, June, August, October, and December. On the other hand,

```
30 12 1-15 3-9 * /usr/sbin/rm -rf /home/user/tmp/*
```

removes all the directories in the user's tmp directory at 12:30 P.M. every day between the first and the fifteenth of every month between March and September. If you tossed in a 5 in the fifth directory, the job would run every Friday as well, even outside the March-through-September range or the first-through-the-fifteenth range.

Note: When the time on a system is changed for any reason, such as correction, Daylight Savings Time, and so on, the crontab files might be affected. If the time is moved forward by less than one hour, any scripts or jobs scheduled to run during that time are still executed. However, if the time is moved ahead by more than an hour, the scheduled jobs are missed.

On the other hand, similar jobs apply to moving time back. If the time is moved backward by less than one hour, the scheduled jobs are not run again. However, if time is moved back by more than an hour, commands are re-executed.

Bash Configuration

Chapter 6 discussed how to configure the bash options for individual users. As a reminder, you should recognize the files .bash_logout, .bash_profile, and .bashrc. These files—which are modeled after the system-wide bash shell configuration files—work interactively with these user files to set up the bash shells for each user. By working interactively, I mean that these files call upon one another for system settings and preferences. Each time a bash shell is executed, three system-wide configuration files are executed and used: /etc/bashrc, /etc/profile, and /etc/profile.d/.

Each time a bash shell is executed, it calls the /etc/profile script, which calls script files that are located under /etc/profile.d. The /etc/profile script calls for a user's .bash_profile (or .profile) file for local settings. The user's .bash_profile file calls for the user's .bashrc file. The user's .bashrc file then calls the system's /etc/bashrc file.

/etc/bashrc

The /etc/bashrc file is the global setup file for the bash shell. Red Hat Linux ships with several shells, including bash, korn, and c, but the standard Red Hat Linux shell is bash. The /etc/bashrc file, by default, simply specifies options for the shell prompt. Here is a sample /etc/bashrc file:

```
# /etc/bashrc

# System wide functions and aliases
# Environment stuff goes in /etc/profile

# are we an interactive shell?
if [ "$PS1" ]; then
    if [ "x`tput kbs`" != "x" ]; then
    # We can't do this with "dumb" terminal
        stty erase `tput kbs`
    fi
    case $TERM in
```

```
        xterm*)
        PROMPT_COMMAND='echo -ne "\033]0;${USER}@${HOSTNAME}: \
        ${PWD}\007"'
                ;;
            *)
                ;;
        esac
        PS1="[\u@\h \W]\\$ "

        if [ "x$SHLVL" != "x1" ]; then # We're not a login shell
            for i in /etc/profile.d/*.sh; do
                if [ -x $i ]; then
                    . $i
                fi
            done
        fi
fi
```

This /etc/bashrc file prints a prompt (indicated by the **PS1=** line). It says to print the default prompt (PS1) with the format within the double quotation marks. The **\u@** indicates to print the username@, and the **\h** indicates to print the host name. The **\W** indicates to print the last directory name within the entered path. The open and close square brackets, [ ], around the statement say to print brackets around the prompt. With the above setting on a system, your default prompt would look something like this:

```
[root@celery root]#
```

You could change the **PS1=** line to become a little simpler. For instance, if you wanted your prompt to simply read the host name but print the full path, your /etc/bashrc file would change the selected line of code from the previous sample to read:

```
PS1='\h:\w\$'
```

This /etc/bashrc file would give you this prompt:

```
celery:~$
```

If you're in a directory other than the home directory, you would get

```
celery:/etc$
```

Note: You might have noticed the difference between the two /etc/bashrc files: One uses double quotation marks ("") around the options, and the other uses single quotation marks ('). The difference is in the way the output is handled. For example, typing echo "$HOME" prints your home directory, whereas typing echo '$HOME' at the prompt prints $HOME exactly.

/etc/profile

The system administrator uses the /etc/profile script to set the global defaults for all users. The /etc/profile script is run by all bash users at login and calls scripts that are saved in /etc/profile.d/ upon system startup. The following is a sample /etc/profile script:

```
# /etc/profile

# System wide environment and startup programs
# Functions and aliases go in /etc/bashrc

PATH="$PATH:/usr/X11R6/bin"
PS1="[\u@\h \W]\\$ "

ulimit -c 1000000
if [ 'id -gn' = 'id -un' -a 'id -u' -gt 14 ]; then
        umask 002
else
        umask 022
fi

USER='id -un'
LOGNAME=$USER
MAIL="/var/spool/mail/$USER"

HOSTNAME='/bin/hostname'
HISTSIZE=1000
HISTFILESIZE=1000

INPUTRC=/etc/inputrc
export PATH PS1 HOSTNAME HISTSIZE HISTFILESIZE USER LOGNAME MAIL
INPUTRC

for i in /etc/profile.d/*.sh ; do
        if [ -x $i ]; then
                . $i
        fi
done

unset i
```

The script starts with the default **PATH** and prompt settings. Next, it specifies the size limit of core files. It then determines the umask of the user shell by determining the user by the user id and whether the user is root. Next, the username, log name, and mail spools are set by determining the login user. Then the host name and history options are set. The **histsize** is the number of commands the history file will remember, and the **histfilesize** is the number of lines the history file can host. The next line specifies where the readline startup file is located. The rest of the script sets the options that use the **export** command, and then runs any scripts located in the /etc/profile.d/ directory.

/etc/profile.d/

The /etc/profile.d/ directory contains any special scripts that the /etc/profile directory should use. This is important because it allows RPM (or you) to add scripts to the directory rather than having you edit the /etc/profile file. Some scripts that you might see in the /etc/profile.d/ directory set up KDE, language, and other shell options. Here is a list of some sample scripts you might find in your /etc/profile.d/ directory:

➤ kde.csh

➤ kde.sh

➤ lang.sh

➤ mc.csh

➤ mc.sh

➤ profile

Practice Questions

Question 1

What script is run for setting bash global defaults for all users?

- ○ a. /etc/profile
- ○ b. /etc/bashrc
- ○ c. /etc/.bashrc
- ○ d. /etc/.profile

Answer a is correct. Answer b is incorrect because it is an invalid file. Answers c and d are incorrect because they configure user-specific aliases and functions, not global defaults.

Question 2

How can a user set up his own crontab file?

- ○ a. **vi /etc/crontab**
- ○ b. **crontab –e**
- ○ c. **vi /user/crontab**
- ○ d. **make cron**

Answer b is correct. Answer a is incorrect because it sets up root's crontab file. Answers c and d are incorrect because they are invalid commands.

Question 3

What does the **0 0 1 1 * /home/kara/.happynewyear** crontab entry do?

This entry in an /etc/crontab file runs the script .happynewyear from the /home/kara directory on the first day of the first month of the year at the zero minute and zero hour.

Question 4

> Which set of commands successfully compiles a new kernel?
>
> ○ a. **make mrproper, make config, make clean, make zImage, make modules_install, make lilo**
>
> ○ b. **make mrproper, make menuconfig, make bzImage, make modules, make modules_install**
>
> ○ c. **make xconfig, make clean, make dep, make bzImage, make modules, make modules_install**
>
> ○ d. **make mrproper dep clean bzImage modules modules_install**

Answer c is correct. Answer a is incorrect because it does not include the **make dep** and **make modules** options. In addition, **make lilo** is not valid. Answer b is incorrect because it does not include the **make clean** and **make dep** options. Answer d is incorrect because it has no .configure file to compile from because **make mrproper** deletes the current .config file.

Question 5

> What format of partition tables does Linux use?
>
> ○ a. Linux
>
> ○ b. BSD
>
> ○ c. Unixware
>
> ○ d. DOS

Answer d is correct. Answer a is incorrect because it isn't a valid partition-table format. Answer b is incorrect because BSD disk labels aren't used by Linux by default. Answer c is incorrect because Unixware slices aren't Linux defaults either.

Question 6

> The **make menuconfig** option is a menu-driven tool that requires X video support.
>
> ○ a. True
>
> ○ b. False

Answer b is correct. The **make menuconfig** tool is menu driven, but it doesn't require X support. The **make xconfig** command, however, does require such X support.

Question 7

> Who created the Linux kernel?
>
> ○ a. Linus Torvalds
>
> ○ b. Richard Stallman
>
> ○ c. Jon "maddog" Hall
>
> ○ d. Bill Gates

Answer a is correct. Answer b is incorrect because Richard Stallman founded the GNU project. Answer c is incorrect because Jon "maddog" Hall is the director of Linux International. Answer d is incorrect because Bill Gates was affiliated with Xenix back in the early 1980s.

Question 8

> To halt a Linux system, what can you do?
>
> ○ a. Ctrl+Alt+Delete
>
> ○ b. **shutdown –t**
>
> ○ c. **shutdown –r now**
>
> ○ d. **init 0**

Answer d is correct. Answers a and c are incorrect because both reboot the system, not halt it. Answer b is incorrect because it isn't complete.

Question 9

> What is the main difference between runlevel 2 and runlevel 3?

Runlevels 2 and 3 are both multi-user runlevels. The biggest difference between the two is simply networking support. Runlevel 2 is full multi-user mode without networking, and runlevel 3 is full multi-user mode with networking support.

Question 10

What command is used to set user and group quotas?

○ a. **/usr/sbin/quota**

○ b. **/sbin/quotaon**

○ c. **/sbin/edquota**

○ d. **/sbin/usrquota**

Answer c is correct. Answers a and d are incorrect because they are not valid commands. Answer b is incorrect because it turns quotas on but doesn't set them up.

Task 1

Recompile your kernel. Use the different **make** configuration tools—such as **make config**, **make menuconfig**, and **make xconfig**—to discover how these **make** options differ and to decide which method you prefer.

Task 2

Set up two new kernels, one monolithic and one modular. Do you notice any differences?

Need to Know More?

 Æleen Frisch. *Essential System Administration*. O'Reilly & Associates, 1995. ISBN 1-56592-127-5. Chapter 14 discusses Unix-style boot processes, and Chapter 15 discusses compiling a Linux kernel.

 http://www.linuxdoc.org/ —The Linux Documentation Project provides an excellent resource on all aspects of Linux, including compiling Linux kernels.

X Window System

Terms you'll need to understand:

✓ Graphical user interface (GUI)

✓ Client/server relationship

✓ Root window

✓ Window manager

✓ Terminal emulator

✓ Desktop environment

✓ Remote host

Techniques you'll need to master:

✓ Understanding X client/server relationships

✓ Selecting the proper XFree86 (XF86) server for specific hardware

✓ Configuring an X server

✓ Understanding desktop environments

✓ Setting up remote X access

The X Window System is the GUI used when Linux is running. Most administration tools used in Linux have a GUI interface that can be used with the X Window System. Most administrators use the X Window System on their Red Hat Linux machines. Therefore, it is imperative that when you are studying for the RHCE 302 exam, you understand the X Window System, X servers, X clients, and remote X applications.

X Concepts

The X Window System is not a new technology. In fact, it was implemented on several Unix systems before Linux was even created. One of the best explanations for where the X Window System came from can be found in the X Window System HOWTO, maintained by Ray Brigleb and found in the LDP (Linux Documentation Project, **http://www.linuxdoc.org/**). The HOWTO explains that the X Window System was developed in the Laboratory for Computer Science at the Massachusetts Institute of Technology and was first released in 1984. The origins of X are based on the W Windowing package developed by Paul Asente at Stanford.

The HOWTO continues to explain that in September 1987, MIT issued the first release of the X11 that we know and use today. As of X11R2, however, development and control passed from MIT to the X Consortium, formed in January 1988.

The X Window System is currently developed and distributed by the X.Org consortium. A liberal license permits the existence of free and low-cost implementations. Linux uses the XFree86 version of the X Window System. The XFree86 version, which can be freely distributed, is a collection of X servers for Unix-based operating systems on Intel x86 platforms. The work is derived from X386, and much of the new work is contributed back into the X11R6 project.

X Window System Components

The X Window System is made up of four main components that interact with one another to function: an X server, an X client, the X protocol, and an X window manager. We'll discuss the server, client, and window managers later in this chapter.

You can establish the X Window System client/server relationship in two ways. Typically, on a Red Hat Linux system, the X client and the X server are located on the same machine. In this scenario, the X application acts as the X client, and the hardware display adapter acts as the X server. In other instances, especially within large Red Hat Linux networks, the client/server relationship is established between two separate machines—a physically separate X client and a separate X server.

With both client/server relationships, however, the X client makes requests to the X server. The X server responds by drawing the windows on the X server display. The X server's response translates the X client's request into hardware instructions, such as to put a pixel here, change this pixel color there, do a screen refresh, and so on.

All the request and response exchanges between the X client and the X server are carried over the X protocol, the X Window System's underlying network transparent protocol. The X protocol is used to enable programs to display graphic images on your monitor.

The traffic that is set up between the X client and the X server does not go by itself between the client and the server. In fact, an X window manager is required. The X window manager, of which there are several types, acts like "middle management" between the X client and the X server.

X Server

The X server is responsible for listening for X client requests for instructions about how to draw windows in a specific way on the X display. If the X server is running without a client that makes requests, your monitor has a gray screen without any features or windows displayed. To understand the X Window System, and to pass the RHCE 302 exam, you must know about the various XF86 servers available and X configuration.

XFree86 Servers

Most Linux distributions use the XFree86 servers supplied by the XFree86 Project. The XFree86 Project, Inc., is a non-profit organization that produces XFree86, a freely distributable implementation of the X Window System that runs on Linux and other x86-based Unix-based operating systems. Red Hat 6.2 is released with XFree86 3.3.6-20. The XFree86 Project for the 3.3.x system currently has over 15 available XFree86 servers. However, all of these servers are being combined into one with the release of XFree86 version 4.0. Upcoming releases of Red Hat will be packaged with both 3.3.6 and 4.0.x versions of XFree86. Until all the video drivers are rewritten for 4.0.x, 3.3.6 will have better hardware support. Using 3.3.6, each server supports a specific type or family of video chipsets. Some of the most common servers are the FBDev, I128, Mach8, Mach32, Mach64, S3 Virge, SVGA, and VGA16. The majority of video cards used today use the SVGA, Mach64, and S3 XF86 servers.

Note: When all servers are compiled into one server with the release of XF86 version 4, individual chipset support will be modularized for use with the single XF86 server.

To see if an XF86 server included in your Red Hat Linux distribution supports your video hardware, check Red Hat Software's hardware compatibility lists (**http://www.redhat.com/**). For hardware support of other versions of XFree86, visit http://www.xfree86.org/, the Web site of the XFree86 Project, Inc. At this Web site, you can also download new versions of the XFree86 server.

X Server Configuration

Setting up the X Window System involves many files, options, and settings. All the configuration files used for the X Window System, as well as several programs and configuration tools, are found in the /etc/X11/ directory. The most important programs and tools include X and xinit, as well as Xconfigurator, XF86Setup, and xf86config.

The X file is actually a symlink to Xwrapper, which runs /etc/X11/X, which is symlinked to the X server you're using. The X server you're using is in the /usr/X11R6/bin/ directory. Therefore, if you were using the XF86_S3 X server, your X file could be symlinked to /usr/X11R6/bin/XF86_S3.

The xinit program is used to start the X Window System. When executed without a specific client program indicated, the xinit program looks for a file named .xinitrc in the user's home directory. The .xinitrc file is a script used to start up client programs as the user has specified. If no .xinitrc file is found in the user's home directory, xinit uses the following by default:

```
xterm -geometry +1+1 -n login -display :0
```

Xconfigurator

Xconfigurator is Red Hat's X Window System configuration program. To invoke this program, enter **Xconfigurator** at the shell prompt. The Xconfigurator program creates a basic XF86Config file that is based on the selections you make within the menu interface. This XF86Config file (on Red Hat systems) is under /etc/X11 (which happens to be symlinked from /usr/X11R6/lib/X11 for compatibility with the default XFree86 directory structure).

When running Red Hat's Xconfigurator program, you are presented with a menu-based screen with a blue, red, yellow, and gray color scheme (as was used during the Red Hat Linux installation). Figure 9.1 shows the interface used with Xconfigurator.

Xconfigurator has two modes of operation: interactive and kickstart. In interactive mode, Xconfigurator prompts you for the type of video card and monitor attached to your computer. Some of this information might be automatically

Figure 9.1 Xconfigurator.

probed and filled in for you. However, if you apply an **expert** option to Xconfigurator, you can override any probed values.

In kickstart mode, Xconfigurator tries to autoprobe all required information. This is most useful when you're using PCI video cards because Xconfigurator typically autoprobes them properly. If no card is detected, you're prompted to select your video card manually.

XF86Setup

The XF86Setup program is the XFree86 Project's GUI configuration tool. You usually use XF86Setup to initially set up the XF86 servers or to adjust current configurations. To invoke the XF86Setup program, enter **XF86Setup** at the shell prompt. When running, XF86Setup presents you with a gray, blue, and teal button-style interface that runs on a generic VGA16 server. Figure 9.2 shows XF86Setup's interface.

As you can see in Figure 9.2, XF86Setup presents you with six buttons used for X Window System configuration. The first button, Mouse, displays a menu that allows you to configure your mouse settings. Within this menu, you can choose the type of mouse protocol to use (such as PS/2, Microsoft, Logitech, and so on) and other mouse options, such as the mouse device (/dev/ttysX or /dev/psaux) and button settings.

The second button in the XF86Setup window is Keyboard. Use this menu to select your keyboard model and language. In addition, you can select options such as Shift/Lock behavior and the position of your Control key.

Figure 9.2 XF86Setup.

The third button in the XF86Setup window is Card. Use this menu to choose the type of XF86 server to use. In addition, you can select specific chipsets, RamDac options, ClockChip, and any other options you would like to have automatically added to the XF86Config file.

The fourth button in the XF86Setup window is Monitor. Use this menu to select your monitor type as well as horizontal and vertical sync rates. This menu lists many common monitor settings that automatically set the horizontal and vertical sync rates. If you know your monitor's capabilities, or if your monitor is not listed, you must specify the horizontal and vertical sync rates manually at the top of the screen. Figure 9.3 shows the monitor configuration interface for XF86Setup.

The fifth button in the XF86Setup window is Modeselection. Use this menu to configure your display resolution and color depth. You can select one of several resolutions (the options differ depending on the server and monitor you choose) that range from (and beyond) 320×200 to 1600×1200. You can also choose at what color depth you want to run the X Window System. Some options include 8bpp (bits per pixel), 16bpp, 24bpp, and 32bpp. If you attempt to select any option that your card or monitor does not support, you receive an error message and are then automatically returned to the configuration menu.

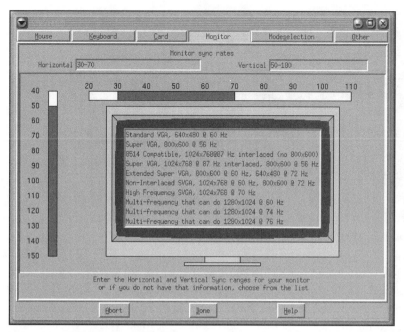

Figure 9.3   XF86Setup monitor configuration.

The final button in the XF86Setup window is Other. Use this menu to select optional server settings. Some of the options available include enabling the hotkey sequence (Ctrl+Alt+Backspace) to kill the XF86 server, enabling video mode switching, and allowing changes from other hosts.

xf86config

The xf86config program is a text-based configuration tool that is used to configure the XF86Config file. To invoke xf86config, enter **xf86config** at a root prompt.

With the xf86config tool, you are prompted to configure your mouse, keyboard, card, and monitor settings with a text-based prompt method. Each of the options prompts you with a list of available numbered options for selection, or prompts you for a yes or no answer. The xf86config tool is the least-used tool for configuring the X Window System. Figure 9.4 shows an example of the xf86config tool's interface.

X Font Server

The standard X Window font server is xfs. This server supplies fonts to the X Window System display servers. Not only does xfs provide fonts for the local X server, but it can also provide large numbers of fonts to other hosts on the network.

Figure 9.4 xf86config.

Font servers are used to provide TrueType fonts to X applications. When an X client makes a request to the X server, the X server binds to the X font server to supply the requested TrueType font. The xfs server is run as a daemon from the /etc/rc.d/init.d/xfs init script. The configuration file for xfs is /etc/X11/fs/config. In the configuration file, you can specify the font servers, the font catalogs, and the font resolution to use. Here's a sample configuration file:

```
#
# Default font server configuration file for Red Hat Linux 6.0
#

# allow a max of 4 clients to connect to this font server
client-limit = 4

# when a font server reaches its limit, start up a new one
clone-self = off

# alternate font servers for clients to use
#alternate-servers = foo:7101,bar:7102

# where to look for fonts
#
catalogue = /usr/X11R6/lib/X11/fonts/misc:unscaled,
            /usr/X11R6/lib/X11/fonts/75dpi:unscaled,
            /usr/X11R6/lib/X11/fonts/100dpi:unscaled,
            /usr/X11R6/lib/X11/fonts/misc,
            /usr/X11R6/lib/X11/fonts/Type1,
            /usr/X11R6/lib/X11/fonts/Speedo,
            /usr/share/fonts/default/Type1,
            /usr/X11R6/lib/X11/fonts/75dpi
```

```
# in 12 points, decipoints
default-point-size = 120

# 100 x 100 and 75 x 75
default-resolutions = 75,75,100,100

# how to log errors
use-syslog = on
```

X Client

An X client is the software that sends requests to the X server. The X server then draws on the X display, returns information, or performs another requested task. An X client can be the software on the same machine as the X server or on a remote host. I'll discuss the remote X applications later in this chapter.

The standard X desktop is made up of many services and programs, which vary depending on the window manager or environment you use. However, several standard terms and applications apply. When using an X client, you should be aware of the following terms and their differences:

➤ *screen* —Your whole desktop. The terms "screen" and "desktop" are often interchanged. Technically, the screen is the primary video display with which you view your X Window System.

➤ *root window* —The background of your screen. The root window doesn't have any of the standard characteristics of any other window, but it does have some unique applications. The root window is where you can customize your background images.

➤ *window manager* —The main interface between the X Window System and the user. The window manager provides functionality such as window borders, menus, icons, desktops, buttons, and toolbars, and it allows the user to customize them all. I'll discuss the various window managers later in this chapter.

➤ *pointer* —The arrow or other indicator that represents the location of your mouse, trackball, glide point, or other pointing device as it corresponds to the location on the screen. Quite often, the shape, color, or size of the pointer changes to indicate that the mouse has a particular function on that specific area of the screen.

➤ *window* —A frame in which any given application resides and is managed by the window manager. The active window, the window you're currently using on your desktop, is usually indicated by being on top, in focus, or highlighted compared to the inactive windows on the screen.

➤ *terminal emulator* —A window that contains just text and that basically simulates a terminal. One example of a terminal emulator is an xterm.

Window Managers

Many window managers—such as AfterStep, Enlightenment, fvwm, and Window Maker—are available for use with your X client. You should not confuse window managers with desktop environments, such as GNU Network Object Model (GNOME) and K Desktop Environment (KDE). I'll discuss these desktop environments later in this chapter.

AfterStep

AfterStep, shown in Figure 9.5, was originally designed to look and feel like the NeXTSTEP interface used on the NeXT operating system.

Enlightenment

Unlike AfterStep or a few of the other window managers, Enlightenment, shown in Figure 9.6, is not modeled to look or feel like any existing window manager or other operating-system environment. Enlightenment is a highly graphical window manager that is changed often.

Figure 9.5   The AfterStep desktop.

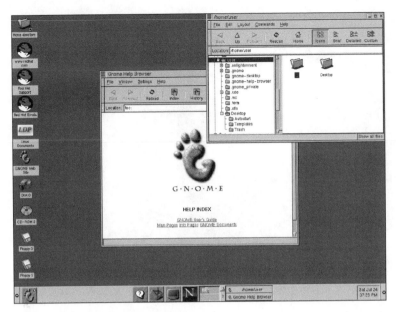

Figure 9.6   The Enlightenment desktop.

fvwm

The fvwm window manager, shown in Figure 9.7, is one of the oldest window managers available for Linux. The fvwm window manager is very small compared to some of the newer ones, such as Enlightenment, and fvwm requires less memory and fewer CPU resources. You can configure the fvwm window manager to look like Motif or even Windows 95. The fvwm manager is based on twm, the standard X window manager.

Window Maker

Window Maker, shown in Figure 9.8, is another window manager modeled to look like NeXTSTEP. Window Maker is designed to give additional integration support for GNUstep applications. Window Maker is relatively fast, easy to use, and popular among many Linux users.

X Server Tools, Tips, and Tricks

Various tools, tips, and tricks are available to assist you in managing and configuring your window manager options. For example, you can set up your Red Hat Linux 6.2 installation to automatically boot into X by default. To do this (assuming that you didn't select the option to start X automatically during installation), edit your /etc/inittab file. To automatically start your window manager, you must

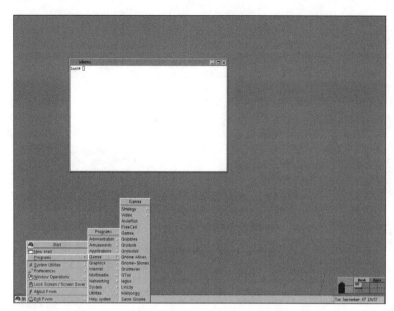

Figure 9.7 The fvwm desktop.

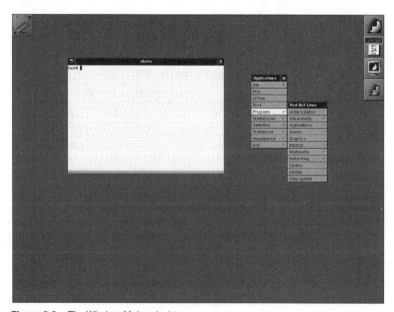

Figure 9.8 The Window Maker desktop.

set your /etc/inittab file to boot into runlevel 5. You set this in one of the first options in the file, in the string

```
id:X:initdefault:
```

where X is the default runlevel at boot-up. To automatically boot into runlevel 5, make sure this configuration string is as follows:

```
id:5:initdefault:
```

If you're running in runlevel 3 (console mode), you have two options to run the X Window System. You can either boot into runlevel 5 with the **init 5** command, or start the X Window System with the **startx** command. Typically, **startx** is the preferred method for starting the X Window System from the console.

The shell script used to specify a user's default environment is Xsession. The default Xsession script, located in the /etc/X11/xdm/ directory, is used if the user does not have an .xsession file or .Xclients file in his home directory. The .xsession and .Xclients files are used to specify certain display environments or window managers for the user—typically if the user wants his setup to be different from the default system setup. The script used to execute the window manager is xinitrc. If a user has an .xinitrc script in his home directory, his personal startup script is used. Otherwise, the default script, /etc/X11/xinit/xinitrc, is used.

Note: If present in a user's home directory, the .xsession, .xinitrc, and .Xclients files must all have the appropriate permissions set before they can be used. Therefore, all three of these files should have the executable permission set (chmod +x).

A final trick for helping to manage window managers is a tool called switchdesk. If you want to change your window manager the next time you start your X Window session, the switchdesk program prompts you for the new window manager. To invoke this program, enter **switchdesk** at a shell prompt. The switchdesk program automatically creates an .Xclients-default that specifies which window manager or environment to run.

Desktop Environments

Over the past couple of years, window managers have escalated to become integrated with entire desktop environments. Desktop environments control not only the look and feel of your desktop but also the tools and applications that are available for your desktop. The two main desktop environments shipped with Red Hat Linux are GNOME and KDE.

GNOME

GNOME is based on CORBA and the GTK+ toolkit, allowing programmers to import and export component type resources of their choice. This means that a program can use any editor it needs as long as the editor supports a standard interface via CORBA. Currently, the GNOME development project is partially funded by RHAD Labs, a division of Red Hat Software, Inc.

GNOME is used primarily as a base desktop environment for other window managers. By default, window managers such as Enlightenment and Window Maker use GNOME as the base environment. In addition to the styles and tools that the window managers add, GNOME offers several GNOME utilities to make the desktop more user-friendly.

One of GNOME's tools is the GNOME Midnight Commander (GMC). GMC is a file manager, similar to the Windows Explorer, that provides capabilities such as drag and drop and file browsing. Another tool GNOME uses is GDM, the GNOME Display Manager. GDM is more robust than the default X Display Manager (XDM). GDM allows the user to log into GNOME, KDE, or AnotherLevel. GDM allows the user to change the environment choice at login. By bringing up an xterm to bypass the window manager, GDM also provides a failsafe mode in case a problem occurs in the user environment.

KDE

Unlike GNOME, KDE is more tightly integrated with the window manager. You can, however, use KDE with other window managers, including AfterStep, Enlightenment, and Window Maker. KDE is based on the Qt toolkit, developed by the Norwegian-based company Trolltech. Figure 9.9 shows a KDE desktop using the default KDE window manager.

KDE provides many KDE tools, applications, and functionality to the window manager. KDE incorporates KDE File Manager (KFM). Like GMC, KFM provides drag-and-drop functionality to the desktop, provides an Explorer-style file manager, and incorporates Web-browsing functionality. Like GNOME, KDE has its own display manager, called KDE Display Manager (KDM).

Other programs that are available for KDE include applications such as killustrator and klyx. The killustrator program is a vector-based graphics program similar to Adobe Illustrator or CorelDRAW. The klyx program is a modern approach to writing documents with a computer, using LyX formatting. Some popular information management tools available for KDE include kalendar and korganizer.

Figure 9.9   KDE.

The kalendar program is a simple KDE-based calendar and to-do-list manager. The korganizer program is a slightly more complex program that involves a calendar and an appointment manager similar to those of Microsoft Outlook and Netscape's NSCAL. You can find many additional applications for KDE at www.kde.org.

Remote X Applications

A very popular feature of the X Window System is that it can display an X application on a remote host, as I mentioned earlier in this chapter. X is an entirely network-transparent system that can provide seamless access from one workstation to another that is running applications. Applications can be displayed on other machines, even if the other machines are not running the same operating system. To set up such access, you must use a host authentication program, such as xhost or xauth, and use a command to export the **DISPLAY** environment variable, such as **export DISPLAY= remotehost:0**.

Setting Up Remote Access

You use the xhost program to grant permission to host applications for other machines. Using xhost is simple. To enable permission to display remote applications, use **xhost** +*remotehost*. To disable permission to display remote applications, use **xhost** –*remotehost*.

To display a shell to another host, use this string:

```
export DISPLAY=remotemachine:0.0
```

After this string is executed, that shell's display is set to the remote machine specified. Any commands executed in that shell are then displayed to the remote machine.

To display a single command to another host, use the

```
command DISPLAY=remotemachine:0 command
```

command, where *remotemachine* is the machine that the application is to be displayed on, and *command* is the command to be exported to the remote machine.

Practice Questions

Question 1

How do you display a single X application on a remote X host?

○ a. **DISPLAY=remoteXhost:0 application**

○ b. **export DISPLAY=remoteXhost:0.0**

○ c. **export xeyes:remoteXhost :0**

○ d. None of the above

Answer a is correct. Answer a instructs the machine to display *application* on the *remoteXhost*. Answer b is incorrect because it simply changes the **DISPLAY** variable to the *remoteXhost* and doesn't send any applications. Answer c is incorrect because it is not a valid option.

Question 2

What is one of the biggest differences between GNOME and KDE?

○ a. One is a window manager and the other is a desktop environment.

○ b. GNOME is an operating system, and KDE is a desktop environment.

○ c. GNOME is an application, and KDE is a desktop environment.

○ d. GNOME is based on GTK+, and KDE is based on Qt.

Answer d is correct. GNOME and KDE are based on different toolkits; GNOME is based on GTK+, and KDE is based on Qt. Answer a is incorrect because both GNOME and KDE are desktop environments, although KDE has a built-in window manager as well. Answer b is incorrect because GNOME is not an operating system. Answer c is incorrect because GNOME is not an application.

Question 3

What tool allows you to change your default X Window desktop?

○ a. xinitrc

○ b. switchdesk

○ c. **Xchange**

○ d. All of the above

Answer b is correct. The switchdesk tool allows you to specify which installed desktop environment will be used by default the next time you run X. Answer a is incorrect because xinitrc is the script that executes the X Window System. Answer c is incorrect because **Xchange** is not a valid command.

Question 4

In what file can you specify that the computer should boot into the X Window System by default?

○ a. Xdefaults

○ b. xinitrc

○ c. /etc/inittab

○ d. .xdefaults

Answer c is correct. In the /etc/inittab file, you can specify the default runlevel in the string **id:5:initdefault:**. Answers a and b are incorrect because they are used when you're starting the X Window System, not to specify boot-time options. Answer d is incorrect because it is not a valid option.

Question 5

What is the difference between a window and a terminal emulator?

A terminal emulator is a type of window. The difference is that a window can display either an X application or a terminal emulator, but a terminal emulator displays only text-based tools and command lines.

Question 6

What X-based tool is available for configuring the X Window System?

○ a. XF86Setup

○ b. Xconfigurator

○ c. xf86config

○ d. All of the above

Answer a is correct. XF86Setup is an X-based tool that invokes a minimum X server, allowing you to use X-based tools to configure XFree86. Although answers b and c configure the X Window System, they are not X-based tools. Therefore, they are incorrect.

Question 7

What project is currently developing X server support?

○ a. RHAD Labs

○ b. XFree86 Project, Inc.

○ c. GNOME Project

○ d. None of the above

Answer b is correct. XFree86 Project, Inc., is primarily responsible for the development of the XF86 X server and support. Answer a is incorrect because RHAD Labs is a division of Red Hat Software. Answer c is incorrect because the GNOME Project is responsible for the development of the GNOME desktop environment, not X server support.

Question 8

What is the difference between an X client and an X server?

The X client is the software located either on a remote machine or on the same machine that sends X display requests to the X server. The X server is the hardware server responsible for responding to drawing requests from the X client.

Question 9

The XFree86 Project develops only the X Window System for Linux.

○ a. True

○ b. False

Answer b is correct. The XFree86 Project is developing X Window System support for all Unix-based operating systems.

Task 1

Set up your X Window System by using each of the available X tools mentioned in this chapter. After setting up a specific desktop, use switchdesk to set your desktop default to another available desktop. View the .Xclients-default file and see what changes were made. Manually edit this file to reflect your original desktop setting. Restart your X session. Did your preferred desktop return?

Task 2

Set up another machine on your network. Set the remote machine to accept remote applications from your machine. Display **xeyes** to the other host. What happened? Log into the other host and display an **xterm** back to your machine. Type **xcalc** in the new xterm displayed on your machine. What happened?

Need to Know More?

 Mui, Linda and Eric Pearce. *X Window System Administrators Guide.* O'Reilly & Associates, 1992. ISBN 0-93717-5838. This book discusses the issues of system administration for X and X-based networks.

 Pennington, Havoc. *GTK+/GNOME Development.* New Riders Publishing, 1999. ISBN 0-73570-0788. This book discusses details about GTK+ and GNOME development.

 Wells, Nicholas. *Using KDE.* Que, 1999. ISBN 0-78972-2143. This book discusses the skills required for programming with KDE, and discusses related skills necessary to gain the advanced knowledge required for administering KDE.

 http://www.linuxdoc.org/HOWTO/HOWTO-INDEX-3.html — This is the Linux Documentation Project Web site, whose links to X, X Window System, and XFree86 supply the latest information regarding the X Window System.

 http://www.afterstep.org/ —This is the AfterStep Web site, which shows the latest developments for the AfterStep window manager.

 http://www.enlightenment.org/ —This is the Enlightenment Web site, which shows current development information and documentation for the popular Enlightenment window manager.

 http://www.gnome.org/ —This is the GNOME Web site, which provides documentation and information about the latest developments and applications for the GNOME environment.

 http://www.kde.org/ —This is the KDE Web site, which provides information about the current development of the KDE environment, and contains links to many applications developed for KDE.

 http://www.windowmaker.org/ —This is the Window Maker Web site, which shows the latest development information and documentation for the window manager Window Maker.

 http://www.xfree86.org/ —This is the XFree86 Project, Inc., Web site, which gives the latest information, documentation, and drivers for the X Window System.

http://www.x.org/ —This is the Web site for X.Org, the worldwide consortium responsible for development of the X Window System standard.

 http://www.helixcode.com/ —This is the Web site that hosts the Helix GNOME project.

 http://www.troll.no/ —This is the Web site for Trolltech, a Norwegian company focused on Qt development.

 http://www.gtk.org/ —This is the official site for the GTK+ toolkit.

Standard
Networking Services

. . . .

Terms you'll need to understand:

✓ Web server

✓ Hypertext Transport Protocol (HTTP)

✓ Virtual hosts

✓ Mail agents

✓ Domain Name Service (DNS)

✓ Forward and reverse DNS

✓ File Transfer Protocol (FTP)

✓ Dynamic Host Configuration Protocol (DHCP)

✓ Proxy server

Techniques you'll need to master:

✓ Configuring an Apache Web server

✓ Configuring virtual hosts

✓ Using sendmail

✓ Configuring and using DNS and BIND

✓ Configuring DNS entries

✓ Setting up anonymous FTP servers

✓ Setting up and using NFS

✓ Setting up Windows client file sharing

✓ Setting up and using DHCP

The largest portion of the RHCE 302 exam centers on setting up Red Hat Linux networking services. The reason for such focus is that the greatest percentage of Red Hat installations is for machines to be used as either clients or servers on a network. Networking support is the strongest feature and most common use of Linux. To be successful not only on the RHCE 302 exam but also as an RHCE, you must be comfortable with installing, configuring, and using many Linux networking services. In this chapter, I'll discuss Apache, email, Domain Name Services (DNS), File Transfer Protocol (FTP), Network File System (NFS), Samba and Server Message Block (SMB), the Dynamic Host Configuration Protocol (DHCP), time services, and the Squid proxy server.

Apache

Apache is the world's most popular Hypertext Transport Protocol (HTTP) server, running on more than 62 percent of the world's Web servers as of this writing. Apache was originally based on the most popular Web server in 1995, NCSA's httpd 1.3. Because the first version of Apache consisted of different patches applied to NCSA's httpd, Apache was often referred to as "a patchy server," which is how Apache got its name (A+PAtCHy). In this section, I'll discuss how to set up Apache and how to set up virtual Apache hosts.

Red Hat Linux 6.2 is shipped with Apache 1.3. You can install it either during the installation of Red Hat Linux or by installing the RPM file apache-1.3.12-2.i386.rpm, which is located on your Red Hat Linux 6.2 CD in the /RedHat/RPMS directory.

The installation of Apache places all the appropriate configuration files in the /etc/httpd/conf/ directory. Apache used to use three main configuration files: access.conf, httpd.conf, and srm.conf. These three files have now been combined into one httpd.conf file.

Configuring Apache

The /etc/httpd/conf/httpd.conf file is the main httpd server configuration file. In previous releases of Apache, the httpd.conf file made calls for information from the access.conf and srm.conf. Due to the size of the httpd.conf file, I'm going to discuss it in sections, explaining the most important configuration options in this file.

The httpd.conf configuration directives are sorted into three basic sections.

➤ Directives that control the operation of the Apache server (global environment).

➤ Directives that define the parameters of the main or default server that responds to requests not handled by a virtual host. (Also provides default values for the settings of all virtual hosts.)

➤ Settings for virtual hosts that allow Web requests to be sent to multiple IP address or host names and then have them handled by the same Apache server process. (I'll discuss setting up virtual hosts in the next section of this chapter.)

Section 1: Global Environment—httpd.conf

The directives in this section of httpd.conf affect the entire operation of Apache. This includes the number of requests that Apache can handle and the location of Apache configuration files.

The following snippet of code specifies whether to run httpd in standalone mode or through **inetd**. The default setting for Apache is to run the server in standalone mode. Running the server through **inetd** is not advised because it causes **inetd** to **fork()** repeatedly, with each **fork()** function running its own instance of httpd. This causes the Web server to be very slow.

```
# ServerType is either inetd, or standalone. Inetd mode is
# only supported on Unix platforms.
#
ServerType standalone
```

The **ServerRoot** directive specifies the top of the directory tree where the server's configuration, error, and log files are kept. Do not add a slash (/) to the end of this directory path. Here's a **ServerRoot** directive:

```
ServerRoot "/etc/httpd"
```

Note: If you intend to place this directive on an NFS (or other network) mounted filesystem, then read the LockFile documentation (http://www.apache.org/docs/mod/core.html).

The following line from httpd.conf sets the number of seconds before **httpd** send and receive requests time out. The numeric setting is set in seconds:

```
# Timeout: The number of seconds before receives and sends time
# out.
#
Timeout 300
```

The following options are used when you're running the Apache server in standalone mode:

```
# Server-pool size regulation. Rather than making you guess
# how many server processes you need, Apache dynamically adapts
# to the load it sees. That is, it tries to maintain enough
# server processes to handle the current load plus a few spare
# servers to handle transient load spikes (e.g., multiple
# simultaneous requests from a single Netscape browser).
#
# It does this by periodically checking how many servers are
# waiting for a request. If there are fewer number than there
# are MinSpareServers, it creates a new spare. If there are
# more than MaxSpareServers, some of the spares die off. The
# default values are probably OK for most sites.
#
MinSpareServers 5
MaxSpareServers 20
```

The settings set how many spare httpd servers are running at any given moment. These spare servers are used to handle sudden rushes of requests or other spikes of HTTP traffic. The **MinSpareServers** directive sets the maximum number of spares to have at any given moment. The following options also regulate the number of httpd servers running:

```
# Number of servers to start initially, should be a reasonable
# ballpark figure.
#
StartServers 8
#
# Limit on total number of servers running, i.e., limit on the
# number of clients who can simultaneously connect -- if this
# limit is ever reached, clients will be LOCKED OUT, so it
# should NOT BE SET TOO LOW.
# It is intended mainly as a brake to keep a runaway server from
# taking the system with it as it spirals down...
#
MaxClients 150
```

The **StartServers** option sets how many servers Apache should be started with. The **MaxClients** option is a little more important because it sets the maximum number of running servers. This limits the number of clients who can simultaneously connect to your server. Therefore, you should not set this option too low, but keep the number reasonable enough to keep your Web server from crashing.

Section 2: Main Server Configuration—httpd.conf

The directives in the second section of httpd.conf set up the values used by the main Apache server that responds to requests not handled by the <**VirtualHost**> definition. The values in this section also provide the default setting for other <**VirtualHost**> containers that you define later in the file.

If you're running Apache as a standalone server, you must specify what port the httpd server should listen on. The default port for httpd is 80:

```
# Port: The port to which the standalone server listens. For
# ports < 1023, you will need httpd to be run as root initially.
#
Port 80
```

The **ServerAdmin** entry sets the email address that appears on pages when Apache reports an error. People receiving errors should use this email address to notify you of the errors. If you don't forward or check your root email often, you should set this address to something you check regularly.

```
ServerAdmin root@localhost
```

The **ServerName** directive is the full domain name of the particular Web site you're hosting. This directive is always the full domain name, such as **www.example.com, web.example.org,** or **another.example.net.** Keep in mind that you cannot simply invent host names unless you set up proper DNS.

```
ServerName www.example.com
```

The **DocumentRoot** directive is the location, on the Apache server, of the files for the entry's Web pages and data. Often, administrators use a single main directory for all Web pages, such as /home/html/, and then create a directory under the /home/html/ directory for each domain. In this case, the **DocumentRoot** would be set to **/home/html/**domain. Other times, administrators link the **DocumentRoot** into a user's home directory, and create a directory in the home directory to contain the documents. In this case, **DocumentRoot** would be set to **/home/**user/domain or something similar.

```
DocumentRoot "/home/httpd/html"
```

When someone attempts to reach a URL such as **http://www.example.com/~kara,** the directory that Apache looks for can be set with the **UserDir** directive. Typically, Linux systems use public_html as this default directory.

```
UserDir public_html
```

The **DirectoryIndex** directive is the default file that is assumed to be loaded first within the Web directory. This means that if you go to **http://www.example.com**, httpd will look in the **DocumentRoot** directive and automatically load the file named index.html, index.shtml, or index.cgi (whichever is present) as specified by the **DirectoryIndex** listing. The index.html file and related files are the default options. If you want to change this, or add files such as home.html, you change the following entry:

```
DirectoryIndex index.html index.htm index.shtml index.cgi
```

The **ErrorLog** directive specifies the location of the error log file. If you don't specify an **ErrorLog** directive within your **<VirtualHost>** container, error messages related to that virtual host will be logged here by default. Many administrators place all their logs under a main logs directory. Therefore, an appropriate setting for **ErrorLog** in the custom scenario would be **ErrorLog logs/www.example.com/error_log**.

```
ErrorLog /var/log/httpd/error_log
```

Note: After configuring Apache, or making changes such as adding virtual hosts, you must restart httpd before your changes go into effect. To restart httpd, use the restart option by running /etc/rc.d/init.d/httpd restart or service httpd restart .

Virtual Hosts

As discussed in the previous section, virtual hosts are configured in the httpd.conf file. Virtual hosts are all the entries for enabling different hosts to be hosted on the same machine. Originally, Web servers could typically host only a single domain on a single machine. Though other Web servers were developing methods to host multiple hosts on a single server, Apache was the first to develop a simple interface for hosting multiple domains on a single machine. The concept of having more than one host on a single machine is called *virtual hosting*.

During the early development of virtual hosting, Apache required individual IP addresses to be assigned to each host. Now Apache allows you to configure multiple hosts to share the same IP address. This means that two domains can be assigned the same IP address but have individual Web sites.

Configuring Virtual Hosts

After you have Apache configured properly, there are eight steps you follow to configure your virtual hosts by editing the httpd.conf file:

1. Set **NameVirtualHost**. The **NameVirtualHost** setting is required only when you're setting up virtual hosts with the same IP address. If you have individual IP addresses for each host, skip this step. The setting for **NameVirtualHost** can be either name-based (**www.example.com**) or IP-based (192.168.0.1). Use this setting to tell httpd that there are multiple hosts under the specific name (**www.domain.com**) or IP address (192.168.0.1). **VirtualHost** entries under the **NameVirtualHost** directive are then indexed by the **ServerName** setting. A request for an IP address or domain listed under the **NameVirtualHost** directive will be matched by **ServerName** and the appropriate **DocumentRoot** settings. For example, **NameVirtualHost 192.168.0.1**.

2. Set **VirtualHost**. The setting for the **VirtualHost** can be either name-based (**www.example.com**) or IP-based (192.168.0.1). Administrators typically prefer to used name-based settings. This method allows the administrator to change IP addresses for the host in DNS without having to change the httpd.conf file. Make sure you have registered the domain and set up DNS to ensure that this option works properly. For example, **<VirtualHost www.example.com>**.

3. Set **DocumentRoot**. The setting for **DocumentRoot** points to the directory where the Web documents for the host can be found. This setting might point to a subdirectory for the host under a larger dedicated directory, such as /home/httpd/*domain*, or to a dedicated subdirectory located under a user's home directory, such as /home/*user*/*domain*, or anywhere else you prefer. Within this dedicated directory, you should put any HTML or other Web files required for the Web site. Make sure the **DocumentRoot** directory, subdirectories, and files are world readable and executable (with permissions set to at least 755 for directories and 644 for files). For example, **DocumentRoot /home/exampleadmin/example/**.

4. Set **ServerName**. The setting for **ServerName** is the name-based reference used by Web browsers to request your host's Web site. For instance, if a user would enter **http://www.example.com/** to access your Web site, your **ServerName** would be **www.example.com**. This option is especially important when IP addresses are being shared among hosts. For example, **ServerName www.example.com**.

5. Set **ErrorLog**. The setting for **ErrorLog** specifies the directory and file in which httpd should store any errors for the specific host. By default, this setting is **logs/error_log**. For example, **ErrorLog logs/error_log**.

6. Set **TransferLog**. The setting for **TransferLog** specifies the directory and file in which httpd should log all access information for the host. The default setting for the TransferLog is **logs/access_log**. For example, **TransferLog logs/access_log**.

7. Close the **VirtualHost** entry. To specify the end of the particular virtual-host entry, you must close it by supplying the **</VirtualHost>** option as the last line of the virtual-host entry. For example, **</VirtualHost>**.

8. Save and restart. Save the changes in the httpd.conf file, and restart httpd (*not* your system). To restart httpd, enter **/etc/rc.d/init.d/httpd restart** or run **service httpd restart**.

There are several other options available for customizing your individual virtual-host entries. Three specific options include the settings for **Alias**, **Redirect**, and **ServerAlias**:

➤ **Alias** */sublocation /alternate_document_root* —Using the **Alias** setting allows you to set an alternative location file for a path below your host. For instance, if you want to have one **DocumentRoot** for **www.example.com**, but have an entirely different path for **www.example.com/example/**, you can supply the **Alias** option within the **www.example.com** virtual-host entry to point **/example** to another directory for its Web files. For example, **Alias /example /home/ example/example**.

➤ **Redirect** */sublocation http://other.new.location* —Using the **Redirect** setting allows you to specify an alternative location for a subdirectory under the specific virtual-host entry. For instance, if you want **www.example.com/***somewhere* to redirect to **www.somewhere.org**, you can add the **Redirect** option to the virtual-host entry for **www.example.com**. For example, **Redirect /somewhere http://www.somewhere.org/**.

➤ **ServerAlias** *example.com *.example.com* —Using the **ServerAlias** setting allows you to specify additional **ServerNames** that can be used to access the same Web data. For example, you can set the **ServerAlias** setting in the **www.example.com** virtual-host entry to allow users to access not only **http://www.example.com/** but also **http://example.com/** and **http://web.example.com/**. For example, **ServerAlias example.com *example.com**.

Sample Virtual Host Scenario

To better understand the layout of the virtual-host entries in the httpd.conf file, please consider the following scenario, and view the following snippet of the scenario's httpd.conf file.

Scenario

Your Web server has been assigned three IP addresses: 123.12.12.1, 123.12.12.2, and 123.12.12.3. You want to host five domains: **www.choc.com**, **www.bar.net**, **www.baz.org**, **www.example.com**, and **www.iluvlinus.com**. You decide to assign **www.choc.com** its own IP address of 123.12.12.1. You decide to share 123.12.12.2 with both **www.bar.net** and **www.baz.org**. You also decide to share 123.12.12.3 with both **www.example.com** and **www.iluvlinus.com**. You want each host to have its files in a home directory dedicated to a user with the same host name (meaning **choc, bar, baz, example**, and **iluvlinus**) in a directory named **web**. You decide to leave the logs in a location beneath the logs directory under /etc/httpd/ conf/. Notice that you need to use the **NameVirtualHost** setting only once above the entries that are sharing the specified IP. (This IP setting can be replaced with a domain name whose address resolves to the shared IP address.) Listing 10.1 lists the sample virtual-hosts entries mentioned in this scenario.

Listing 10.1 Virtual-hosts entries in httpd.conf.

```
<VirtualHost www.choc.com>
DocumentRoot /home/choc/web
ServerName www.choc.com
ErrorLog logs/www.choc.com/error_log
TransferLog logs/www.choc.com/access_log
</VirtualHost>

NameVirtualHost 10.12.12.2
<VirtualHost www.bar.net>
DocumentRoot /home/bar/web
ServerName www.bar.net
ErrorLog logs/www.bar.net/error_log
TransferLog logs/www.bar.net/access_log
</VirtualHost>

<VirtualHost www.baz.org>
DocumentRoot /home/baz/web
ServerName www.baz.org
ErrorLog logs/www.baz.org/error_log
TransferLog logs/www.baz.org/access_log
</VirtualHost>

NameVirtualHost 10.12.12.3
<VirtualHost www.example.com>
DocumentRoot /home/example/web
ServerName www.example.com
ErrorLog logs/www.example.com/error_log
```

```
TransferLog logs/www.example.com/access_log
</VirtualHost>

<VirtualHost www.iluvlinus.com>
DocumentRoot /home/iluvlinus/web
ServerName www.iluvlinus.com
ErrorLog logs/www.iluvlinus.com/error_log
TransferLog logs/www.iluvlinus.com/access_log
</VirtualHost>
```

Email Services

Email services comprise three main parts: the mail transport agent (MTA), the mail delivery agent (MDA), and the mail user agent (MUA). The MTA is responsible for the physical sending and receiving of user and system email. The MDA receives the incoming email from the MTA and delivers it to the appropriate user. The MUA retrieves the mail delivered by the MDA and allows the user to read it. In addition to incoming mail relaying from MTA to MDA to MUA, outgoing mail is submitted by the MUA, transferred to the MTA, and sent to the appropriate recipient server. In this section, I'll briefly discuss the default Red Hat Linux MTA (sendmail), MDA (procmail), and popular MUAs (Elm, Pine, and Netscape Messenger).

sendmail

The most popular (default Red Hat Linux) mail transport agent (MTA) is sendmail. The sendmail program is typically installed by default during the Linux installation; when installed via the Red Hat 6.2 CD-ROM, sendmail requires no configuration to work properly.

If sendmail is not installed during your Red Hat Linux installation, you can install the RPM found on your Red Hat Linux 6.2 CD-ROM. The sendmail RPM file on the Red Hat 6.2 CD is sendmail-8.9.3-20.i386.rpm; it's found in the /RedHat/RPMS/ directory on your Red Hat 6.2 CD-ROM.

Configuring sendmail

The main configuration file for sendmail is /etc/sendmail.cf. The /etc/sendmail.cf file is machine-readable code used to run sendmail. Because /etc/sendmail.cf is machine-readable code, it is not very administrator- or reader-friendly. Because of the complexity and sensitivity of this file, editing this file by hand is not recommended. For this task, there is a macro preprocessor available, m4, which should be used to re-create the sendmail.cf file from an edited source (/etc/sendmail.mc).

To use m4, you must install the sendmail-cf RPM file, sendmail-cf-8.9.3-20.i386.rpm, found on your Red Hat 6.2 CD in the /RedHat/RPMS/ directory. To change your /etc/sendmail.cf file, follow these instructions:

1. Make backups. Make backups of your /etc/sendmail.cf and /etc/sendmail.mc files. Copy these files from sendmail.cf to sendmail.cf.old, and from sendmail.mc to sendmail.mc.old, or something suitable.

2. Edit /etc/sendmail.mc. Edit the /etc/sendmail.mc file to make any changes you need. If an option is in single quotes, be sure the first quote around the option is a back tick (') and the last quote around the item is a forward tick ('). To disable (or comment) a line, insert **dnl** at the front of the line.

3. Generate a new /etc/sendmail.cf file. Generate the new /etc/sendmail.cf list from the edited /etc/sendmail.mc by using the m4 macro processor. To do this, execute: **m4 sendmail.mc > sendmail.cf**. (Please double-check to see that you have a backup of your current running sendmail.cf before overwriting your current one.)

4. Restart sendmail. Restart **sendmail** by running **/etc/rc.d/init.d/sendmail restart** or **service sendmail restart**.

procmail

The mail delivery agent used by default with Red Hat Linux 6.2 and sendmail is procmail. The procmail MDA is used to handle the mail between the MTA (sendmail) and the MUA (mail reader). Typically, procmail is installed during Red Hat Linux 6.2 installation. If necessary, however, you can install procmail via RPM. The RPM file included with Red Hat Linux 6.2 for procmail is procmail-3.14-2.i386.rpm, located in the /RedHat/RPMS/ directory on your Red Hat Linux 6.2 CD-ROM.

Configuring procmail

For the MDA services of procmail, there is nothing you need to configure. This means that after installation, procmail is ready to go "out of the box." You can, however, customize how procmail handles each user's mail; you do this by editing a .procmailrc file within each user's home directory. By editing a user's home .procmailrc, you can enable mail sorting, blocking, and more. For an in-depth description of filtering options available through procmail, run **man procmailrc**.

Email Clients

Email clients are the mail user agents used by the user to read her mail. There are a variety of MUAs available. Any MUA can be used as long as the MUA supports the POP or IMAP (discussed in Chapter 4) protocols to receive mail remotely. Some popular email clients used on Linux include **elm**, **pine**, and the Netscape mail reader.

Elm

The MUA Elm is a popular text-based mail reader used on Unix systems. The interface is text-based, and commands are given by simple key commands as prompted by the mail reader. The text of the email is derived by editing a text file with your default editor (emacs, vi, and so on), which is automatically spawned when running Elm. To install Elm, install elm-2.5.3-6.i386.rpm from the /RedHat/RPMS/ directory of your Red Hat Linux 6.2 CD-ROM. Figure 10.1 shows the interface used with the ElmMUA.

Pine

Another popular text-based MUA is Pine. The Pine mail reader is a little more user-friendly than Elm key-combination menu-based options; Pine uses a simpler text editor. To install Pine from the Red Hat Linux 6.2 CD, install the pine-4.21-8.i386.rpm file. Figure 10.2 shows the text-menu-based interface for Pine.

Netscape

In addition to the multiple text-based MUAs that are found on most Unix systems, other graphical MUAs exist as well. Remember, any MUA that supports POP and IMAP (as discussed in Chapter 4) should work on your Red Hat Linux

Figure 10.1 Elm.

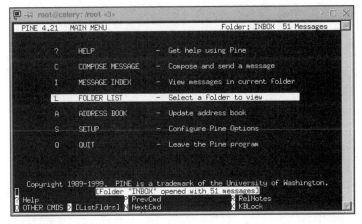

Figure 10.2 Pine.

system. One popular GUI MUA is the Netscape mail reader that is included in Netscape Communicator. The Netscape MUA has a graphical window interface with directory-style options for mailboxes on the left, and mail list indexes and mail content text on the right. Buttons at the top of the Netscape mail reader allow you to maneuver through the MUA program. To install the Netscape mail reader found on your Red Hat Linux 6.2 CD, you must install Netscape Communicator 4.72 from the RPM file netscape-communicator-4.72-.i386.rpm, located in the /RedHat/RPMS/ directory on your CD. Figure 10.3 shows the graphical interface of the Netscape mail reader.

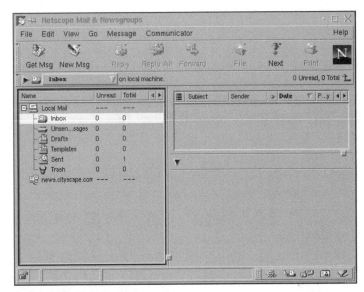

Figure 10.3 Netscape Mail.

Domain Name Service (DNS)

DNS is the service responsible for managing the host and domain name conversion to and from the mapped IP addresses. Therefore, DNS is responsible for converting an IP address to its domain name and converting a domain name to its assigned IP address. The server that is run on a Linux DNS server is **named**. The **named** server is a part of the BIND (Berkley Internet Name Domain) package used on more than 85 percent of all DNS servers in the world.

Configuring BIND 8.x

During the Red Hat Linux 6.2 installation, you're given the option of installing BIND automatically. However, if BIND isn't installed during the Linux installation, you can install it from the Red Hat Linux 6.2 CD-ROM. There are three RPMs you should install. The first, and most important, is the bind-8.2.2_P5-9.i386.rpm file, which is the main BIND RPM. The second is recommended to be installed on every machine, even if a machine isn't being used as a DNS server, because it is the BIND utilities package. The BIND utilities package is installed with bind-utils-8.2.2_P5-9.i386.rpm. An optional (but highly recommended) package to be used with BIND is the caching name-server package that configures your DNS server to cache DNS entries, making name lookups and DNS access faster. The caching name-server package to install is caching-nameserver-6.2-2.noarch.rpm.

The main configuration file for BIND 8.x is /etc/named.conf. In the /etc/named.conf file, you can specify options, such as the default directory for **named** files, and specify the zones for the **named** entries you're hosting. There are two types of **named** files that you host. The first is the database (db) entry specified for each domain you host. These db entries are typically named either db.*domain.com* or *domain.com*.db, depending on the naming scheme you use. The db entries are the forward DNS entries for your domain. The second type of **named** file you host is the reverse DNS file, denoted typically by db.x.x.x.in-addr.arpa where x.x.x is the reverse subnet you're hosting. For example, if you host the 192.168.1.x subnet, you have a db.1.168.192.in-addr.arpa reverse DNS file.

Some DNS servers do not host the entire subnet. Therefore, the subnet provider (Internet Service Provider) hosts the reverse DNS information, and the in-addr.arpa entries are not required on your machine.

named.conf

The /etc/named.conf file is the main configuration file for **named**. Within the named.conf file, you specify options such as the default directory for **named** entries (the Red Hat Linux 6.2 default is /var/named/) and zone entries for individual **named** files. The following is a sample /etc/named.conf file:

```
options {
        directory "/var/named";
};

zone "." {
        type hint;
        file "named.ca"'
};

zone "1.168.192.in-addr.arpa" {
        type master;
        file "db.1.168.192.in-addr.arpa";
};

zone "example.com" {
        type master;
        file "db.example.com";
};

zone "example.net" {
        type slave;
        file "db.example.net";
        masters {
                192.168.0.100;
        };
};
```

This sample /etc/named.conf file has five types of entries. (For clarity, each entry is highlighted separately.) The first two entries are mandatory configuration options for BIND. The first entry specifies BIND options. In this example, the specified option sets where all **named** files will be placed. By default, this option is set to **/var/named/**. Many DNS administrators are accustomed to keeping named files under /etc/named/ and thus change this directory option to "**/etc/named**".

The second entry is a default zone entry to specify which file can be used as a "hint" for where to find root name servers. By default, BIND 8 uses **/var/named/ named.ca**. This second entry is required, and editing this entry or file is not recommended unless it's absolutely necessary.

The third entry in the example is a reverse DNS zone entry. The zone specified is the "**1.168.192.in-addr.arpa**" zone. The reverse DNS is a primary DNS record, so the **type** entry is set to **master**. The file with the reverse DNS information is in /var/named/db.1.168.192.in-addr.arpa, so the file is set to "**db.1.168.192.in-addr.arpa**".

The fourth entry in the example is a primary DNS zone entry. The zone specified is the "**example.com**" zone. Because the entry is a primary DNS entry, the **type** is set to **master**. The file for the entry is found in /var/named/db.example.com, so the file is set to "**db.example.com**".

The fifth entry in the example is a sample secondary DNS zone entry. The zone specified in the example is "**example.net**". Because the entry is a secondary DNS entry, the **type** is set to **slave**. The file for this secondary entry is found in /var/named/db.example.net, so the file option is set to "**db.example.net**". Because this entry is a secondary DNS entry, you must provide the primary DNS server information from which to retrieve the DNS information. In this entry's case, the primary DNS server is 192.168.0.100; therefore, the **masters** option is set to **192.168.0.100**.

Forward DNS Files

Forward DNS files are used to resolve domain names to the domains' assigned IP addresses. These files, by default, are found under the /var/named/ directory and are typically named db.*domain.com* or *domain.com*.db. In these examples, I'll use db.example.com. The following is a sample forward DNS file for a master (primary) record:

```
$TTL 86400
@            IN      SOA     ns.example.com.  root.example.com. (
                            1999080101     ; serial
                            10800   ; refresh (3 hours)
                            3600    ; retry (1 hour)
                            604800 ; expire (7 days)
                            86400 ) ; minimum (1 day)

             IN      NS      ns1.example.com.
             IN      NS      ns2.example.com.

             IN      MX      0      mail.example.com.
             IN      A       192.168.0.212
localhost    IN      A       127.0.0.1
www          IN      A       192.168.0.212
ns1          IN      A       192.168.0.10
ns2          IN      A       192.168.0.11
```

```
ftp        IN        CNAME        www
mail       IN        CNAME        www
irc        IN        CNAME        irc.example.net.
```

For clarity, the sections of the /var/named/db.example.com file have been high-lighted. The first section is the SOA (Start of Authority) entry. The SOA entry contains the domain of the originating host, the domain address of the main-tainer, the file serial number, and various time parameters (refresh, retry, expire, and minimum TTL).

The second highlighted section of the sample /var/named/db.example.com file specifies the domain's primary and secondary DNS server. These servers are de-noted by the **NS** tokens. The first **NS** entry is the primary DNS server, and the second **NS** entry specifies the secondary DNS server. You can also add tertiary DNS servers and so forth with the same **NS** entries.

The third highlighted section includes other references, options, and settings for the domain entry. The **MX** (mail exchange) token points to the mail exchange server for the domain. The **A** tokens point to host addresses. For example, the **A** token in this example sets the domain **example.com** to 192.168.0.212. Another **A** token sets the domain **www.example.com** to 192.168.0.212 as well. An addi-tional token used in this example section is **CNAME** (canonical name). The **CNAME** token points an alias to the appropriate IP address or domain. In the example, **ftp.example.com** is pointed to the same address as **www**, which was already defined as 192.168.0.212. Also, **mail.example.com** is directed to **www**. There is also a **CNAME** pointer for **irc.example.com** that redirects the request to a real IRC (Internet Relay Chat) server, which in this example is located at **irc.example.net**.

Reverse DNS Files

Reverse DNS files are used to resolve IP addresses to their assigned host names. Reverse DNS is set up per subnet, meaning that all 192.168.0.x addresses would have a single reverse DNS file defined, as would 192.168.1.x, 192.168.2.x, and so on (where x is equal to all nodes from .0 through .255).

Reverse DNS files are named by the subnet address (in reverse order) followed by the in-addr.arpafilename. For instance, the reverse DNS file for the 192.168.100.x subnet would be db.100.168.192.in-addr.arpa, and the reverse DNS file for the 205.23.12.x subnet could be db.12.23.205.in-addr.arpa.

Although the subnet and in-addr.arpa file names are always used, many adminis-trators replace the db. with rev., simply for clarification (for instance, rev.12.23.205.in-addr.arpa or 12.23.205.in-addr.arpa.rev). Regardless of which naming convention you use, keep the same naming convention throughout your system, and make sure that all appropriate references (such as in /etc/named.conf) match appropriately.

The following is an example of the reverse DNS file (db.0.168.192.in-addr.arpa). You'll notice that it looks similar to the forward DNS files, with the same SOA head entry, but has different tokens used in the body of the file.

```
@       IN      SOA     ns.example.com. root.example.com. (
                        1999080101     ; serial
                        10800   ; refresh (3 hours)
                        3600    ; retry (1 hour)
                        604800 ; expire (7 days)
                        86400 ); minimum (1 day)
        IN      NS      ns.example.com.
1       IN      PTR     gateway.example.com.
2       IN      PTR     boss.example.com.
3       IN      PTR     node3.example.com.
;4      IN      PTR     node4.example.com.
212     IN      PTR     www.example.com.
254     IN      PTR     router.example.com.
```

In this example, the first six lines are identical to the forward DNS files. The first six lines of the file are the SOA entry information, which includes the host information, file serial number, and various time settings. The remaining body of the example differs greatly from the forward DNS file, however. The remaining entries use the **PTR** (pointer) token. The **PTR** token resolves the specific node on a subnet to a domain name. The first column in this example of **PTR** entries specifies the node number on the subnet. For instance, 1 refers to 192.168.0.1, 2 refers to 192.168.0.2, and so forth. Either nodes that aren't assigned are not listed, or nodes that are disabled are commented out. (For example, the entry for 4 is commented out with the semicolon at the beginning of the line.) Therefore, the entry for 1 will resolve 192.168.0.1 to **gateway.example.com**, the entry for 212 will resolve 192.168.0.212 to **www.example.com**, and so forth.

Primary DNS

When you have a domain registered with your DNS server specified as the primary DNS server, you'll need to set up your **named** files by following these steps:

1. Add **zone** to /etc/named.conf. As a primary entry, your **zone** entry in /etc/named.conf will look like this:

```
zone "example.com" {
    type master;
        file "db.example.com";
    };
```

2. Edit db.example.com. Create a file under /var/named named db.example.com. Add any necessary token entries, and change the file serial number (highlighted in the next code section) to reflect the current date.

 The serial number (by standard convention) should be 10 characters. The first four (1999) reflect the year; the next two (08) reflect the current month; the next two (01) reflect the current day; and the last two (01) reflect the number of times you changed that file that day. (For instance, if this was the first time you made a change, the digits would be 01, the second 02, the third 03, and so on.)

3. Set your primary and secondary DNS servers. Add any hosts for this domain with appropriate tokens. Your db.example.com should look something like this:

```
@          IN      SOA     ns.example.com.  root.example.com. (
                           1999080101     ; serial
                           10800   ; refresh (3 hours)
                           3600    ; retry (1 hour)
                           604800 ; expire (7 days)
                           86400 ) ; minimum (1 day)
           IN      NS      ns1.example.com.
           IN      NS      ns2.example.net.
           IN      A       192.168.0.212
www        IN      A       192.168.0.212
ftp        IN      CNAME   www
node2      IN      A       192.168.0.2
router     IN      A       192.168.0.254
ns1        IN      A       192.168.0.10
```

4. Set up reverse DNS. Create the db.0.168.192.in-addr.arpa file under /var/named/. Set up any and all reverse entries for each node, as specified in the forward DNS file. (Remember to change your file serial number accordingly!) Your reverse DNS file should look something like this:

```
@          IN      SOA     ns.example.com. root.example.com. (
                           1999080101     ; serial
                           10800   ; refresh (3 hours)
                           3600    ; retry (1 hour)
                           604800 ; expire (7 days)
                           86400 ) ; minimum (1 day)
           IN      NS      ns1.example.com.
2          IN      PTR     node2.example.com.
10         IN      PTR     ns1.example.com.
254        IN      PTR     router.example.com.
```

5. Verify changes and restart **named.** Verify that your IPs, hosts, and serial number information are correct. Then restart **named** by running **/etc/rc.d/init.d/ named restart** or **service named restart.** To verify that you have your domain running properly, use **nslookup** (discussed in the "DNS Tools" section of this chapter) by running **nslookup www.example.com** and **nslookup 192.168.0.212.** You should receive the appropriate IP and domain information if DNS is set up properly.

Secondary and Tertiary DNS

When a domain is registered, it should be registered with not only a primary DNS server but with a secondary DNS server as well. Therefore, if the primary server is down, the secondary server will take over. For even more fail-over, a tertiary DNS server can be set up.

Setting up secondary DNS for a domain is even more simple than setting up primary DNS. Essentially, you have to do only Steps 1 and 4 from the previous example of setting up primary DNS. There is a difference, however, from Step 1 in the previous example. The following steps explain how to set up secondary DNS.

1. Add **zone** to /etc/named.conf. As a secondary entry, your **type** is **slave.** With a **slave** entry you have to specify the master (used to pull the DNS information for the domain), which in this example is 192.168.2.50. As a secondary entry, your **zone** entry in /etc/named.conf will look like this:

```
zone "example.com" {
        type slave;
        file "db.example.com";
        masters {
                192.168.2.50;
        };
};
```

2. Verify changes and restart **named.** Verify that your IPs and host information are correct. Then restart **named** by running **/etc/rc.d/init.d/named restart.**

DNS Tools

There are a variety of DNS tools available to help you utilize and examine the DNS service. DNS tools should be installed on every Linux workstation, not just DNS servers. Tools such as nslookup are a great help for even users who want to look up an IP address or domain using a name server.

Table 10.1	DNS tools.	
Tool	**Usage**	**Description**
dig	**dig @nameserver** domain	Queries the name server for domain name packet information
dnsquery	**dnsquery –n nameserver host**	Queries the domain name server for the host using resolver
host	**host domain**	Looks up the host for the domain name
nslookup	**nslookup domain** or **nslookup ipaddress**	Queries Internet name servers for IP and domain information

DNS tools can be installed on your system with the bind-utils-8.2-2_P5-9.i386.rpm file found on your Red Hat Linux 6.2 CD in the /RedHat/RPMS directory. Some of the popular DNS tools included in this package are dig, dnsquery, host, and nslookup. Table 10.1 briefly explains these tools and gives an example of their usage.

File Transfer Protocol (FTP)

FTP is the File Transfer Protocol used to connect two machines (a server and a client) in order to transfer files from one to the other. Typically, FTP works by a client connecting to a server (via an FTP client) and then either uploading files to the server or downloading files from the server to the client.

Two general types of FTP servers are *user access* and *anonymous access*. User-access FTP servers require that the client accessing the FTP server have a valid user account (username and password) on the system. Anonymous-access FTP servers allow any client to connect without needing a specific username or password to access the system. In this section, I'll discuss how to set up the default Red Hat Linux FTP server (**wu-ftpd**) and how to set up the anonymous FTP.

Setting Up wu-ftpd

The default Red Hat Linux 6.2 FTP server is **wu-ftpd**. By default, you can install the **wu-ftpd** package during the Red Hat Linux 6.2 installation. If you did not install **wu-ftpd** during your Red Hat Linux installation, you can install it from the Red Hat 6.2 CD with the RPM wu-ftpd-2.6.0-3.i386.rpm.

After the installation of **wu-ftpd** is finished, there is nothing to configure. With the default **wu-ftpd** installation, any user can then **ftp** to your server and, with his username and password authentication, gain FTP access to his own home directory (unless otherwise specified). The **wu-ftpd** package sets up three configuration files: /etc/ftpaccess, /etc/ftphosts, and /etc/ftpusers.

The /etc/ftpaccess File

The /etc/ftpaccess file is the main **ftpd** configuration file. There are a number of options you can configure and customize in the /etc/ftpaccess file. With the **loginfails** option, you can specify the number of attempts to successfully log into the FTP server. (The default is **loginfails 5**, which allows five attempts before the FTP server refuses connection.) You can also allow or deny specific tool access (such as compress, tar, and chmod) to specific types of connections (such as **all**, **guest**, and **anonymous**). For more information about /etc/ftpaccess options, read the ftpaccess man page (**man 5 ftpaccess**).

The /etc/ftphosts File

The /etc/ftphosts file is used to allow or deny access to specific accounts from specified hosts. There are two types of entries in the /etc/ftphosts file. The first is **allow**, and the second is **deny**. The syntax used is **allow** *username host* or **deny** *username host*. For example, **allow kara 192.168.0.*** would allow only the user "kara" to log in from 192.168.0.* hosts. The entry **deny anonymous 192.168.1.*** would deny all anonymous user connections from any 192.168.1.* host. For more information about setting up the /etc/ftphosts file, read the ftphosts man page (**man 5 ftphosts**).

The /etc/ftpusers File

The /etc/ftpusers file is used to specify exactly which system user accounts cannot log into the server via **ftp**. By default, system users such as root, bin, deamon, adm, lp, sync, shutdown, halt, mail, news, uucp, operator, games, and nobody are automatically added to this list. If you create any users to whom you want to deny FTP access, add them to the /etc/ftpusers file as well.

Setting Up Anonymous FTP

An anonymous FTP server does not require a user to enter a specific user ID or password to access the server. This means the FTP server can be reached with anonymous FTP clients (such as Netscape Navigator) and by simply passing the generic usernames (such as "anonymous" and "ftp") along with the email address as the password.

To configure your FTP server as an anonymous FTP server, you can install the anonftp RPM, and the **wu-ftpd** server will be configured automatically. This RPM can be found on your Red Hat Linux 6.2 CD as /RedHat/RPMS/ anonftp-3.0-3.i386.rpm.

Network File System (NFS)

NFS is the Network File System, the standard method for sharing files between Unix (and Unix-like) systems. Linux can be an NFS server to other Linux (or Unix) systems, as well as an NFS client to other Linux (or Unix) systems.

The NFS Server

The NFS server can be installed by default during the Red Hat Linux 6.2 installation. If NFS was not installed during your Red Hat installation, you can use the RPM on the Red Hat installation CD. The NFS RPM can be found at /RedHat/RPMS/knfsd-1.2.2-4.i386.rpm.

Red Hat 6.2 uses the new kernel **nfsd** feature of the 2.2 Linux kernels. Therefore, in order to use the NFS server, the kernel must be configured with the appropriate kernel support. With the stock Red Hat 6.2 kernel, the kernel **nfsd** requires the nfsd.o module (which then requires the lockd.o and sunrpc.o modules). In addition, the NFS server requires the following specific user-space daemons and utilities.

➤ *Portmap* —The NFS server system must be running the **portmap** daemon. It is included in the **portmap** package portmap-4.0-19.i386.rpm.

➤ *RPC* —RPC daemons from the **knfsd** package must be running. They include **rpc.statd, rpc.rquotad, rpc.mountd,** and **rpc.nfsd.** (These can be started by running /etc/rc.d/init.d/nfs start.)

Note: If for some reason the nfsd.o module is not available, rpc.nfsd will continue to run with the same behavior as the old user-space unfsd. Normally, it will pass control to the kernel nfsd and exit.

Configuring NFS Server Exports

The **knfsd** server uses /etc/exports to configure exported NFS filesystems. The format of the file entries is typically

```
/path/to/export host(options)
```

The first field (/path/to/export) is the path that you want to make available via NFS. An example would be /mnt/cdrom. The second field (host) is the host name (IP address or address/netmask) to which you want the filesystem to be made available. If nothing is supplied for host, the filesystem is exported to the world. The last field (options) is a comma-separated list of export options. Some standard examples are **ro** for read-only and **rw** for read-write. An example of the options field can be **(ro)** specifying that the exported filesystem is read-only or (**rw**) specifying that the exported filesystem is readable and writable. The following is an example of an /etc/exports file:

```
/mnt/cdrom          (ro)
/tmp                (rw)
/home               192.168.0.0/255.255.255.0(rw)
```

The first line in this example exports /mnt/cdrom read-only to the world. The second line exports /tmp read-write to the world. The third line exports /home read-write to only the 192.168.0.0 network. For more information about the format and options of /etc/exports, view the **exports** man page (**man 5 exports**).

After you have added your filesystem entries to /etc/exports, you must take the following steps:

1. Run **exportsfs –av**. To initially add all your entries in /etc/exports to the list of exported filesystems (assuming that **mountd** is already running), run **exportfs -av**. The **a** option specifies **exportfs** to add the entries, and the **v** option specifies to print the output verbosely.

2. Run **exportfs –rv**. After changing /etc/exports, you must update the NFS server by using **exportfs -rv**. This command re-exports all directories in /etc/ exports, synchronizing the server's list of exports (maintained by **mountd** in /var/lib/nfs/xtab) with the /etc/exports file.

To remove a filesystem from **mountd**'s list of exportable filesystems, use **exportfs -u**. More information about **exportfs** can be found in the **exportfs(8)** man page (**man 8 exportfs**).

The NFS Client

The NFS client is included in the NFS RPM nfs-utils-0.1.6-2i386.rpm. It contains useful NFS client tools such as showmount. The default NFS client on Linux consists of several parts. Some of the most important parts include the specific kernel modules **portmap** and **mount**.

Kernel Modules

The NFS client requires a specific set of kernel modules. These modules include nfs.o, lockd.o, and sunrpc.o. These kernel modules are installed in the default Red Hat 6.2 kernel installation and will automatically load when you start the user-space daemons by the kernel module loader.

portmap

The NFS client (as well as the server) requires the system to be running the **portmap** daemon. The **portmap** daemon must be running for the NFS **lockd** (file locking over NFS) daemon to work properly. The **portmap** daemon is installed as /sbin/portmap on Red Hat 6.2 (included in the portmap RPM portmap-4.0-19.i386.rpm). To start **portmap,** run **/etc/rc.d/init.d/portmap start** or **service portmap start.**

mount

The utility required to use NFS as a client is the mount utility. The mount utility is used to mount a remote NFS filesystem. Common use of the mount utility is **mount remotehost:/path /local/path.** There are several commonly used mount options for NFS. Table 10.2 lists the most common mount options used on NFS.

Using the previous mount options, you could mount the filesystem /export on the NFS server **linux.example.com** with an 8K blocksize on /mnt/nfs by issuing the following:

```
mount linux.example.com:/export /mnt/nfs -o rsize=8192,wsize=8192
```

NFS Tools

In addition to the **mount** command used to **mount** the NFS filesystems, there are a few other useful NFS tools to help you use and administer NFS filesystems. Table 10.3 lists a few extra tools to make your life with NFS easier.

Table 10.2   NFS mount options.

Mount Option	Description
rsize=num	Read **num** bytes at a time (instead of the default 1024 bytes).
wsize=num	Write **num** bytes at a time (instead of the default 1024 bytes).
soft	If a timeout occurs, return an I/O error to the calling program.
hard	If a timeout occurs, send a "Server not responding" message to the console and continue to retry. (This is the default behavior.)
intr	For a hard mount that has timed out, allow I/O to be interrupted with a signal to the calling program. (The default is to not allow I/O on a hard mount to be interrupted.)

Table 10.3   NFS tools.

NFS tool	Usage	Description
df	**df**	Lists the filesystems mounted on your machine
showmount	**showmount –e host**	Shows export mount information for the host
rpcinfo	**/usr/sbin/rpcinfo –p host**	Lists all RPC services running on the host

Samba (SMB)

Samba is the open source server that implements SMB (Server Message Block). SMB allows you to set up your Red Hat Linux 6.2 machine to act as a server for Windows 95/98/NT for services such as file- and print-sharing.

Setting Up SMB

With Red Hat Linux 6.2, you can install Samba during the installation (use the Set Up Windows File And Print Sharing option). If Samba wasn't installed during your Red Hat installation, you can install the Samba RPM from the Red Hat Linux 6.2 CD. The CD contains the RPM in /RedHat/RPMS/samba-2.0.6-9.i386.rpm.

Installing the Samba RPM sets up the main configuration file for SMB as /etc/smb.conf. In addition to the main configuration file, a number of additional configuration files and tools are installed. Table 10.4 lists all the configuration files and tools installed by the Samba RPM file.

Table 10.4	SMB files.	
File	**Path**	**Description**
smb.conf	/etc/smb.conf	Configuration file for Samba
smbpasswd	/etc/smbpasswd	Configuration file for Windows password file for server
smbuser	/etc/smbuser	Unix-to-NT user mapping
nmdb	/usr/sbin/nmbd	Windows NetBIOS names for sending and receiving names of machines on the network
smbd	/usr/sbin/smbd	SMB daemon for server shares
swat	/usr/sbin/swat	Web-based configuration tool for SMB
smbadduser	/usr/bin/smbadduser	Tool for adding users to your system
smbclient	/usr/bin/smbclient	Client-side program to connect to SMB server from Linux
smbmount	/usr/bin/smbmount	Utility to mount SMB shares
smbpasswd	/usr/bin/smbpasswd	Utility used to add users to /etc/ smbpasswd, allowing for Windows encrypted passwords
smbprint	/usr/bin/smbprint	Script used for printing
smbrun	/usr/bin/smbrun	Script used to start SMB server
smbstatus	/usr/bin/smbstatus	Tool used to print status information for the running SMB server
smbtar	/usr/bin/smbtar	Script used for backing up Windows machines to your SMB server
smbumount	/usr/bin/smbumount	Tool used to unmount SMB service

Setting Up a Samba Share

When you're setting up a Samba share, there are roughly five steps to follow (after the basic installation). To set up a Samba share for a specific directory (for this example /home), go through the following steps.

1. Check the workgroup setting in /etc/smb.conf. The default setting is **WORKGROUP**. To set the workgroup (or domain) to **MYGROUP**, add a line in the **[globals]** section like this:

```
workgroup = MYGROUP
```

2. Add the share to the /etc/smb.conf. You first need to add the share entry beneath the **Share Definitions** section of /etc/smb.conf. The entry will have six lines. The first line names your share—for example, **[USER_HOME]**. The second line sets the comment that is the part seen by the Windows client. A sample comment could be **Home Directories**. The third line specifies the path to the shared directory. For this example, the setting would be **/home**. The fourth line specifies public access (also known as *guest ok*). The fifth line specifies whether the share is printable (used only for printer shares). The sixth line specifies whether the share is writable. A sample entry for a Share Definition might look like this:

```
[USER_HOME]
        comment = User Home Directories
        path = /home
        public = yes
        printable = no
        writable = yes
```

3. Check your /etc/smb.conf syntax. After you have saved your changes to /etc/smb.conf, you should check your smb.conf syntax. A tool that allows you to do that is testparm.

4. Restart Samba. After your /etc/smb.conf has been set up appropriately, you need to restart the SMB server. To do this, run **/etc/rc.d/init.d/smb restart** or **service smb restart**.

5. Test your SMB shares. First check to make sure that SMB is running (**/etc/rc.d/init.d/smb status** or **service smb status**). If SMB seems to be running properly, attempt to mount your own SMB share via **smbclient**. To do this, use **smbclient −L localhost**. (When you're prompted with a password, press Enter.) If your system is working properly, you should see everything your machine is offering as a SMB share.

Dynamic Host Configuration Protocol (DHCP)

DHCP is a superset of **bootp**, which is used to assign IP addresses to clients on a network. DHCP is used for dynamic hosts that can move, connect, and disconnect from networks. DHCP can dynamically assign IP addresses from preassigned IP addresses in /etc/dhcpd.leases and set up static IP addresses based on the NIC MAC (Media Access Control) address. DHCP can even restrict access by accepting requests from only specified MAC addresses.

Setting Up a DHCP Server

To set up a DHCP server, make sure that you have installed the DHCP RPM. The DHCP RPM packaged with Red Hat Linux 6.2 is dhcp-2.0-5.i386.rpm. To finish setting your DHCP server, follow these steps:

1. Check to see that you have MULTICAST support in your kernel. To do this, run **ifconfig –a**. If you already have MULTICAST support, you will have a line that says "UP BROADCAST RUNNING MULTICAST MTU:1500 Metric:1" in the **eth0** section of the **ifconfig** output. If MULTICAST is not in your configuration, you must reconfigure your kernel to support MULTICAST, replace your NIC (if not supported), or change your interface settings.

2. Add a route for 255.255.255.255 (required by Microsoft clients). To do this, type **route add –host 255.255.255.255 dev eth0** (where **eth0** is the device of your Ethernet card).

   Note: If you get an "unknown host" error when adding this route, add the following entry to your /etc/hosts file: 255.255.255.255 all-ones.

3. Start the DHCP server. To start the server, type **/etc/rc.d/init.d/dhcpd start**.

4. Verify that DHCP is working properly. Type **/usr/sbin/dhcpd –d –f**.

5. Configure your /etc/dhcpd.conf file (an example for setting random IPs for clients follows).

Configuring dhcpd for Random IP Assignment

To set up DHCP to assign random IP addresses to DHCP clients on the network, you'll need to configure the /etc/dhcpd.conf file, which is the main configuration file for DHCP. The following list contains sample settings for the /etc/dhcpd.conf file. These settings will allow DHCP to randomly assign IP addresses on your network that are between 192.168.1.10 and 192.168.1.100, as well as in the range 192.168.1.150 through 192.168.1.200. Listing 10.2 is a sample /etc/ dhcpd.conf configuration.

Listing 10.2   Sample /etc/dhcpd.conf file.

```
default-lease-time 500;
max-lease-time 6000;
option subnet-mask 255.255.255.0;
option broadcast-address 192.168.1.255;
option routers 192.168.1.254;
option domain-name-servers 192.168.1.1, 192.168.1.2;
option domain-name "example.com";
subnet 192.168.1.0 netmask 255.255.255.0 {
            range 192.168.1.10 192.168.1.100;
            range 192.168.1.150 192.168.1.200;
}
```

Using a DHCP Client

The DHCP client used on Red Hat Linux is called **pump**. If you did not install **pump** during the Red Hat Linux installation, you can install the **pump** RPM from the Red Hat Linux 6.2 CD-ROM. The file is pump-0.7.8-1.i386.rpm; it can be found in the /RedHat/RPMS/ directory on the Red Hat 6.2 CD-ROM. To configure your Linux DHCP client, take the following steps:

1. Execute netcfg by typing **netcfg** at the root prompt.

2. Choose the Interfaces button.

3. Select the Ethernet interface of your network connection (typically eth0).

4. Choose the Edit button to open the configuration window for the Ethernet interface.

5. Using the down arrow next to Interface Configuration Protocol, choose the dhcp option.

6. Enable the option to Activate Interface At Boot Time.

7. Choose Done.

8. Select the eth0 (or appropriate Ethernet) interface, and choose the Activate Button.

9. Choose the Save button to ensure that your configuration is saved, and then choose the Quit button.

10. To make sure that you're connected to the DHCP server, run **ifconfig**. The eth0 section of the output should have an **inet addr:** entry with your DHCP-assigned network address.

Time Services

A number of services available in Red Hat Linux allow you to configure and synchronize time services on your machine. These tools are made available because few machines have atomic clocks attached to them; therefore, computers often lose accurate time. There are three main time-related tools included in Red Hat Linux 6.2—they are the time configuration tool timetool and the time synchronization tools xntpd and rdate.

Time Configuration

A GUI tool for time configuration, timetool, is packaged with Red Hat Linux 6.2. The RPM available for timetool on the Red Hat Linux 6.2 CD is timetool-2.7.3-1.noarch.rpm.

To change system time with timetool, execute it as root by typing **timetool** at the root prompt. In the GUI window, select the time setting you want to change (hour, minute or second), and then use the up and down arrows to change the setting. When the time is set appropriately, choose the Set System Clock button to save the time setting to the system. Then choose the Exit Time Machine button to exit.

Time Synchronization

Some administrators choose to use time synchronization tools to set the system time based on a specified host machine. One (older) tool used for this is rdate. A more popular package used to set up a continuously running synchronization daemon is **xntp3**.

rdate

The Red Hat Linux tool rdate is a tool used to synchronize the system time with a specified machine. The rdate tool synchronizes only once when the tool is being used. The RPM used to install rdate on the Red Hat Linux 6.2 CD is rdate-1.0-1.i386.rpm.

To use rdate, run **rdate –p –s** *host* where *host* is the machine with which you want to synchronize your time. The **-p** option prints the time set on the remote host you specify. The **-s** option synchronizes the time on your machine with the host you specify.

The rdate tool uses port 37 to send and receive **rdate** requests. Many administrators disable this port and service; therefore, finding a good rdate host might be troublesome unless it is on your own network.

xntp3

The most popular package used for time synchronization is the **xntp3** package. The **xntp3** package contains several time-related tools such as **ntpdate** and the popular **xntpd** time daemon, which runs continuously to synchronize your system time. The RPM used to install **xntp3** on the Red Hat Linux 6.2 CD is xntp3-5.93-14.i386.rpm, and it is found in the /RedHat/RPMS/ directory.

➤ ntpdate —Similar to **rdate**. The **ntpdate** tool is used to retrieve the date and time from the network by polling the Network Time Protocol Servers as specified in the command. The **ntpdate** command is often placed in /etc/rc.local's startup script, or it can be run from the system cron.

➤ xntpd —Time synchronization daemon used to continuously adjust system time. Configuration for **xntpd** is done through /etc/ntp.conf.

Squid Proxy Server

Squid is a caching proxy server. Proxy servers are used to cache data streams such as FTP, gopher, and HTTP. Network clients can then be directed to the proxy server to aid in pulling up cached HTTP documents.

Setting Up Squid

To install Squid via RPM from the Red Hat Linux 6.2 CD, use squid-2.3.STABLE1-5.i386.rpm from the /RedHat/RPMS/ directory. The main configuration file that is automatically set up from the RPM is /etc/squid/squid.conf. The squid.conf file consists of every configuration setting needed to run Squid; this file contains excellent comment explanations for each setting available.

After you install the Squid RPM, the default configuration file (squid.conf) is already configured with default settings that allow you to run Squid "out of the box." To start Squid, type **/etc/rc.d/init.d/squid start** or **service squid start**. When you start Squid for the first time, you automatically create the Squid cache files as specified in the /etc/squid/squid.conf settings. The **squid** daemon will automatically listen on port 3128 for proxy requests.

Using Squid

The most popular use for Squid is as a Web proxy server. A Web proxy server caches HTTP request information (such as images, HTML pages, and so on) on a local machine to speed browsing download times for clients on the network. This feature is especially useful when a specific Web site is requested numerous times on a specific network.

When configuring a client to use a proxy server (such as Netscape), you simply set the client to point its HTTP traffic to the proxy server's IP address and port (3128). For instance, if your proxy server was on 192.168.0.1 and the network client was running Netscape, you would take the following steps:

1. Load Netscape Navigator. From the menu at the top of the window, choose Edit and then Preferences. In the Preferences menu, you can set up everything from identification information to advanced options, such as using a proxy server.

2. Select the Advanced option in the left frame of the Preferences window by selecting the arrow to the left of the Advanced option. Select the Proxies option from beneath the Advanced directory. In the right frame of the window, select Manual Proxy Configuration and choose the View button. An Edit Manual Proxy Configuration window then appears.

3. In the HTTP: setting box, set the IP address to the Squid server on your network (in this example, the server is set to 192.168.0.1), and set the port to send to (by default, this is set to 3128).

Practice Questions

Question 1

Which daemon is used for the Apache server?

○ a. **apached**

○ b. **httpd**

○ c. **htmld**

○ d. **ftpd**

Answer b is correct. The server used to set up an Apache Web server is httpd. Answers a and c are incorrect because they are not valid servers. Answer d is incorrect because ftpd is the FTP server.

Question 2

What is the main Apache configuration file?

○ a. httpd.conf

○ b. apache.conf

○ c. access.conf

○ d. conf.apache

Answer a is correct. The main Apache configuration file is /etc/httpd.conf. Answers b and d are incorrect because they are not valid options. Answer c is incorrect because although it is an Apache configuration file, it is deprecated.

Question 3

What is a **DocumentRoot**?

○ a. The file characteristics that indicate the root settings for the document

○ b. The header files of a document that indicate where the document should be kept

○ c. The default location where httpd files for a domain are to be kept

○ d. None of the above

Answer c is correct. The **DocumentRoot** setting is given in the httpd.conf file for setting up the default location for domain httpd files (such as HTML, CGI, and so forth).

Question 4

What are the three required parts of a default Red Hat Linux email system? [Check all correct answers]

❏ a. The MTA

❏ b. The MUA

❏ c. procmail

❏ d. Pine

❏ e. The MBA

Answers a, b, and c are correct. The three main ingredients of a default Red Hat Linux system are the MTA (sendmail), the MDA (procmail), and the MUA (mail reader). Answer d is incorrect because although Pine is an MUA, the particular program Pine can be replaced by other MUAs on the system, such as Elm or Netscape. Answer e is incorrect because it is not a valid option.

Question 5

Which server is used with the BIND package?

O a. **httpd**

O b. **bind**

O c. **dnsd**

O d. **named**

Answer d is correct. The server used with BIND (DNS) is **named**. Answer a is incorrect because httpd is the Apache server. Answers b and d are incorrect because they are not valid entries.

Question 6

What is an FTP server used for?

An FTP server is a File Transfer Protocol server. The FTP server is used to transfer files between a client and a server. The FTP server is capable of both uploading files from the client to the server, and downloading files from the server to the client.

Question 7

NFS is used to share information between Unix servers and Windows clients.

O a. True

O b. False

Answer b is correct. NFS is used to share data and mounted directories between multiple Unix and Linux machines. To share data between a Linux client or server and a Windows client, you must use Samba.

Question 8

What is xntpd?

○ a. An X Window server

○ b. An X FTP server

○ c. A time synchronization server

○ d. An X-based NT administration tool

Answer c is correct. The xntpd is part of the **xntpd3** package that includes tools for time synchronization between a client and a host machine. Answers a, c, and d are all invalid answers.

Question 9

What is Squid?

○ a. An HTTP proxy

○ b. An NIS proxy

○ c. A DNS caching proxy

○ d. The Linux mascot

Answer a is correct. Squid is a proxy server that is capable of caching HTTP, FTP, and gopher requests. Answer b is incorrect because there is no such thing as an NIS proxy. Answer c is incorrect because the DNS caching is handled by the name server. Answer d is incorrect because Tux (a penguin) is the Linux mascot.

Question 10

What port does Squid listen to (by default)?

○ a. 3620

○ b. 3128

○ c. 6619

○ d. None of the above

Answer b is correct. The default port Squid listens to is 3128. Answers a, c, and d are incorrect because they are not valid answers.

Task 1

Install the DNS (BIND) server on your machine. Configure it to set up three primary domains and a secondary domain. Set up the reverse files for your subnet. Use nslookup to see that your three primary domains each have the appropriate IP addresses and domains assigned to them.

Task 2

Install the Apache Web server. Configure Apache to host three different virtual hosts, each with its own IP on your subnetwork. Create unique **DocumentRoot** entries for each so that, when displayed on your system, each has a unique Web site. Now change the configuration files for the three to have the same IP address but still have the three unique Web sites. Don't forget to set up any DNS and host files.

Task 3

Install the **wu-ftpd** FTP server. Set up a new user on your system to FTP from another machine on your network (if available). Upload a test file into the user's home directory. Now change to ftpaccess files to deny that user from the remote host. Try to connect again. What happens? Next configure the FTP server for anonymous user connections by using the **anon-ftp** package. Now connect from the same remote system as an anonymous user. What happens? Why?

Task 4

Install the NFS server on your machine. Set up an NFS share for the /tmp directory on your system. Mount the NFS share from another machine on your network. Try to write a file to the /tmp directory. What happens? Change the NFS mount entry to **(ro)**. Try to write another file to the /tmp directory from the remote host. What happens?

Task 5

Install the SMB server on your machine. Set up an SMB share to /usr/docs. Make sure that the docs are not writable. Mount the SMB share from a Windows client on your network. Browse the /usr/docs/ entries and open a file. Try to write to it. What happens? Add another share to the /mnt/cdrom directory. Mount a Windows or Microsoft-related CD-ROM in the SMB server CD-ROM. Access the /mnt/cdrom share from a Windows machine. Execute an .exe from the CD-ROM. Did it work?

Task 6

Set up two machines on your network. Set up the first machine to be a DHCP server. Set up the second machine to be a DHCP client. Bring the Ethernet interface on the client up and down a few times, checking the IP address assigned to the machine each time. What happens? Why?

Need to Know More?

 Albitz, Paul and Cricket Liu. *DNS and BIND*. O'Reilly & Associates, 1998. ISBN 1-56592-512-2. This book covers the implementation and usage of DNS and BIND.

 Baines, Dominic. *Samba Black Book*. The Coriolis Group, 1999. ISBN 1-57610-455-9. This book covers the implementation and usage of Samba.

 Costales, Bryan and Eric Allman. *Sendmail*. O'Reilly & Associates, 1997. ISBN 1-56592-222-0. This book covers all the technical aspects of compiling, configuring, and using sendmail.

 Kabir, Mohammed J. *Apache Server Bible*. IDG Books Worldwide, 1999. ISBN 0-76453-218-9. This book covers every aspect of Apache Web server administration, including configuration. This book also includes a CD-ROM with utilities covered in the book and third-party applications to assist with Apache installation and administration.

 Kelly, Petter, P. Donham, and David Collier-Brown. *Using Samba*. O'Reilly & Associates, 1999. ISBN 1-56592-449-5. This book covers the implementation and usage of Samba.

 Laurie, Ben and Peter Laurie. *Apache: The Definitive Guide, Second Edition*. O'Reilly & Associates, 1999. ISBN 1-56592-528-9. This book is a complete guide to obtaining, configuring, and securing Apache on Unix and other operating systems.

 Stern, Hal and Mike Loukides. *Managing NFS and NIS*. O'Reilly & Associates, 1991. ISBN 0-93717-575-7. This book provides required information for system administrators who need to set up and administer either NFS or NIS in a Unix environment.

 http://squid.nlanr.net/ —For more information about the current development of and documentation for Squid, visit the Squid Web site.

 http://www.samba.org/ —For more information about the current development of and documentation for Samba, visit this Web site.

http://www.sendmail.org/ —For more information about the current development of and documentation for sendmail, visit this Web site.

 http://www.linuxdoc.org/ —The Linux Documentation Project contains links, HOWTOs, and other documentation.

System Security and Administration

· ·

Terms you'll need to understand:

✓ Database

✓ Query

✓ Pluggable modules

✓ tty devices

✓ Daemon

✓ Firewall

✓ Route

Techniques you'll need to master:

✓ Using NIS

✓ Implementing Name Server Switching options

✓ Using Pluggable Authentication Modules (PAM)

✓ Setting up secure tty sessions

✓ Using INET services

✓ Implementing tcp_wrappers

✓ Setting up routing

✓ Configuring a firewall

Security is an essential part of networking. Keeping your system secure from crackers and available for only authorized use is a must. Some very basic security problems can arise from standard daily activities. With such emphasis placed on network security today, it's important for an RHCE in the workplace to be comfortable with setting up network security. With this in mind, a working knowledge of network security concepts, tools, and configuration is essential. In this chapter, I'll discuss security concepts, NIS (Network Information Service), LDAP (Lightweight Directory Access Protocol), PAM (Pluggable Authentication Modules), inetd, and tcp_wrappers. I'll also discuss some advanced network options, including routing, firewalling, and IP masquerading and SSH (Secure Shell).

NIS

NIS is Sun Microsystems' Network Information Service. It was formerly known as Yellow Pages, but after a trademark dispute with British Telecom, Sun changed the name to Network Information Service. The original name, Yellow Pages, is why all the NIS-related commands begin with **yp**.

NIS is a simple directory service whose main purpose is to allow remote authentication of systems on local network systems. NIS allows configuration information—such as passwd and group files, sendmail aliases, automount maps, and hosts files—to be kept on a central server. Each system in the NIS domain runs the NIS client, ypbind, to find a server and retrieve the appropriate maps on it.

NIS uses a master/slave server configuration that resembles DNS. The master NIS server holds the NIS map files. Changes in the maps are then pushed to the slave server(s). Although an NIS domain can operate with only one server, it's best to have at least one slave server for redundancy.

You must run the RPC portmapper (/usr/sbin/portmap) to run NIS. The RPC portmapper servers convert the RPC program numbering to TCP/IP or UDP/IP protocol port numbers.

NIS on Red Hat Linux

Red Hat Linux 6.2 ships with NIS-v.2-compliant clients, servers, and tools. The three NIS packages in Red Hat Linux 6.2 include ypbind (the NIS client), ypserv (the NIS server), and yp-tools (the utilities for querying the NIS server). NIS is used only when specified by the /etc/nsswitch.conf file and ypbind. In this section, I'll discuss the NIS client and NIS server commands.

NIS Client

The NIS client is responsible for querying the NIS server for information from the NIS system maps and for other NIS information. NIS clients use six main tools:

➤ *ypbind* —Finds and stores information about an NIS domain and server. Information is stored in /var/yp/binding. This tool runs during boot-up.

➤ *ypwhich* —Returns the name of the NIS server used by the NIS client.

➤ *ypcat* —Prints the values of all keys in the specified NIS map.

➤ *yppoll* —Returns the version and master server of the specified NIS map.

➤ *ypmatch* —Prints the values of keys from an NIS map.

➤ *ypdomainname* —Prints the name of the NIS domain.

NIS Server

The NIS server is responsible for hosting the NIS maps responding to NIS client requests, for managing changes to NIS maps (especially the NIS password map), and, in the case of a master NIS server, for pushing map changes to slave servers. In addition to the NIS client commands, the NIS server uses NIS commands such as:

➤ **ypserv** —Starts the NIS server program.

➤ **yppasswd** —Starts the server that handles the NIS password changes.

➤ **makedbm** —Translates ASCII databases, such as /etc/passwd, to DBM databases.

➤ **yppush** —Notifies the slave servers when master databases are changed.

/etc/nsswitch.conf

NIS is used only when specified by the /etc/nsswitch.conf file. The GNU C library includes support for the Name Server Switch file (/etc/nsswitch.conf), which is patterned after the nsswitch.conf file on Solaris 2. The Name Server Switch file configures the order of lookups for various system services. The following code is the /etc/nsswitch.conf file that is shipped with Red Hat 6.2.

```
#
# /etc/nsswitch.conf
#
# An example Name Service Switch config file. This file should be
# sorted with the most-used services at the beginning.
```

```
#
# The entry '[NOTFOUND=return]' means that the search for an
# entry should stop if the search in the previous entry turned
# up nothing. Note that if the search failed due to some other
# reason (like no NIS server responding) then the search continues
# with the next entry.
#
# Legal entries are:
#
# nisplus or nis+    Use NIS+ (NIS version 3)
# nis or yp          Use NIS (NIS version 2), also called YP
# dns                Use DNS (Domain Name Service)
# files              Use the local files
# db                 Use the local database (.db) files
# compat             Use NIS on compat mode
# hesiod             Use Hesiod for user lookups
# [NOTFOUND=return] Stop searching if not found so far
#
# To use db, put the "db" in front of "files" for entries you want
# to be looked up first in the databases
#
# Example:
#passwd:    db files nisplus nis
#shadow:    db files nisplus nis
#group:     db files nisplus nis

passwd:     files nisplus nis
shadow:     files nisplus nis
group:      files nisplus nis

#hosts:     db files nisplus nis dns
hosts:      files nisplus nis dns

# Example - obey only what nisplus tells us...
#services:   nisplus [NOTFOUND=return] files
#networks:   nisplus [NOTFOUND=return] files
#protocols:  nisplus [NOTFOUND=return] files
#rpc:        nisplus [NOTFOUND=return] files
#ethers:     nisplus [NOTFOUND=return] files
#netmasks:   nisplus [NOTFOUND=return] files

bootparams: nisplus [NOTFOUND=return] files

ethers:     files
netmasks:   files
networks:   files
```

```
protocols:  files
rpc:        files
services:   files

netgroup:   nisplus

publickey:  nisplus

automount:  files nisplus
aliases:    files nisplus
```

The format of the preceding nsswitch.conf file uses the layout, database: location [result=action], where *database* is the name of the requested database, *location* is the location of the database, *result* is the requested result, and *action* is the action that occurs if the requested result is matched. Therefore, as in the stock Red Hat 6.2 nsswitch.conf file, passwd lookups with the getpw*C library calls will first go to the local passwd file, and if the passwd lookups are not located, will next try NIS+, and if they are still not located, will finally try NIS if it's configured.

Tables 11.1 through 11.3 list the databases, locations, and results that the GNU C library can recognize.

Note: The action for any result will always be either RETURN or CONTINUE.

Table 11.1 NIS databases.	
Database	**Description**
aliases	Mail aliases that are used by sendmail
ethers	Ethernet numbers
group	User groups used by **getgrent()** functions
hosts	Host names and numbers; used by **gethostbyname()** and similar functions
netgroup	Network-wide list of hosts and users; used for access rules
network	Network names and numbers; used by **getnetent()** functions
passwd	User passwords; used by **getpwent()** functions
protocols	Network protocols; used by **getprotent()** functions
publickey	Public and secret keys for **secure_rpc**; used by NIS+ and NFS
rpc	Remote-procedure-call names and numbers; used by **getrpcbyname()** and similar functions
services	Network services; used by **getservent()** functions
shadow	Shadow user passwords; used by **getspnam()** functions

Table 11.2	NIS locations.
Location	**Location Description**
nisplus (nis+)	Lookup via NIS+
nis (yp)	Lookup via NIS
compat	Lookup via NIS in manner compatible with older versions of glibc
db	Lookup via local database files
files	Lookup via local text files
dns	Lookup via DNS

Table 11.3	NIS results.	
Result	**Result Description**	**Default Action**
SUCCESS	The error occurred, and the wanted entry is returned.	**RETURN**
NOTFOUND	The lookup process works OK, but the needed value was not found.	**CONTINUE**
UNAVAIL	The service is permanently unavailable. This can mean that the needed file is not available, or, for DNS, that the server is not available or does not allow queries.	**CONTINUE**
TRYAGAIN	The service is temporarily unavailable. This can mean that a file is locked or that a server cannot accept any more connections.	**CONTINUE**

Lightweight Directory Access Protocol (LDAP)

LDAP is an open standard protocol for accessing directory information services. The LDAP protocol runs over TCP protocols and other Internet transport protocols. LDAP can be used to access either standalone directory services or X.500 directories.

Combined with SSL (Secure Sockets Layer), LDAP is intended to be an alternative directory service for NIS. Many of SSL's features include encryption support and the ability to access control lists.

LDAP directory service is based on a client/server model, quite similar to NIS. One or more LDAP servers contain the data used to make up the LDAP directory tree or back-end database. An LDAP client connects to the LDAP server to make a request. The server responds to the request with either an answer or a pointer to where the client can get an answer to its request. One of the biggest advantages of LDAP over NIS is that with LDAP, server synchronization occurs in increments, so data is pushed immediately to slave servers, whereas NIS synchronizes its data transfers periodically.

OpenLDAP

The OpenLDAP project is a collaborative effort to provide an open-source LDAP suite of applications and tools. Like Netscape Communications' Directory Server, OpenLDAP also bases its project on the original University of Michigan LDAP server project.

The OpenLDAP package uses the server daemon *slapd*. The slapd server runs in a standalone environment. The OpenLDAP X.500 gateway is called *ldapd*. The OpenLDAP replication server is called *slurpd*. The configuration file used to set up LDAP client behavior is /etc/openldap/ldap.conf.

OpenLDAP can be installed from the openldap-1.2.9-5.i386.rpm off your Red Hat 6.2 installation CD, or downloaded from OpenLDAP's Web site at **http://www.openldap.org/**.

Pluggable Authentication Modules (PAM)

PAM is the Pluggable Authentication Modules system that enables ruleset implementation without having to recode individual services. All security-conscious programs (such as login, su, and ftp) are configured by PAM to do a variety of authentication and security checks.

When a service such as login is used, PAM checks its configuration files to determine how to authenticate the user. For instance, PAM might authenticate by checking /etc/passwd, kerberos, or NIS. After the method of authentication is determined, PAM then returns an answer to the service to indicate whether the user was authenticated.

PAM Configuration

All the PAM configuration files are located in /etc/pam.d/. Every application or service that can use PAM has a file entry in /etc/pam.d/ as well. Some of the most common entries that can be found in /etc/pam.d/ include **chfn, chsh, halt, linuxconf, login, passwd, ppp, reboot, rexec, rlogin, rsh, shutdown, su, xdm,** and **xscreensaver.** If they're installed, you might find entries for **kde, samba,** and **ssh** here as well. Looking at these files, you will see four columns of information.

They include module-type, control-flag, module-path, and arguments. Take a look at the following example of the login entry in /etc/pam.d/:

```
#%PAM-1.0
auth       required    /lib/security/pam_securetty.so
auth       required    /lib/secuirty/pam_pwdb.so        shadow nullok
auth       required    /lib/security/pam_nologin.so
account    required    /lib/security/pam_pwdb.so
password   required    /lib/security/pam_cracklib.so
password   required    /lib/security/pam_pwdb.so nullok use_authtok
session    required    /lib/security/pam_pwdb.so
session    optional    /lib/security/pam_console.so
```

module-type

The module-type column in your PAM configuration files contains four types of modules. These include auth, account, session, and password.

➤ *auth* —This module type provides two ways of authenticating the user. First, it establishes that the user is indeed who the user claims to be. It does this by instructing the application to prompt the user for a password. The module can then grant group membership (independent of /etc/groups) or other privileges through its credential granting properties.

➤ *account* —This module performs non-authentication-based account management. This module is typically used to restrict or permit access to a service based on the time of day, the maximum number of users, or even the location of the user (for instance, allowing user "root" to log in from only the console).

➤ *session* —This module performs duties that need to be done for the user before they can be given service. Services that are affected by this module include the logging of information about a user opening and closing data, mounting directories, and so on.

➤ *password*—This module is required for updating the authentication token associated with each user. There is typically one module for each challenge- or response-based authentication (auth) module-type.

control-flag

The control-flag is used to indicate how the PAM library will react to the success or failure of the module with which it is associated. The four flags that are used to specify the module actions are **required, requisite, sufficient,** and **optional,** described here:

➤ **required** —Indicates that the success of the module is required for the module-type facility to succeed. If this module fails, the failure will not be apparent to the user until all the modules of the same module-type have been executed.

➤ **requisite** —Similar to **required,** but if this module fails, control is immediately returned to the application. This flag is useful to protect against the possibility of a user being allowed to enter a password over an unsafe medium.

➤ **sufficient** —Indicates that the Linux-PAM library is satisfied that this module-type has succeeded in its purpose. If no previous module has failed, no more stacked modules of this type are invoked. If this module fails, the result is not deemed fatal to the application.

➤ **optional** —Marks the module as not being critical to the success or failure of the user's application for service. In fact, Linux-PAM will ignore such a module when determining if the module stack succeeds or fails.

module-path and Arguments

The **module-path** is the path name to the dynamically loadable module. The default path to the module is set to /lib/security/ unless another path is mentioned. Typically, the full path /lib/security/ is listed regardless.

The **argument** column of each entry lists arguments that are passed to the module when the module is invoked. Typically, these arguments are optional and are listed specifically to each given module. If an argument is invalid, the module ignores it. If such an error is made, the module is required to write the error to **syslog,** the system log daemon. The five generic arguments that are often used and understood by most modules are **debug, no_warn, use_first_pass, try_first_pass,** and **use_mapped_pass,** described here:

➤ **debug** —Use the **syslog** call to log debugging information to the system log files.

➤ **no_warn** —Instructs the module to not give warning messages to the application.

➤ **use_first_pass** —The module should not prompt the user for a password. Instead, the module should obtain the previously typed password from the preceding auth module. If that does not work, the user will not be authenticated.

➤ **try_first_pass** —The module should attempt authentication with the previously typed password from the preceding auth module. If that does not work, the user is prompted for a password.

➤ **use_mapped_pass** —Instructs the module to take the clear text authentication token entered by a previous module and use it to generate an encrypted (or decrypted) key to safely store or retrieve the authentication token required for the module.

The **use_mapped_pass** argument is not currently supported by any of the modules in the Linux-PAM distribution because of possible consequences associated with US encryption restrictions. Developers within the United States (or their own countries) can implement it freely within their countries.

Note: A special argument listed in the example for auth was shadow. This refers to support for shadow passwords, a feature that's is supported by pam_pwdb.so. Shadow passwords utilize several methods to increase system security. Shadow passwords make it more difficult to extract system password information from system password files, by replacing the password field of /etc/passwd (with an "x") and creating the file /etc/shadow to contain the password hash.

Red Hat 6.2 can be set to use shadow passwords during installation. If shadow passwords were not enabled during installation, you can convert the system to use shadow passwords by running the pwconv program. If necessary, you can later convert it back to regular passwords by using pwunconv. The change should be transparent to all programs that use PAM.

/etc/securetty

The /etc/securetty file is used by **login** to determine which tty devices root can log in on. Typically, only the local consoles are listed. By limiting access to only local consoles, you disable direct login superuser privileges from anywhere except the console. This is not fail-safe, however, because disabling virtual terminal console login does not restrict the user from using **su** to log in as root from the user account. Also, some programs such as SSH and xdm can be configured to allow root logins over the network regardless of securetty-file settings. The output of the /etc/securetty file is very simple because it lists only the tty devices that allow root logins. Figure 11.1 shows a sample output of a default Red Hat 6.2 /etc/ securetty file.

inetd

The daemon **inetd** is the Internet "superserver" daemon that controls most of the network services that listen for incoming connections on your machine. The **inetd**

Figure 11.1   A default Red Hat 6.2 /etc/securetty file.

daemon runs in the background, binding all relevant ports and calling the appropriate servers when necessary.

The /etc/inetd.conf configuration file controls the **inetd** daemon. This inetd.conf file specifies which services **inetd** manages, and it contains a list of entries composed of seven fields. The seven fields are as follows:

➤ *Service Name*—The service name is translated to a port number by looking up the service name in the /etc/services file.

➤ *Socket Type*—This specifies either the stream for TCP or the dgram for UDP.

➤ *Protocol*—This specifies the name of the transport protocol used by the service.

➤ *wait/nowait*—This specifies the **wait** or **nowait** option for dgram sockets (it does not affect stream sockets).

➤ *User*—Login ID of the user under whom the process will execute.

➤ *Server Program*—Full path name to the server program to be executed.

➤ *Arguments*—Command and arguments to be passed to the server.

When a connection is requested from another machine over a network, the request is initially handled by **inetd**. The **inetd** daemon looks up the service by its port number in /etc/services/. It then starts the appropriate server listed in the /etc/inetd.conf file to connect with the incoming request.

To disable a network service handled by inetd is very simple: using a hash (#) mark, comment the specific line in /etc/inetd.conf that corresponds to the service. The following is a snippet from a sample inetd.conf file. Notice that there can be multiple entries for services that can be used with both TCP and UPD. In addition, notice that this /etc/inetd.conf file has several services disabled, such as finger and talk:

```
#
ftp     stream  tcp   nowait   root    /usr/sbin/tcpd    in.ftpd -l -a
telnet  stream  tcp   nowait   root    /usr/sbin/tcpd    in.telnetd
#
# Shell, login, exec, comsat and talk are BSD protocols.
#
shell   stream  tcp   nowait   root    /usr/sbin/tcpd    in.rshd
login   stream  tcp   nowait   root    /usr/sbin/tcpd    in.rlogind
#exec   stream  tcp   nowait   root    /usr/sbin/tcpd    in.rexecd
#talk   dgram   udp   wait     root    /usr/sbin/tcpd    in.talkd
ntalk   dgram   udp   wait     root    /usr/sbin/tcpd    in.ntalkd
#
# Pop and imap mail services et al
#
#pop-2  stream  tcp   nowait   root    /usr/sbin/tcpd    ipop2d
#pop-3  stream  tcp   nowait   root    /usr/sbin/tcpd    ipop3d
#imap   stream  tcp   nowait   root    /usr/sbin/tcpd    imapd
#
# Finger, systat and netstat give out user information which may
# be valuable to potential "system crackers." Many sites choose
# to disable some or all of these services to improve security.
#
finger stream tcp  nowait    root  /usr/sbin/tcpd   in.fingerd
#cfinger stream tcp nowait    root  /usr/sbin/tcpd   in.cfingerd
#systat stream tcp  nowait    guest /usr/sbin/tcpd/bin/ps   -auwwx
#netstat stream tcp nowait    guest /usr/sbin/tcpd /bin/netstat -f
inet
#
# Authentication
#
auth   stream  tcp   nowait   nobody /usr/sbin/in.identd in.identd -l
#
# End of inetd.conf
```

Shadow Passwords

Shadow passwords have several purposes. First, the password field of /etc/passwd is removed (replaced by an "x"). The file /etc/shadow then contains the password hash. The permissions on the shadow file make it unreadable by anyone but root (and, in some distributions, the "shadow" group). This makes it more difficult to extract password hashes to run through crack or other similar password-guessing programs. The shadow file also contains password aging information.

You can convert a system to shadow passwords by running the pwconv program. If necessary, you can later convert the system back by using pwunconv. The change should be transparent to all programs that use PAM. Password aging can be controlled with the chage program.

tcp_wrappers

The use of tcp_wrappers on your system allows you to perform specific actions when another machine connects to your own. With the use of the /etc/hosts.allow and /etc/hosts.deny configuration files, you can and cannot use specific services. The use of tcp_wrappers can affect only services that are controlled by inetd (as previously discussed in the section on inetd).

When a connection request is sent from another machine to your machine, inetd first checks to see that the service is enabled and all permissions are set properly. If so, inetd then passes off the request to tcp_wrappers. Next, tcp_wrappers checks the /etc/hosts.allow file to see if permission is granted specifically for that service to the requested user. If tcp_wrappers finds that the specific user is granted access to the service, the connection is granted. If no setting in the /etc/hosts.allow file is specified, then tcp_wrappers checks the /etc/hosts.deny file. If tcp_wrappers finds that the specific service has been denied to that user, the connection is refused. However, if no setting in /etc/hosts.deny specifies that the service to the requested user is denied, the connection is granted.

/etc/hosts.allow

The /etc/hosts.allow file is the first file that tcp_wrappers checks for allowed connections to specific services by specific users. If a service or user is specifically granted access in /etc/hosts.allow, the /etc/hosts.deny file is ignored.

In the /etc/hosts.allow file, permission is granted to either a specific service or to all services. The service setting is then granted to individual IP blocks, IP ranges, domains, local, or to all. The entries in the /etc/hosts.allow file are set up by *service:granted_to* where *service* specifies the name of the services and *granted_to* specifies who (or what location) has permission to use the service.

Specifying Services

When specifying a service to provide access to, you can specify the particular service, such as ftpd, or specify all services. To specify a particular service, you use the syntax **in.**_service_, where _service_ is the service to be specified. To specify all services, you use the syntax **ALL**.

To grant a specific service, such as ftpd, to everyone on your local 192.168.x.x network, you would have an entry in your /etc/hosts.allow file that looked like this: **in.ftpd: 192.168.0.0/255.255.0.0**. With this entry, tcp_wrappers allows access to the ftp daemon that is connecting from any IP from 192.168.0.0 through 192.168.255.255.

To grant all services to everyone on your local 192.168.x.x network, you would have an entry in your /etc/hosts.allow file that looked like this: **ALL: 192.168.0.0/255.255.0.0**. With this entry, tcp_wrappers allows access to all services granted by inetd that are connecting from any IP from 192.168.0.0 through 192.168.255.255.

Specifying User Access

When granting a user access to a service, you can specify a specific domain, an IP, a range of IPs, or all. In addition, you can use an **EXCEPT** argument that allows you to specify specific domains and IPs to which access should not be granted.

To allow all services access to a specific domain, such as redhat.com, you would use the following entry: **ALL: .redhat.com**. With this entry, any user from redhat.com can access all available services on your machine. To specify an additional domain, such as coriolis.com, you would use the following: **ALL: .redhat.com, .coriolis.com**.

To grant a specific IP, such as 192.168.0.1, access to all services, IP, such as 192.168.0.1, you would use the following: **ALL: 192.168.0.1**. With this entry, only users from 192.168.0.1 can access all services on the machine. To specify an additional IP, such as 192.168.0.100, you would use the following: **ALL: 192.168.0.1, 192.168.0.100**.

To grant all users access to all services, you would use **ALL: ALL**. You can specify **EXCEPT** cases with any of the previously mentioned arrangements. For instance, **ALL: ALL EXCEPT LOCAL** would grant access to everyone except users on your local connection. In addition, **ALL: ALL EXCEPT .redhat.com** would grant access to everyone except users connecting from redhat.com. An additional use of **EXCEPT** is in the services specification **ALL EXCEPT in.ftpd: ALL**. Any combination of services and hosts can be used in the /etc/hosts.allow file. A sample /etc/hosts.allow file follows:

```
#
# hosts.allow   This file describes the names of the hosts which
#               are allowed to use the local INET services, as
#               decided by the '/usr/sbin/tcpd' server.
```

```
#
in.ftpd:ALL EXCEPT 10.28.2.23, 10.28.0.1
in.telnetd: .examcram.com
```

/etc/hosts.deny

If a service or user is not specified to have direct access in the /etc/hosts.allow file, tcp_wrappers checks to see if the service or user is denied in the /etc/hosts.deny file. The format for the entries in /etc/hosts.deny is identical to the entries found in /etc/hosts.allow. To refer to online syntax for /etc/hosts.deny, refer to the previous section, "/etc/hosts.allow."

Any entry in /etc/hosts.deny can be overridden in the /etc/hosts.allow file. Therefore, if access is granted to **ALL:ALL** in /etc/hosts.allow, then an entry of **in.ftpd: .redhat.com** in /etc/hosts.deny will be ignored. However, if /etc/hosts.allow contains an entry such as **in.ftpd: 192.168.0.0/255.255.0.0**, and /etc/hosts.deny contains an entry such as **ALL:ALL**, the only service that can be accessed on your system is ftpd. The service can be accessed by only those users on IPs ranging from 192.168.0.0 through 192.168.255.255. All other service requests or requests from any other IP will be rejected by the /etc/hosts.deny entry.

Linux Routing

Linux fully implements TCP/IP routing. There are several routing services available in addition to simple "router" services. With routing on Linux, you can also set up Linux firewalls and IP masquerading (discussed in the "Linux Firewalling" and "IP Masquerading" sections later in this chapter).

Routing

To set up IP routing on Linux, you must have installed the net-tools packages. The net-tools package (net-tools-1.54-4.i386.rpm) can be found on your Red Hat Linux 6.2 CD under the /RedHat/RPMS/ directory. The main tools found in the net-tools package are ifconfig, route, and netstat.

The **ifconfig** command is used to configure network interfaces. Using **ifconfig** without any options will print the status of the given interface. For example, if you want to see the current status of your first Ethernet interface, eth0, use **ifconfig eth0**. Some options available when you're using **ifconfig** are: **add** for adding an address to the interface, **del** for deleting an address from an interface, **netmask** for specifying the address netmask, and **up, down** for bringing the interface up or down.

The **route** command is used to add routes to your routing system. For example, let's say you have a system on the network with an IP address (192.168.1.1) on the Ethernet interface (eth0). The router on your network has the IP address

192.168.2.1. If you wanted to send all traffic (that wasn't destined to 192.168.1.0) to the 192.168.2.1 "gateway" host, you could issue

```
route add default gw 192.168.2.1 dev eth1
```

The **netstat** command is used to list network connections and the routing tables used on your system. By viewing the routing table, you can print all the routes that are set up on your system. To view the routing table, use the command **netstat −rn**. The Kernal IP routing table, shown in Listing 11.1, is one example.

Listing 11.1   The Kernel IP routing table.

Destination	Gateway	Genmask	Flags	Metric	Ref	Use	Iface
192.168.1.1	0.0.0.0	255.255.255.255	UH	0	0	0	eth0
192.168.1.0	0.0.0.0	255.255.255.0	U	0	0	0	eth0
192.168.2.100	0.0.0.0	255.255.255.255	UH	0	0	0	eth1
192.168.2.0	0.0.0.0	255.255.255.0	U	0	0	0	eth1
127.0.0.0	0.0.0.0	255.0.0.0	U	0	0	0	lo
0.0.0.0	192.168.2.1	0.0.0.0	UG	0	0	0	eth1

Listing 11.1 has six routing entries. The first two entries specify that traffic destined for the 192.168.1.0 network should be sent through the eth0 interface. The second two entries specify that network traffic destined for the 192.168.2.0 network should be sent through the eth1 interface. The fifth entry specifies a route to the loopback interface. The sixth entry specifies that all other traffic should be routed to 192.168.2.1, and the host on that IP will have to decide where to route the information from there.

IP Forwarding

A router uses IP forwarding to route packets originating from a separate host to another host on the network. For instance, a system (without IP forwarding set up) using the previous routing table would get a "host unreachable" error if a host on the 192.168.1.0 network sent a packet to any host other than 192.168.1.1. To enable this sample system to forward the packet as if it were originating from the system itself, you would enable network pack forwarding (IPv4). There are three methods you can use to enable packet forwarding:

➤ Edit the /etc/sysctl.conf file; change or add the line **net.ipv4.ip_forward=1**; and run **sysctl -p**.

➤ Issue a command to the ip_forward script to enable the proc file forwarding. You can do this manually by typing

```
echo 1 >/proc/sys/net/ipv4/ip_forward
```

➤ Use netcfg. Execute netcfg to bring up the network configurator window. Under the Routing option, enable the option that says Network Packet Forwarding (IPv4). This sets the option in sysctl.conf.

Routes

Two types of routes can be established with Linux TCP/IP routing—static and dynamic. Static routes are hard-coded routes that are assigned on a router. They will not change, whether there is a failure on a network or an alternate route is available. This means that a static route is the only path from one host to another. The most popular static route on a Linux network is the route to the machine's default gateway.

A dynamic route is a route that is assigned "on the fly," meaning that no definitive route is set, and a route for a packet is assigned each time a packet is sent (not predetermined). A typical type of dynamic route is the route established with standard dial-up access to an ISP. When the client makes a request for a particular Web site, for instance, the packet is sent from the client to the ISP router. The ISP router then looks for the next router that can accept the packet for the requested recipient. If that router does not respond, the ISP router then looks for an alternate router that can reach the host (or an additional router), until the host is reached. The ability to use an alternate route is the main difference between dynamic and static routes. A dynamic route can use a separate route each time a specific host is requested, whereas a static route will use the exact same route for the specified host.

Linux Firewalling

The Linux kernel can be set up to do firewalling, meaning that certain kinds of TCP/IP traffic are allowed, but other traffic is not. Firewall support is configured using ipchains. Support for ipchains is a feature of 2.2.x (and very late 2.0.x kernels). Earlier kernels used the ipfwadm utility (which is now obsolete).

In the latest kernel, 2.4.x, the kernel firewalling code has been rewritten. Firewalling in 2.4.x is controlled with a program called iptables. The 2.4.x kernel also contains compatibility modules for ipchains and ipfwadm. As of the publish date of this book, a stable version of 2.4.x has not been released, so I'll cover ipchains here. Because ipchains and iptables are similar, the same concepts will apply to both. The iptables HOWTO, available from **http://netfilter.kernelnotes.org/**, contains a section on the differences between ipchains and iptables. Consult that documentation for more information if you're trying to do firewalling with a 2.4.x kernel.

In order to perform firewalling on a Red Hat Linux system, you must have compiled the Linux kernel with firewalling support. To check whether your kernel is already compiled for firewalling, issue the following command:

```
ls -l /proc/net/ip_fwchains
```

If the file exists, then your kernel already has compiled support for firewalling. If not, then you need to compile a kernel with firewalling support. If you need (or choose) to compile a new kernel for firewalling support, enable (or modularize) at least the following support:

➤ Networking support (**CONFIG_NET**)

➤ Network firewalls (**CONFIG_FIREWALL**)

➤ TCP/IP networking (**CONFIG_INET**)

➤ IP: firewalling (**CONFIG_IP_FIREWALL**)

➤ IP: always defragment (required for masquerading) (**CONFIG_IP_ ALWAYS_DEFRAG**)

ipchains

The ipchains tool specifies firewall policies to the Linux kernel. With ipchains, you can filter depending on IP address, port, network, destination, source, subnet, connection state, domain names, sub-domain names, and so on. You can install ipchains from the **ipchains** package on the Red Hat Linux 6.2 CD-ROM. The RPM for ipchains is ipchains-1.3.9-5.i386.rpm.

There are three categories of rules in ipchains: the IP input chain, the IP output chain, and the IP forwarding chain. For each category, an individual table of rules is maintained:

➤ *IP input chain (input firewall)* —The IP input rules regulate the acceptance of incoming IP packets. All packets coming in via one of the local network interfaces are checked against the input firewall rules. A rule that matches a packet will cause the rule's packet and byte counters to be incremented appropriately.

➤ *IP output chain (output firewall)* —The IP output rules define the permissions for sending IP packets. All packets that are to be sent via one of the local network interfaces are checked against the output firewall rules. A rule that matches will cause the rule's packet and byte counters to be incremented appropriately.

➤ *IP forwarding chain (forwarding firewall)* —The IP forwarding rules define the permissions for forwarding IP packets. All packets sent by a remote host having another remote destination are checked against the forwarding firewall rules. A rule that matches will cause the rules packet and byte counters to be incremented appropriately.

Using ipchains

Multiple options and rules can be used for issuing **ipchains** commands. The standard syntax for using **ipchains** is:

```
ipchains -command chain [rule specification] [target]
```

Several commands can be issued to **ipchains**. Table 11.4 lists the six most common commands, their usage, and descriptions of what the commands do. (For a complete list, view the **ipchains(5)** man page—**man 5 ipchains**.)

Rule specifications are required when you add (-A) or delete (-D) a rule. Several parameters can be used for rule specifications (for a complete list, view **man 5 ipchains**). Three popular rule specifications are −p (protocol), −s (source), and −j (jump), described here:

➤ -p—Specifies the protocol. The protocol can be TCP, UDP, ICMP, or all. For example, a sample rule would be **ipchains −A input −p icmp −s** *source* **−j** *target*.

➤ -s—Specifies the source. The source can be the name of a host or a network, or an IP address. For example, a sample rule would be **ipchains −A input −s 192.168.100.0 −j** *target*.

Table 11.4	Commands for ipchains.	
Command	**Usage**	**Description**
-A	**ipchains −A chain rule**	Appends a rule specification to the end of the specified chain.
-D	**ipchains −D chain rule**	Deletes a rule from the specified chain.
-L	**ipchains −L chain**	Lists all rules in the selected chain. (If no chain is specified, all rules are listed.)
-F	**ipchains −F chain**	Flushes all rules from the selected chain.
-P	**ipchains −P chain target**	Sets a policy of the specified chain to the given target (see Table 11.5).
-h	**ipchains −h**	Displays Help for the command.

➤ -j—Specifies a target to a rule; that is, what to do if the packet matches the specified source. For example, a sample rule would be **ipchains –A input –s 192.168.100.0 –j DENY**.

When specifying your rule, you can specify several types of targets. The target is what happens when your rule specifications are matched. Five of the most common target values are **ACCEPT, DENY, REJECT, MASQ,** and **REDIRECT**. Table 11.5 lists and explains each of the five targets.

Sample ipchains

The following are some sample **ipchains** rules and their explanations. The sample scenario is being set up on a router (192.168.0.254) controlling a 192.168.0.x network:

➤ **ipchains –P input -j REJECT** —Rejects all incoming packets unless otherwise specified with an **ALLOW** in the input chain.

➤ **ipchains –A input –p icmp –j DENY** —Adds to the input chain a rule that drops all ICMP packets coming into the network.

➤ **ipchains –A output –p tcp –j ALLOW** —Adds to the output chain a rule that **ALLOW**s all TCP packets to go out of the network.

➤ **ipchains –A input –s 192.168.50.2 –j REJECT** —Adds to the input chain a rule that rejects all packets from 192.168.50.2 coming into the network.

Table 11.5	ipchains targets.
Target	**Description**
ACCEPT	Allows the packet through.
DENY	Drops the packet.
REJECT	Similar to **DENY**, but sends an ICMP message back to the sender, stating that the packet was dropped.
MASQ	Used only in forward chains (or user-defined chains). Requires **CONFIG_IP_MASQUERADE** to be compiled in the Linux kernel. Packets are masqueraded as if they originated from the local host. (Reverse packets are also demasqueraded automatically, bypassing the forwarding chain.) See the section titled "IP Masquerading" for more information.
REDIRECT	Used only in forward chains (or user-defined chains). Requires **CONFIG_IP_TRANSPARENT_PROXY** to be compiled in the Linux kernel. Packets are redirected to a local socket.

IP Masquerading

IP masquerading is a specialized version of NAT (Network Address Translation), in which all packets on a network are forwarded through a firewall and modified to appear as if the packet originated from the firewall itself. IP masquerading relies on the firewalling and **ipchains** packages to be installed (explained in the section titled "Sample ipchains").

Setting Up IP Masquerading

In addition to the support for firewalling and the **ipchains** package installation, you must have specific options compiled (or modularized) into the Linux kernel. The three options required are as follows:

➤ IP: transparent proxy support (**CONFIG_IP_TRANSPARENT_PROXY**)

➤ IP: masquerading (**CONFIG_IP_MASQUERADE**)

➤ IP: masquerading special modules support (**CONFIG_IP_MASQUERADE _MOD**)

Using ipchains for IP Masquerading

Setting up an ipchains rule to masquerade is simple. Let's say you have an internal network assigned with 192.168.0.x addresses. You want to give each machine in your internal network access to the Internet through a single gateway server (a Linux router dialed in via modem to the Internet). You can forward all traffic from the internal Ethernet interface (eth0) to the external network interface (ppp0), masquerading all the packets to look as if they were generated by the router with the following **ipchains** command (all on one line):

```
ipchains -A forward -p all -s 192.168.0.0/24 -d 0.0.0.0/0 -i ppp0
        -j MASQ
```

Secure Shell (SSH)

SSH is the Secure Shell utility used to securely connect and transfer data between two machines over a network. SSH provides secure replacement for utilities such as rsh, telnet, rlogin, ftp, and rcp.

SSH also runs in a server/client environment using **sshd** server and **ssh** client. The SSH client connects with the **sshd** server and authenticates the connection, allowing the connection or data transportation to occur over an encrypted tunnel. For data transactions such as rcp or ftp, the secure replacement tool with SSH is **scp**.

In addition to simple data transactions, SSH can also provide transparent X authentication and redirection. With SSH, you can start an X client on the remote machine, and the display will travel encrypted over your connection and appear on your local machine without using systems such as **xhost** or **xauth**, as I discussed in Chapter 9.

Because of export encryption technology laws, SSH is not shipped on your Red Hat 6.2 CD. You should either obtain SSH from **http://www.zedz.net/** or acquire an open-source version from **http://www.openssh.com/**.

Practice Questions

Question 1

What line in /etc/hosts.allow would specifically grant access to ftpd for users
from redhat.com?

○ a. **ALL EXCEPT in.ftpd: .redhat.com**

○ b. **in.ftpd: ALL EXCEPT .redhat.com**

○ c. **ALL: in.ftpd**

○ d. None of the above

Answer d is correct. Answer a is incorrect because it specifies permission for all
services except ftpd to redhat.com. Answer b is incorrect because it specifies access to ftpd from all except redhat.com. Answer c is incorrect because it is an
invalid format.

Question 2

What command do you use to add routes to a Linux router?

○ a. **addroute**

○ b. **route**

○ c. **netstat**

○ d. **net**

Answer b is correct. The **route** command is used for adding routes to a Linux
router. Answers a and d are incorrect because they are invalid options. Answer c
is incorrect because **netstat** is used to print network information, such as routing
tables and so forth, but does not add routes to the system.

Question 3

> In what file could you deny all INET services from all network connections?
> [Check all correct answers]
>
> ❑ a. /etc/hosts.allow
>
> ❑ b. /etc/hosts.deny
>
> ❑ c. /etc/inetd.conf
>
> ❑ d. /etc/pam.d

Answers b and c are correct. In answer b, you could deny all services to all users with an **ALL:ALL** entry. However, with answer c, you could simply disable all network services that would deny access to all INET services to all users as well. Answer a is incorrect because /etc/hosts.allow only specifies permission, not denial. Answer d is incorrect because pam.d sets up authentication for services, not permissions for them.

Question 4

> How do you disable a service in /etc/inetd.conf?

To disable a service in /etc/inetd.conf, simply insert a hash (#) mark in front of the line that specifies the service.

Question 5

> It is invalid to have duplicate services listed under /etc/inetd.conf.
>
> ○ a. True
>
> ○ b. False

Answer b is correct. A service can be listed twice under /etc/inetd.conf, once for the TCP protocol and once for the UDP protocol, if applicable.

Question 6

PAM authentication is used by:

○ a. passwd

○ b. ppp

○ c. su

○ d. All of the above

Answer d is correct. All the above answers—passwd, ppp, and su—use PAM for authentication.

Question 7

What is IP forwarding?

IP forwarding is the process of forwarding a packet from one source and redirecting it to the appropriate destination host.

Question 8

What is used to convert RPC programming numbering to TCP or UDP protocol port numbers?

○ a. /etc/inetd.conf

○ b   /etc/pam.d

○ c. /usr/sbin/proto

○ d. None of the above

Answer d is correct. The program used to convert the RPC programming numbering to TCP or UDP protocol port numbers is /usr/sbin/portmap.

Question 9

> What can be used to set up a firewall on a Linux system?
>
> ○ a. tcp_wrappers
>
> ○ b. route
>
> ○ c. ipchains
>
> ○ d. NIS

Answer c is correct. When setting up a firewall on a Red Hat Linux system with a 2.2 (or newer) kernel, you use ipchains. Answer a is incorrect because tcp_wrappers is used to allow or deny services on a single system to specific hosts, but it does not apply a firewall to traffic from (or to) a network. Answer b is incorrect because it is used to establish routes, not manage them. Answer d is incorrect because it is used in authentication, not firewalling.

Question 10

> How is a network connection request handled when you're using tcp_wrappers?

When a network connection request is made to a server, the request is accepted by inetd. If access is passed by inetd, inetd then starts tcpd with the argument for which program to start. Then tcp_wrappers checks the service and the user-access grant permissions in /etc/hosts.allow. If no specifications are made in /etc/hosts.allow, then tcp_wrappers checks for any deny entries for the service or user in /etc/hosts.deny. If no deny entry is found in /etc/hosts.deny, the connection is granted.

Task 1

Set up some basic security options on your machine. Disable any tools that you don't want anyone to use in inetd. Disable telnet in inetd, and attempt to connect via telnet from another system. What happens?

Task 2

Set up tcp_wrappers to deny connections from all except your local network. Attempt to connect to your machine from another network. What happens?

Need to Know More?

 Anonymous. *Maximum Linux Security: The Hacker's Guide to Protecting Your Linux Server and Network.* Sams, 1999. ISBN 0-67231-170-6. This book provides specifics regarding securing Internet and intranet servers.

 Stern, Hal. *Managing NFS and NIS.* O'Reilly & Associates, 1991. ISBN 0-93717-575-7. This book details how to configure and administer NIS systems for Unix system administrators.

 Ziegler, Robert. *Linux Firewalls.* New Riders, 1999. ISBN 0-73570-900-9. This book provides all the steps that a small business using Linux should take to secure its Linux machines from outside intruders.

 http://www.linuxdoc.org/ —The Linux Documentation Project. Excellent resource for finding guides, HOWTOs, and more Linux-related information.

 http://www.linuxdoc.org/HOWTO/IPCHAINS-HOWTO.html — The ipchains (firewalling) HOWTO. Excellent guide for using ipchains.

 http://netfilter.kernelnotes.org/—The Web site for the netfilter project, used for firewalling with 2.4.x kernels.

 http://www.kernel.org/pub/linux/libs/security/pam/ —The Web site for the Linux-PAM project.

The Installation and Configuration Exam

As I discussed in the first chapter, the majority of the RHCE 302 Exam is performance-based. This means that sections of the exam are hands on and are graded by how well you do (or don't) perform the tasks.

There are many things to manage when you're taking performance-based examinations such as the RHCE 302. Not only do you need to be fluent with the skills at hand, but you need to manage your time well, know where to go when the going gets tough, and know what to do when things are not going well.

One of the hands-on portions of the RHCE 302 centers on the installation and configuration of Red Hat Linux. This chapter discusses methods, planning, and skills relating to the installation and configuration of Red Hat Linux.

Installation and Configuration

The root of one of the two hands-on portions of the RHCE 302 exam is the installation and configuration of a networked Red Hat Linux system. Topics at hand will cover everything from the base Red Hat Linux installation to software configuration (covered in the next section). Until you get started, you won't be sure what is available for you to use (equipment, media, software, man pages, and so on), how you'll have to install the system, and what (if any) documentation will be available. In addition, the installation and configuration portion of the performance-based exam is time-limited. By default, you are given only two and a half hours to perform the system installation and to configure whatever hardware and software options are specified.

What You Can Expect

When you go in for the installation and configuration portion of the exam, try to feel prepared. Feel confident that you can successfully achieve all the primary goals of each section in this book. Don't walk in expecting any surprises. You shouldn't find any surprises or extenuating circumstances in this exam.

For the exam, you'll be presented with all the tools you can use (if any) for your installation. What types of tools could you be presented with? You might have scratch paper, writing utensils, floppy disks, CD-ROMs, network information, server information, and more.

You'll then be given your list of objectives. Nope, you can't start yet! When all test-takers have received their objectives, you'll be asked to turn over the objective packet to fill out the front information. On the first sheet of the packet, you'll fill out your name, other basic information, and the time you start (provided by the instructor). In addition, you'll be asked to sign a nondisclosure agreement stating that you will not share the contents of your exam.

When you're finished with the exam, you place your objectives sheet upside down on your desk and check in with your instructor before leaving the exam room. The instructor will then check whether and how you completed your objectives.

How to Handle It

Your installation and configuration exam objectives will be straightforward. Remember, don't expect anything tricky for this part of the exam. When your instructor signals for you to begin, follow these steps:

1. Read each objective.

2. Note which objectives you can perform most easily and which ones you'll find difficult.

3. Make any quick notes that you might find useful as reminders later in the exam. (Especially write notes that you might not have media, documentation, or **man** pages for.)

4. Make note of any objectives that you can meet simultaneously. Remember, this is a timed exam. If any objective requires you to wait for a result, do something else at the same time. Also, if any objectives can be related, finish both in one step (rather than returning to a subject and finishing later).

5. Don't spend more than five minutes doing this. Pick your first obvious objective and begin. With this exam, you'll have a few more minutes to plan the rest of your test during the software installation.

Software Configuration Objectives

The biggest (and most difficult) parts of this exam are the software configuration objectives. The largest percentage of your software configuration test is covered in Chapter 10 with networking services. In addition, you can expect objectives to cover subjects ranging from installation and configuration options in Chapter 6, to advanced configuration options in Chapter 8, X options in Chapter 9, and security features in Chapter 11. You should expect to see objectives (and probably more than one) from each of these chapters. Spend your time wisely.

Managing Your Time

You are given two and a half hours for the installation and configuration portion of the exam. Use the following guidelines, and budget your time so you can finish all objectives in the exam.

➤ *Plan* —While previewing your objectives, make a mental (or paper) note of how long each task should take you. Objectives that take longer, or that make you wait, can probably be done at the same time as another objective, saving overall time. Make sure to leave the last 15 minutes of the exam available to double-check your work.

➤ *Begin* —Begin your exam within five minutes of receiving your objectives. Do not preview too long, or you'll risk running out of time to complete the exam. Installation and configuration take time.

➤ *When you get stuck* —If you're stuck on an objective, or it just isn't working right, spend no longer than five minutes trying to work on it. If you're unable to solve the problem, concentrate on getting through the rest of the objectives, and then go back to the ones you had problems with.

Sample Lab Objectives

Please review and complete the following objectives. (In addition, you'll want to review the tasks from each chapter and feel comfortable completing them.) The following objectives, like the objectives of the exam, are performance-based. This means that there are no right-or-wrong, yes-or-no answers. The credit is given for making the objective work, and making it work right, not necessarily for the steps you took to get there or the tools you used. Therefore, you will not find an answer key for this section in the back of the book (as you will for the multiple-choice element of the exam in Chapter 14).

Objective 1

Install Red Hat Linux with the CD-ROM media provided. Set up the machine with separate partitions dedicated for /boot, /home, /(root), /var, and swap. Configure the Red Hat machine to support networking via DHCP, X Window System, and printing.

Objective 2

Your mom wants an account on your machine. Set her up with a nonprivileged account where she can browse the Internet and receive email. Well, Linux is catching on at your house—Dad and little sister Pam want accounts, too. Set dad up with an account. He wants his email forwarded to his dad@example.com account. Pam wants an email-only account on your machine. That way she can download her email to her computer at school.

Objective 3

Compile a custom modularized kernel. Customize options such as machine type and hardware support, and disable options, such as ISDN and Infrared, that might not be available on your machine. The main objective is to have a kernel configured specifically for your machine. Set up the machine so that you have a choice to boot from either your new kernel or your old kernel.

Objective 4

Your mom is really tired of using WindowMaker. She wants to try KDE instead. Your little sister Pam decides she wants to browse the Internet when she's at home, too, but she prefers fvwm95. Dad just doesn't like change, so he wants to keep WindowMaker. Set each of these users up to automatically start up their favorite desktop or window managers when they log in.

Objective 5

It's time to start setting up a network server. You want to set up a family Web site to help keep you, your mom and dad, and your sister in contact while Pam is off to school and you move away from home. Set up an FTP server that allows each family member to **ftp** their Web files into their own home directories. Set up Apache for the Web site **http://family.example.org/**. Set up /mom, /dad, and /pam under the domain to point to their Web entries in their own home directories that you set up for FTP. Set up your FTP server to allow anonymous connections to download photos of you and your family.

Objective 6

Guess what? Your boss saw what you set up for home, and he wants you to set it up for him, too. Set up another domain, **http://boss.example.org/**, to access Web files that your boss can upload to his own Web directory. Don't forget to set up your DNS.

Objective 7

Your boss decides he wants you to share your Linux box as a file server with the Windows clients on the network. Set up Samba on your system to share your /home directory with all Windows clients on your network.

Objective 8

Your sister has been using your server to connect to chat rooms. Some kids in the chat rooms saw her connection information and decided to start trying to access your Linux server. The kids are trying to connect from **cracker.example.com** as well as from an unknown network IP of 192.168.250.250. On your system, set up some low-level security that denies all access from people on either **cracker.example.com** or 192.168.250.250. Take that a step further and deny access to everyone except your boss (from **boss.example.org**) and family (from **family.example.org**). Also allow your sister to connect from school from her static IP address of 192.168.2.23. Allow only your family to have FTP access.

The Debugging Exam

As I discussed in Chapter 12, the majority of the RHCE 302 exam is performance-based. Whereas the installation and configuration exam is graded by your completion of objectives and goals as specified in your objectives sheet, the debugging exam is different. You're not presented with a list of specific tasks to accomplish. Instead, you're presented with an end goal (what needs to work), and you have to work your way through a number of (unspecified) problems to get to your end goal.

There are many things to manage when you're taking a performance-based examination such as the debugging element. Not only do you need to be fluent with the skills at hand, but you also need to manage your time well, know where to go when the going gets tough, and know what to do when things are not going well.

This hands-on portion of the RHCE 302 focuses on the troubleshooting of Red Hat Linux. This chapter discusses methods, planning, and skills relating to the debugging of Red Hat Linux.

Preparing for this section of the exam is difficult because you cannot be sure which element of Red Hat Linux will be broken, you won't be sure exactly which tools you'll have to fix the problems, and under no circumstances can you simply reinstall the broken component (or system). The debugging portion of the RHCE 302 exam allows you two and a half hours (total) to fix two separate debugging issues.

What to Expect

When you go to take the debugging element of the exam, remain calm. Your debugging skills work best when you have a clear mind. The biggest mistake people make during the debugging element is to worry about what will be broken on the system and to be stressed about the exam before taking it. Don't make any assumptions about what you can or cannot do for the exam.

When you enter the examination room, you'll be seated at your machine and asked to stow away any tools, books, or other materials you brought with you. You'll then be presented with any tools you're allowed to use during the exam. As with the installation and configuration exam, you'll be issued an objectives sheet, and when instructed to do so, you'll turn it over and sign the nondisclosure agreement on the front page. When permitted, you can open the objectives handout and start the exam.

When you're finished with the first objective, you'll document what the problem was and how you fixed it. The instructor will then come to your machine, sign off on your objectives sheet, verify that you did or did not fix the problem, and send you off for a quick break while he or she prepares your system for the next debugging objective.

How to Handle It

After opening your objectives sheet, you'll be given a result to work toward. A sample result could be something similar to "establish a networking connection from the workstation to the server by using DHCP." This might sound simple, but the machine has been "sabotaged" to make the task more difficult. First, the machine might not boot properly, and second, it might have something configured improperly in networking that doesn't allow a simple configuration for DHCP (or it might not).

Regardless of what your objectives will be or what part of your system will be broken, there are several steps you can follow to help you determine the problem and recover your system. Not all of the following steps will be required each time you troubleshoot a machine (in real life or on the exam):

1. Boot your machine. See what happens, what errors you get, and where the system seems broken. Do you know where the error is? Can you fix the machine as is? If not, perhaps you need to boot the system into single-user mode and fix the problem. You might need to use system rescue disks.

2. Obtain boot disks.

This set is created from your system and a boot image from the Red Hat 6.2 CD-ROM. (You'll either create these disks from your installation and configuration exam or have them supplied by the instructor.)

Use **mkbootdisk** for the first disk. This creates a boot disk for your system (used for emergencies, to boot without LILO, and such). To create your boot disk, type **mkbootdisk** *image* where *image* is the image of your bootable kernel located in /boot.

Use the boot.img or bootnet.img image from the Red Hat 6.2 CD-ROM for the second rescue disk. Type:

```
dd if=/mnt/cdrom/images/boot.img of=/dev/fd0
```

3. Boot your machine. If you can fix your problem by booting from single-user mode, type **linux single** at the LILO prompt, and proceed to the next step. Otherwise, check the system BIOS to see that it's set to boot from floppy disk as its first option. Then boot with either your boot disk or your bootable CD-ROM.

4. Do you need to check your filesystem? First, use **fdisk –l** to print your partition table. Verify what you believe to be the filesystem partitions. After you've decided which is your root filesystem (it will most likely be the largest one), you can use **fsck** to check the filesystem. If /(**root**) is /dev/hda4, then use **fsck /dev/hda4**.

5. Do you need to mount your filesystems? (If you booted via the rescue disks, then yes, you do.) You can mount your filesystems by using **mount**. Be sure to verify your partition table by using **fdisk –l**. You must mount your devices in a specific order.

First, create a mount directory to mount your file systems. For instance, if you want to mount root (/) and /boot, then create directories called /mnt/harddrive (for root) and /mnt/harddrive/boot (for /boot). Next, mount your file systems. You must always mount your root (/) file system first, and the remaining file systems beneath the root file system mountpoint. If /dev/hda4 is your root (/) file system and /dev/hda2 is your /boot file system, mount root (**mount /dev/hda4 /mnt/harddrive**) and then /boot (**mount /dev/hda2 /mnt/harddrive/boot**).

6. Regardless of boot method (single-user mode or with rescue disks), you'll need to make any appropriate changes to your system to fix the problem (if the problem was something other than a corrupt filesystem, which is most likely the case for the RHCE 302 exam).

7. Did you have to change LILO? If you did, you have to rerun **lilo** to save the changes to the system. Run **/sbin/lilo** if you are in single-user mode. If you are in rescue boot mode, you will have to use **lilo –r** to specify where the root filesystem is (because you mounted it to /mnt/harddrive). To use **lilo** on the separate mounted filesystem, use **/mnt/harddrive/sbin/lilo –r /mnt/harddrive**.

8. Have you changed the disk? If so, then you need to synchronize your disk to ensure that the system buffers (changes you made) are written to the hard disk. To do this, use **sync**. From the prompt, run **sync**. You might want to run this another time or two to be absolutely positive that all of your system buffers were flushed and written to the disk.

9. Are you ready to reboot? Well, if you're in single-user mode, go for it. If you're in rescue mode, you have to unmount your mounted filesystem. You have to do this in a specific order as well. Whereas when you mounted them, you mounted root (/) first, when you unmount them, you have to unmount root (/) last. To unmount the /boot partition (from these examples), use **umount /mnt/harddrive/boot**. Next, unmount the root (/) partition by using **umount /mnt/harddrive**.

10. Now remove all disks (if necessary), and exit from the system. Power the system off, and try out the repaired system.

Does your system boot properly now? Good. You might not be through, however. Your objective sheet might list something in particular (such as networking, video, or sound) that isn't working right on the system. Because your system is now booting properly, you can fix whatever is specified, using your knowledge of setting up and configuring the item (covered in previous chapters, such as items discussed in Chapters 6, 8, 9, and 10).

Managing Your Time

You're given two and a half hours to complete two separate sets of objectives in the debugging portion of the exam. Try to use the following guidelines, and budget your time so that you can finish all objectives in the exam.

➤ *Plan* —While previewing your objectives, make a mental (or paper) note of how long each task should take you. Try to budget only 1.25 hours (half the exam time) for each objective sheet. (Remember, you won't know what the second set of objectives is until you have completed the first.)

➤ *Begin* —Begin your exam within five minutes of receiving your objectives. Do not preview too long, or you'll risk running out of time to complete the exam. Installation, configuration, and debugging all take time.

➤ *When you get stuck* —Each set of objectives will have two types of debugging elements involved. With this in mind, try to budget 25 percent of your time for each mini-objective. If you've spent more than half of your total time (50 percent of two and a half hours) on the first mini-objective, then you might want to consult the instructor for help. Consulting for help on a mini-objective, however, means that you don't get credit for that mini-objective. (If there are two mini-objectives in an objective, and you get help on one of them, you lose 50 percent for the single objective.) Although completing each mini-objective is critical to your score, running out of time and not completing the remaining objectives is detrimental.

Sample Written Test

This chapter provides pointers to help you develop a successful test-taking strategy. I'll discuss how to choose proper answers, how to decode ambiguity, how to work within the Red Hat testing framework, how to decide what you need to memorize, and how to prepare for the test. At the end of the chapter are 50 questions on subject matter pertinent to the RHCE 302 exam. Good luck!

Questions, Questions, Questions

There should be no doubt in your mind that you are facing a test full of specific and pointed questions. The written element of the RHCE 302 exam will consist of 50 questions and take somewhere between 30 and 60 minutes.

When taking the exam, you might be presented with various types of questions, such as:

➤ Multiple-choice with a single answer

➤ Multiple-choice with multiple answers

➤ Statement with a choice of "true" or "false"

Always take the time to read a question at least twice before selecting an answer. Remember, not every question has only one answer; many questions require "the best" answer. Therefore, you should read each question carefully, determine how many answers are valid, and look for hints in the question when selecting answers.

Choosing Proper Answers

The only way to pass any exam is to select enough of the right answers to obtain a passing score. However, Red Hat's exams are not standardized like the SAT and GRE exams; they are far more diabolical and convoluted. In some cases, questions are strangely worded, and deciphering them can be a real challenge. In those cases, you might need to rely on answer-elimination skills. Almost always, at least one answer out of the possible choices for a question can be eliminated immediately because it matches one of these conditions:

➤ The answer does not apply to the situation.

➤ The answer describes a nonexistent issue, an invalid option, or an imaginary state.

➤ The answer can be eliminated because of information in the question itself.

After you eliminate all answers that are obviously wrong, you can apply your retained knowledge to eliminate further answers. Look for items that sound correct but refer to actions, commands, or features that are not present or not available in the situation that the question describes.

If you're still faced with a blind guess among two or more potentially correct answers, reread the question. Try to picture how each of the remaining answers would alter the situation. Be especially sensitive to terminology; sometimes the choice of words, such as "remove" instead of "disable," can make the difference between a right answer and a wrong one.

Only when you've exhausted your ability to eliminate answers but remain unclear about which of the remaining possibilities is correct should you guess at an answer. An unanswered question offers you no points, but guessing gives you at least some chance of getting a question right. Just don't be too hasty when making a blind guess.

 If you're taking a multiple-choice test, you can wait until the last round of reviewing questions (just as you're about to run out of time or out of unanswered questions) before you start making guesses. Guessing should be a last resort.

Working within the Framework

The test questions appear in random order, and many elements or issues that receive mention in one question might also crop up in other questions. It's not uncommon to find that an incorrect answer to one question is the correct answer to another question, or vice versa. Take the time to read every answer to each question, even if you recognize the correct answer to a question immediately. That extra reading might spark a memory or remind you about a Linux feature or function that will help you on another question in the exam.

For the multiple-choice exam, you can revisit any question as many times as you like. If you're uncertain of the answer to a question, circle it and come back to it later.

 For written tests, we strongly recommend that you first read the entire test quickly, before getting caught up in answering individual questions. This will help to jog your memory as you review the potential answers, and it can help identify questions that you want to mark for easy access to their contents. It will also let you identify and mark the tricky questions for easy return. The key is to make a quick pass over the territory to begin with—so that you know what you're up against—and then to survey that territory more thoroughly on a second pass, when you can begin to answer all questions systematically and consistently.

Preparing for the Test

The best way to prepare for the test—after you've studied—is to take at least one practice exam. We've included one in this chapter for that reason. The test questions are located in the pages that follow. (Unlike the preceding chapters in this book, the answers don't follow the questions immediately; you'll have to flip to Chapter 15 to separately review the answers).

Give yourself an hour to take the exam, and keep yourself on the honor system—don't look at earlier chapters in the book or jump ahead to the answer key. When your time is up or you've finished all the questions, you can check your work in Chapter 15. Pay special attention to the explanations for the incorrect answers; these can also help to reinforce your knowledge of the material. Knowing how to recognize correct answers is good, but understanding why incorrect answers are wrong can be equally valuable.

Taking the Test

Relax. Once you're sitting in front of the test, there's nothing more you can do to increase your knowledge or preparation. Take a deep breath, stretch, and start reading that first question.

You don't need to rush, either. You have plenty of time to complete each question and to return to those questions that you skip or mark for return. If you read a question twice and remain clueless, you can circle it and come back to it later. Both easy and difficult questions are intermixed in random order throughout the test. When taking a multiple-choice test, don't cheat yourself by spending too much time on a hard question early in the test, thereby depriving yourself of the time you need to answer the questions at the end of the test.

On the multiple-choice test, you can read the entire test, and, before returning to circled questions for a second visit, you can figure out how much time you've got per question. As you answer each question, move on to the next. Continue to review the remaining marked questions until you run out of time or complete the test.

That's it for pointers. Here are some questions for you to practice on.

Sample Written Test

Question 1

In order to increase the amount of memory available for a system, what is the maximum size of a swap partition (with kernel version 2.2.x)?

○ a. 32MB

○ b. 64MB

○ c. 128MB

○ d. 512MB

○ e. 2GB

Question 2

For you to create a swap partition by using fdisk, what must the partition's system ID type be?

○ a. 4

○ b. 5

○ c. 82

○ d. 83

○ e. c

Question 3

How many primary partitions can exist on one drive?

○ a. 1

○ b. 2

○ c. 4

○ d. 16

○ e. None of the above

Question 4

How many extended partitions can exist on one drive?

○ a. 1

○ b. 2

○ c. 4

○ d. 16

○ e. None of the above

Question 5

How many logical partitions can exist on one drive?

○ a. 1

○ b. 12

○ c. 4

○ d. 16

○ e. None of the above

Question 6

In Linux, hard drives and their partitions have a specific naming convention. What would the device name be for the first IDE hard drive's first primary partition?

○ a. hda

○ b. hda1

○ c. sda

○ d. sda1

○ e. hda5

Question 7

What is the device name for the first logical partition on the first IDE hard drive?

○ a. hda1

○ b. hda2

○ c. sda

○ d. sda1

○ e. hda5

Question 8

To create a boot disk for Linux by using DOS or Windows, what command could you use?

○ a. **transdisk**

○ b. **fdisk**

○ c. **copy**

○ d. **diskcopy**

○ e. **rawrite**

Question 9

To create an installation boot floppy disk from Linux (or another Unix) machine, what command could you use?

○ a. **rawrite**

○ b. **dd**

○ c. **fsck**

○ d. **fdisk**

○ e. **copy**

Question 10

Which of these types of installations requires a special installation boot image other than boot.img?

○ a. NFS

○ b. FTP

○ c. Hard disk

○ d. Both answers a and b

○ e. All of the above

Question 11

You install the Linux bootloader to the first sector of the boot partition when:

○ a. Multiple operating systems are on the system.

○ b. This is a trial run for installing Linux.

○ c. There is a fear of losing data or the superblock.

○ d. Another boot loader is already on the system.

○ e. Booting by floppy is used.

Question 12

To build a modularized kernel, the kernel-headers and kernel-source packages must first be installed. Where will you find the kernel-headers and kernel-source?

○ a. /usr/bin

○ b. /usr/src/redhat

○ c. /usr/src/linux

○ d. /usr/local

○ e. /usr/local/src

Question 13

What command do you use to build a kernel configuration file? [Choose the best answer]

○ a. **make config**

○ b. **make menuconfig**

○ c. **make xconfig**

○ d. Both answers a and c

○ e. All of the above

Question 14

After you have compiled your kernel, what do you have to edit to boot your new kernel image?

○ a. /etc/lilo.conf

○ b. /etc/named.boot

○ c. /etc/conf.modules

○ d. /boot/lilo.conf

○ e. /boot/conf.modules

Question 15

What file specifies the order in which to use specified name services?

○ a. /etc/hosts

○ b. /etc/nsswitch.conf

○ c. /etc/nsorder

○ d. /etc/services

○ e. /etc/inetd.conf

Question 16

What file contains the list of port numbers (and associated names) monitored by **inetd**?

- ○ a. /etc/hosts
- ○ b. /etc/nsswitch.conf/
- ○ c. /etc/nsorder
- ○ d. /etc/services
- ○ e. /etc/inetd.conf

Question 17

What service is not monitored by **inetd**?

- ○ a. finger
- ○ b. ntalk
- ○ c. time
- ○ d. SSH
- ○ e. Telnet

Question 18

In which tcp_wrappers file can you specify to allow all connections from all hosts?

- ○ a. /etc/tcp.conf
- ○ b. /etc/hosts
- ○ c. /etc/hosts.deny
- ○ d. /etc/hosts.allow
- ○ e. None of the above

Question 19

What are the three types of chain rulesets defined by default in ipchains?

- ○ a. **accept, deny, reject**
- ○ b. **accept, deny, forward**
- ○ c. **deny, forward, masq**
- ○ d. **input, output, forward**
- ○ e. None of the above

Question 20

Which command allows you to print your routing table?

- ○ a. **route-add**
- ○ b. **netstat-rn**
- ○ c. **print route**
- ○ d. Both answers a and b
- ○ e. None of the above

Question 21

You just added a new user, kara, to the system. What group is kara added to by default?

- ○ a. user
- ○ b. group
- ○ c. kara
- ○ d. root
- ○ e. None of the above

Question 22

How do you change the group setbit on a directory?

○ a. **chmod +x**

○ b. **chmod +s**

○ c. **chmod +b**

○ d. **setbit +1**

○ e. None of the above

Question 23

Which command can you use to view a system log continuously (in real time)?

○ a. **cat**

○ b. **head**

○ c. **view**

○ d. **tail**

○ e. **tail –f**

Question 24

How would you create a boot disk for a specific kernel image on your system?

○ a. **dd**

○ b. **mkbootdisk**

○ c. **mkkickstart**

○ d. **cp**

○ e. **cat**

Question 25

Which command can you use to view your system's partition table?

○ a. **fdisk**

○ b. **df**

○ c. **du**

○ d. **dd**

○ e. **fdisk −l**

Question 26

Which command can force all buffers to disk?

○ a. **flush**

○ b. **edbuff**

○ c. **sync**

○ d. **save**

○ e. None of the above

Question 27

Which methods can you use to install Red Hat Linux?

○ a. CD-ROM

○ b. FTP

○ c. Samba

○ d. Both answers a and b

○ e. All of the above

Question 28

Which boot image is required for a network installation?

○ a. boot.img

○ b. netboot.img

○ c. bootnet.img

○ d. network.img

○ e. None of the above

Question 29

Which file is used to configure which filesystems are mounted?

○ a. /etc/fstab

○ b. /etc/sysconfig

○ c. /etc/filesys

○ d. /etc/mount.sys

○ e. None of the above

Question 30

With which file can you edit your systems' virtual console specifications?

○ a. /etc/consoles

○ b. /etc/inittab

○ c. /etc/inetd.conf

○ d. Both answers a and b

○ e. None of the above

Question 31

Which tool can be used to add a user to the system?

- ○ a. adduser
- ○ b. linuxconf
- ○ c. useradd
- ○ d. Both answers b and c
- ○ e. All of the above

Question 32

In which directory can you store system user default files used for creating user directories?

- ○ a. /etc/users
- ○ b. /etc/skel
- ○ c. /etc/default
- ○ d. /usr/tmp
- ○ e. None of the above

Question 33

How could you install the file ipchains-1.3.9-5.i386.rpm?

- ○ a. **rpm –e ipchains-1.3.9-5.i386.rpm**
- ○ b. **rpm –i ipchains*.i386.rpm**
- ○ c. **rpm –Uvh ipchains**
- ○ d. **rpm –qip ipchains**
- ○ e. None of the above

Question 34

What could you use to list all the files in an RPM package?

○ a. **rpm –qa**

○ b. **rpm –qi**

○ c. **rpm –ql**

○ d. **rpm –L**

○ e. None of the above

Question 35

Which boot image would you need to use a PCMCIA network card during installation?

○ a. bootnet.img

○ b. pcmcia.img

○ c. boot.img

○ d. Both answers a and b

○ e. None of the above

Question 36

Which runlevel reboots the system?

○ a. 1

○ b. 2

○ c. 3

○ d. 4

○ e. None of the above

Question 37

Which option can you pass at the "LILO:" prompt to boot into single-user mode?

- a. **linux 1**
- b. **init 1**
- c. **linux single**
- d. Both answers a and c
- e. All of the above

Question 38

Which is the system initialization script that is run at boot time?

- a. /etc/rc.d/rc0.d
- b. /etc/rc.d/init.d
- c. /etc/rc.d/start
- d. /etc/rc.d/rc.sysinit
- e. None of the above

Question 39

Which type of kernel has all support compiled into the kernel image?

- a. Monolithic
- b. Modular
- c. bzImage
- d. zImage
- e. Boot

Question 40

Which program is used to automatically install Red Hat Linux on identical hardware?

- ○ a. mkkickstart
- ○ b. ghost
- ○ c. tar
- ○ d. bzImage.img
- ○ e. None of the above

Question 41

Which program is used to schedule particular jobs or programs at particular times on the system?

- ○ a. cron
- ○ b. Scheduler
- ○ c. Outlook
- ○ d. vi
- ○ e. None of the above

Question 42

Which is the main sendmail configuration file?

- ○ a. /etc/pine.conf
- ○ b. ~/.sendmail.rc
- ○ c. /etc/sendmail.cf
- ○ d. Both answers a and c
- ○ e. None of the above

Question 43

In what file can you specify which users are not allowed to access a system via FTP?

○ a. /etc/ftpaccess

○ b. /etc/hosts.deny

○ c. /etc/ftpusers

○ d. All of the above

○ e. None of the above

Question 44

Which command is used to see which services an NFS server is running?

○ a. **nfserv**

○ b. **getnfs**

○ c. **rpcinfo**

○ d. **nfsmount**

○ e. None of the above

Question 45

Which command is used to mount NFS filesystems?

○ a. **nfsmount**

○ b. **knfsd**

○ c. **mount**

○ d. Both answers a and b

○ e. None of the above

Question 46

Which is used to access an SMB share on a Linux system?

- a. NFS
- b. SMBD
- c. smbclient
- d. smbserver
- e. None of the above

Question 47

Which cannot be assigned by a DHCP server?

- a. IP address
- b. Gateway
- c. Netmask
- d. DNS
- e. None of the above

Question 48

Which command lists your configured network interfaces and information such as IP address, broadcast address, and netmask?

- a. **netstat –rn**
- b. **route**
- c. **ichains**
- d. **ifconfig**
- e. None of the above

Question 49

What symbolic link points to the pathed filename of the system-preferred display manager?

○ a. Xdefaults

○ b. /etc/X11/prefdm

○ c. Xclients

○ d. Xdisplay

○ e. None of the above

Question 50

What is the main Apache configuration file?

○ a. /etc/srm.conf

○ b. /etc/httpd/conf/httpd.conf

○ c. /etc/httpd/conf/apache.conf

○ d. Both answers a and b

○ e. None of the above

Answer Key
to Written Test

This chapter is an answer key to Chapter 14's multiple-choice exam. Please note that no answer keys are available for exam situations in Chapters 12 and 13. The performance-based exams do not have answer keys because they are graded by the outcome result of the required objective (as specified in the exam) and not by a specific answer or method.

1. e	14. a	27. d	40. a
2. c	15. b	28. c	41. a
3. c	16. d	29. a	42. c
4. a	17. d	30. b	43. c
5. b	18. d	31. e	44. c
6. b	19. d	32. b	45. c
7. e	20. b	33. b	46. c
8. e	21. c	34. c	47. e
9. b	22. b	35. b	48. d
10. d	23. e	36. e	49. b
11. d	24. b	37. d	50. b
12. c	25. e	38. d	
13. e	26. c	39. a	

Question 1

Answer e is correct. Kernel versions 2.2 and higher can support up to 2GB on Intel machines; therefore, answers a, b, c, and d are incorrect.

Question 2

Answer c is correct. ID type 82 is Linux swap. Partition ID type 4 is FAT16; therefore, answer a is incorrect. ID type 5 is Extended; therefore, answer b is incorrect. ID type 83 is Linux native; therefore, answer d is incorrect. ID type c is Win95 FAT32; therefore, answer e is incorrect.

Question 3

Answer c is correct. A Linux system uses the DOS-style partition table, which limits the system to a maximum of four primary partitions; therefore, answers a and b are incorrect. The total number of partitions that can be used (including extended and logical) is 16, so answer d is incorrect.

Question 4

Answer a is correct. A Linux partition table can support up to four primary partitions, one of which can be extended.

Question 5

Answer b is correct. A Linux partition table can support a total of 16 partitions. This includes 3 primary, 1 extended (which counts as the fourth supported primary partition), and 12 logical partitions.

Question 6

Answer b is correct. The first primary partition on the first IDE hard drive would be hda1. Answer a, hda, refers to the first hard drive, but not to the first primary partition on the first IDE hard drive; therefore, a is incorrect. Answers c and d are sda and sda1, which refer to the first SCSI hard drive and the first SCSI hard-drive partition; therefore, both c and d are incorrect. Answer e, hda5, refers to the first logical partition and therefore is incorrect.

Question 7

Answer e is correct. The device name for the first logical partition on the first IDE hard drive is hda5. The answers hda1 and hda2 refer to the first and second (primary or extended) partitions; therefore, answers a and b are incorrect. The answers sda and sda1 refer to the first and second (primary or extended) partitions, making answers c and d incorrect.

Question 8

Answer e is correct. To create a boot disk for Linux by using DOS or Windows, you use **rawrite**. The command **transdisk** is not valid; therefore, answer a is incorrect. The **fdisk** command is used for disk partitioning; therefore, answer b is incorrect. Answer c, **copy**, is used for copying files, not creating images, and therefore is incorrect. The option **diskcopy** is not a valid command; therefore, answer d is incorrect.

Question 9

Answer b is correct. To create a boot disk from Unix, you would use **dd**. The **rawrite** command is used to write images on a DOS or Windows machine; therefore, answer a is incorrect. Answer c, **fsck,** is used to check Unix filesystems and therefore is incorrect. Answer d, **fdisk,** is used for manipulating partitions and therefore is also incorrect. The **copy** command is used for copying files; therefore, answer e is incorrect.

Question 10

Answer d is correct. Special installation diskettes are required when an installation is to be performed either over the network or via a PCMCIA device (such as CD-ROM or NIC). NFS is a network service. FTP is also a network service; therefore, answer b is also correct. Answer c does not require a boot disk other than boot.img; therefore, answer c is incorrect. Answer d selects both answers a and b; therefore, answer d is correct. Answer e selects all of the above and (because c is incorrect) is incorrect.

Question 11

Answer d is correct. You should install the Linux bootloader within the first sector of the boot partition only when you're planning to use an alternative bootloader (such as NT) to manage the multiboot system. The Linux bootloader is capable of booting multiple operating systems; therefore, answer a is incorrect. The bootloader has nothing to do with the trial run of Linux; therefore, answer b is incorrect. Installing the Linux bootloader to the superblock (MBR) does not lose data; therefore, answer c is incorrect. If you're using another bootloader instead of Linux, you install Linux to the boot partition; therefore, answer d is correct. Using a boot floppy bypasses the installed Linux bootloader, so installing in the MBR or the boot partition is irrelevant; therefore, answer e incorrect.

Question 12

Answer c is correct. To build a modularized kernel, you'll find the installed kernel-headers and kernel-source packages in /usr/src/linux. Answer a, /usr/bin, contains system binaries; therefore, it is incorrect. Answer b, /usr/src/redhat, stores information for source RPMs and therefore is incorrect. Answer d, /usr/local/, contains various user tools and information and therefore is incorrect. Answer e, /usr/local/src/, does not contain data, by default, and is incorrect.

Question 13

Answer e is correct. To build a kernel configuration command, you use **make** and the configuration option. Answer a, **make config**, presents you with a text-based configuration and therefore is correct. Answer b, **make menuconfig**, presents you with a menu-based configuration and therefore is correct. Answer c, **make xconfig**, presents you with an X-based configuration tool and is also correct. Answer d leaves out one correct answer and is therefore incorrect. Answer e, all of the above, encompasses all the answers and therefore is the best answer.

Question 14

Answer a is correct. To boot your new kernel image, you must edit /etc/lilo.conf. Answer b, /etc/named.boot, is the BIND 4 configuration file and is therefore incorrect. Answer c, /etc/conf.modules, lists kernel modules and is incorrect. Answers d and e are invalid options and are incorrect.

Question 15

Answer b is correct. To specify the order in which to use specified name servers, you must add them appropriately to /etc/nsswitch.conf; therefore, answer a is incorrect. Answer b, /etc/nsswitch.conf, is therefore correct. Answer c is invalid and therefore is incorrect. Answer d, /etc/services, configures network services and therefore is incorrect. Answer e, /etc/inetd.conf, manages network services and therefore is incorrect.

Question 16

Answer d is correct. The file /etc/inetd.conf contains the list of port numbers monitored by **inetd**. The /etc/hosts file specifies hosts used by the system and is therefore incorrect. The /etc/nsorder option is invalid; therefore, answer c is incorrect. Answer e, /etc/inetd.conf, specifies which services are enabled, but not their port numbers, and therefore is incorrect.

Question 17

Answer d is correct. **inetd** monitors a great number of services. The programs finger, ntalk, time, and Telnet (answers a, b, c, and e, respectively) are incorrect. SSH is not monitored via **inetd**; therefore, answer d is correct.

Question 18

Answer d is correct. The file /etc/hosts.allow is where you can specifically allow all connections from all hosts using tcp_wrappers. Answer a, /etc/tcp.conf, is an invalid option and is therefore incorrect. Answer b, /etc/hosts, specifies system hosts and therefore is incorrect. Answer c, /etc/hosts.deny, specifies whom to deny and therefore is incorrect.

Question 19

Answer d is correct. The three main chains defined by default in ipchains are **input, output,** and **forward.** The options **accept, deny,** and **masq** are invalid because they are used as targets, not chains. This makes answers a, b, c, and e incorrect.

Question 20

Answer b is correct. To print your routing table, use **netstat -rn**. Answer a, **route -add**, is used to add a route to the routing table and therefore is incorrect. Answer c, **print route**, is invalid. Answer d includes answer a and therefore is incorrect.

Question 21

Answer c is correct. When you create a user, the user is automatically added to a group by the same name. Therefore, new user "kara" will be added to group "kara" by default. Unless otherwise specified, "kara" will not be added to groups named "user," "group," or "root"; therefore, answers a, b, and d are incorrect.

Question 22

Answer b is correct. To change the group setbit on a directory, use the **+s** option with **chmod**. Answer a, **chmod +x**, makes the file (directory) executable; therefore, answer a is incorrect. Answer c, **chmod +b**, is invalid and is therefore incorrect. Answer d, **setbit +1**, is invalid and is therefore incorrect.

Question 23

Answer e is correct. To view a system log continuously (in real time), use the **–f** command option with tail. Answer a, **cat**, is used to concatenate a file and therefore is incorrect. Answer b, **head**, prints the first 10 lines of a file and therefore is incorrect. Answer c, **view**, is invalid. Answer d, **tail**, is incorrect because it prints only the last 10 lines of a file, but with the **–f** option (answer e), continuously prints the file (in real time) and therefore is correct.

Question 24

Answer b is correct. To create a boot disk for your running system, use **mkbootdisk**. While **dd** is used to create boot disks for installation, you cannot create a system disk with it, and therefore answer a is incorrect. Answer c, **mkkickstart**, creates kickstart installation disks and therefore is incorrect. Answer d, **cp**, is used to copy files and is incorrect. Answer e, **cat**, is used to concatenate files and is incorrect.

Question 25

Answer e is correct. To view your system's partition table, use the command **fdisk** –l, making answer e the best answer. Answer a, **fdisk**, by itself, only opens fdisk, where you have the option to view your partition table but must enter the command to do so; therefore, answer a is incorrect. Answer b, **df**, is used to print the disk space available on the machine and therefore is incorrect. Answer c, **du**, is used to print disk space used on the system and is incorrect. Answer d, **dd**, is used for converting and copying a file and is incorrect.

Question 26

Answer c is correct. When you need to flush the system buffers to disk, use the **sync** command, making answer c incorrect. Answer a, **flush**, is a Tcl command and therefore incorrect. Answer b, **edbuff**, is invalid and therefore incorrect. Answer d, **save**, is invalid and incorrect.

Question 27

Answer d is correct. There are various ways you can install Red Hat Linux. You can install via CD-ROM; therefore, answer a is correct. You can also install via FTP; therefore, answer b is also correct. Answer c, Samba, is not supported and therefore is incorrect. Answer d selects both answers a and b and therefore is the best answer.

Question 28

Answer c is correct. When you're performing a network-based installation, a boot disk using the bootnet.img image is required. Answer a, boot.img, is used for a standard installation disk. Answer b is invalid. Answer d is invalid.

Question 29

Answer a is correct. To configure mounted filesystems, edit the /etc/fstab file. Answer b, /etc/sysconfig/, is a directory and incorrect. Answers c and d are invalid.

Question 30

Answer b is correct. To edit your virtual console setting, edit the /etc/inittab file. Answer a is invalid. Answer c, /etc/inetd.conf, configures **inetd** settings and is incorrect.

Question 31

Answer e is correct. When adding a user, you can use adduser, linuxconf, and useradd (equivalent to adduser), which makes answers a, b, and c correct. Answer e includes all the answers and is the single best answer.

Question 32

Answer b is correct. Default user files (used when creating user directories) are kept in /etc/skel, making answer b correct. Answer a is invalid. Answer c, /etc/default, contains only the command **useradd** (by default), and answer d, /usr/tmp, is used for temporary user files; therefore, both are incorrect.

Question 33

Answer b is correct. To install an RPM, use **rpm –i** or **rpm –U**. Answer a, **rpm -e ipchains-1.3.9-5.i386.rpm**, deletes the file and therefore is incorrect. Answer b, **rpm –i ipchains*.i386.rpm**, installs the package (which fits the * wildcard) and is correct. Answer c, **rpm –Uvh ipchains**, doesn't specify a valid package and is incorrect. Answer d, **rpm –qip ipchains**, queries a package for information and is incorrect.

Question 34

Answer c is correct. To list all files in an RPM package, use **rpm –ql**; therefore, answer c is correct. Answer a, **rpm –qa**, lists all files installed on a system and is incorrect. Answer b, **rpm –qi**, queries for information and is incorrect. Answer d, **rpm –L**, is invalid.

Question 35

Answer b is correct. To use a PCMCIA device during installation, you must use a pcmcia.img boot image. Answer a, bootnet.img, is used for network installations and is incorrect. Answer c, boot.img, is used for regular installation and is incorrect.

Question 36

Answer e is correct. The runlevel to reboot the system is runlevel 6, and therefore answer e, none of the above, is correct. Runlevel 1 boots the system in single-user mode, 2 into multi-user mode (no networking), and 3 into multi-user full networking mode (4 is invalid); therefore, answers a, b, c, and d are incorrect.

Question 37

Answer d is correct. To boot into single-user mode from the "LILO:" prompt, use either answer a, **linux 1**, or answer c, **linux single**. This makes answer d the best answer. Answer b, **init 1**, is used to boot the system into single-user mode from runlevels 2 through 5, but it is invalid for the "LILO:" prompt.

Question 38

Answer d is correct. The rc.sysinit script is the system initialization script run during boot-time. Answer a, /etc/rc.d/rc0.d/, is a runlevel directory and incorrect. Answer b, /etc/rc.d/init.d/, is a daemon directory and incorrect. Answer c is invalid.

Question 39

Answer a is correct. A monolithic kernel has all support compiled into the kernel image. Answer b, modular, is a kernel that makes use of modules for support. Answers c and d are types of kernel images, but not types of kernels, and are therefore incorrect. Answer e is invalid.

Question 40

Answer a is correct. When installing Red Hat Linux on multiple (identical) machines, you can use kickstart to automate the installation. Answer a, mkkickstart, is used to create the boot floppy for kickstart, but isn't the program that runs, and therefore is invalid. Answer b, ghost, is a commercial software package not used by Linux to create hard-drive images; therefore, it's not correct. Answer c, tar, is a compression tool, but is not used to install Red Hat Linux and is incorrect. Answer d is invalid. Therefore, the answer is a, none of the above.

Question 41

Answer a is correct. To schedule jobs or to make programs run at specific times, use cron. Answers b and c are invalid. Answer d, vi, is a Linux editor and is incorrect.

Question 42

Answer c is correct. The main sendmail configuration file is /etc/sendmail.cf. Answers a and b are invalid (which also makes d invalid).

Question 43

Answer c is correct. To specify which users are not allowed to access a system via FTP, edit the /etc/ftpusers file. Answer a, /etc/ftpaccess, is used to configure FTP access options and is not correct. Answer b, /etc/hosts.deny, specifies which domains and networks cannot access FTP, but does not deny individual users, and therefore is incorrect.

Question 44

Answer c is correct. To see which services an NFS server is using, use **rpcinfo**. Answers a, b, and d are invalid.

Question 45

Answer c is correct. To mount an NFS filesystem, use the command **mount** in answer c. Answer a is invalid. Answer b, **knfsd**, is an NFS daemon and therefore is incorrect.

Question 46

Answer c is correct. To view an SMB share from a Linux (or other Unix) system, use smbclient. Answer a is a separate network service and is incorrect. SMBD is the SMB server and is incorrect. Answer d is invalid.

Question 47

Answer e is correct. Many settings can be assigned with a DHCP server. Some of these items include the IP address (answer a), the gateway (answer b), the netmask (answer c), and DNS (answer d). The best answer is e, none of the above.

Question 48

Answer d is correct. To view your configured network interfaces, use **ifconfig**. Answer a, **netstat –rn**, prints the routing table and is incorrect. Answer b, **route**, prints the routing table and is used for route configuration, and therefore is incorrect. Answer c is invalid.

Question 49

Answer b is correct. The symbolic link used to link to the path for the system-preferred display manager is /etc/X11/prefdm. Answers a and c, .Xdefaults and .Xclients, are used to configure a user's X Window System. Answer d is invalid.

Question 50

Answer b is correct. The main Apache configuration file is /etc/httpd/conf/httpd.conf. Answers a and c are invalid.

Appendix
GNU General
Public License

The GPL is the license that most open source projects use for their software. Developed in the late 1980s, it has not been revised since its publication in 1991. The GPL is quite extensive, and many of its users interpret the document in different ways. Read on for a better understanding of the foundation of the open source community.

Version 2, June 1991
Copyright (C) 1989, 1991 Free Software Foundation, Inc.
59 Temple Place - Suite 330, Boston, MA 02111-1307, USA

Everyone is permitted to copy and distribute verbatim copies of this license document, but changing it is not allowed.

Preamble

The licenses for most software are designed to take away your freedom to share and change it. By contrast, the GNU General Public License is intended to guarantee your freedom to share and change free software—to make sure the software is free for all its users. This General Public License applies to most of the Free Software Foundation's software and to any other program whose authors commit to using it. (Some other Free Software Foundation software is covered by the GNU Library General Public License instead.) You can apply it to your programs, too.

When we speak of free software, we are referring to freedom, not price. Our General Public Licenses are designed to make sure that you have the freedom to distribute copies of free software (and charge for this service if you wish), that you receive source code or can get it if you want it, that you can change the software or use pieces of it in new free programs; and that you know you can do these things.

To protect your rights, we need to make restrictions that forbid anyone to deny you these rights or to ask you to surrender the rights. These restrictions translate to certain responsibilities for you if you distribute copies of the software, or if you modify it.

For example, if you distribute copies of such a program, whether gratis or for a fee, you must give the recipients all the rights that you have. You must make sure that they, too, receive or can get the source code. And you must show them these terms so they know their rights.

We protect your rights with two steps: (1) copyright the software, and (2) offer you this license which gives you legal permission to copy, distribute and/or modify the software.

Also, for each author's protection and ours, we want to make certain that everyone understands that there is no warranty for this free software. If the software is modified by someone else and passed on, we want its recipients to know that what they have is not the original, so that any problems introduced by others will not reflect on the original authors' reputations.

Finally, any free program is threatened constantly by software patents. We wish to avoid the danger that redistributors of a free program will individually obtain patent licenses, in effect making the program proprietary. To prevent this, we have made it clear that any patent must be licensed for everyone's free use or not licensed at all.

The precise terms and conditions for copying, distribution and modification follow.

Terms and Conditions for Copying, Distribution, and Modification

This License applies to any program or other work which contains a notice placed by the copyright holder saying it may be distributed under the terms of this General Public License. The "Program", below, refers to any such program or work, and a "work based on the Program" means either the Program or any derivative work under copyright law: that is to say, a work containing the Program or a portion of it, either verbatim or with modifications and/or translated into another language. (Hereinafter, translation is included without limitation in the term "modification".) Each licensee is addressed as "you".

Activities other than copying, distribution and modification are not covered by this License; they are outside its scope. The act of running the Program is not restricted, and the output from the Program is covered only if its contents constitute a work based on the Program (independent of having been made by running the Program). Whether that is true depends on what the Program does.

1. You may copy and distribute verbatim copies of the Program's source code as you receive it, in any medium, provided that you conspicuously and appropriately publish on each copy an appropriate copyright notice and disclaimer of warranty; keep intact all the notices that refer to this License and to the absence of any warranty; and give any other recipients of the Program a copy of this License along with the Program.

   You may charge a fee for the physical act of transferring a copy, and you may at your option offer warranty protection in exchange for a fee.

2. You may modify your copy or copies of the Program or any portion of it, thus forming a work based on the Program, and copy and distribute such modifications or work under the terms of Section 1 above, provided that you also meet all of these conditions:

   a) You must cause the modified files to carry prominent notices stating that you changed the files and the date of any change.

   b) You must cause any work that you distribute or publish, that in whole or in part contains or is derived from the Program or any part thereof, to be licensed as a whole at no charge to all third parties under the terms of this License.

   c) If the modified program normally reads commands interactively when run, you must cause it, when started running for such interactive use in the most ordinary way, to print or display an announcement including an appropriate copyright notice and a notice that there is no warranty (or else, saying that you provide a warranty) and that users may redistribute the program under these conditions, and telling the user how to view a copy of this License. (Exception: if the Program itself is interactive but does not normally print such an announcement, your work based on the Program is not required to print an announcement.)

   These requirements apply to the modified work as a whole. If identifiable sections of that work are not derived from the Program, and can be reasonably considered independent and separate works in themselves, then this License, and its terms, do not apply to those sections when you distribute them as separate works. But when you distribute the same sections as part of a whole which is a work based on the Program, the distribution of the whole must be on the terms of this License, whose permissions for other licensees extend to the entire whole, and thus to each and every part regardless of who wrote it.

Thus, it is not the intent of this section to claim rights or contest your rights to work written entirely by you; rather, the intent is to exercise the right to control the distribution of derivative or collective works based on the Program.

In addition, mere aggregation of another work not based on the Program with the Program (or with a work based on the Program) on a volume of a storage or distribution medium does not bring the other work under the scope of this License.

3. You may copy and distribute the Program (or a work based on it, under Section 2) in object code or executable form under the terms of Sections 1 and 2 above provided that you also do one of the following:

   a) Accompany it with the complete corresponding machine-readable source code, which must be distributed under the terms of Sections 1 and 2 above on a medium customarily used for software interchange; or,

   b) Accompany it with a written offer, valid for at least three years, to give any third party, for a charge no more than your cost of physically performing source distribution, a complete machine-readable copy of the corresponding source code, to be distributed under the terms of Sections 1 and 2 above on a medium customarily used for software interchange; or,

   c) Accompany it with the information you received as to the offer to distribute corresponding source code. (This alternative is allowed only for noncommercial distribution and only if you received the program in object code or executable form with such an offer, in accord with Subsection b above.)

The source code for a work means the preferred form of the work for making modifications to it. For an executable work, complete source code means all the source code for all modules it contains, plus any associated interface definition files, plus the scripts used to control compilation and installation of the executable. However, as a special exception, the source code distributed need not include anything that is normally distributed (in either source or binary form) with the major components (compiler, kernel, and so on) of the operating system on which the executable runs, unless that component itself accompanies the executable.

If distribution of executable or object code is made by offering access to copy from a designated place, then offering equivalent access to copy the source code from the same place counts as distribution of the source code, even though third parties are not compelled to copy the source along with the object code.

4. You may not copy, modify, sublicense, or distribute the Program except as expressly provided under this License. Any attempt otherwise to copy, modify, sublicense or distribute the Program is void, and will automatically terminate your rights under this License. However, parties who have received copies, or rights, from you under this License will not have their licenses terminated so long as such parties remain in full compliance.

5. You are not required to accept this License, since you have not signed it. However, nothing else grants you permission to modify or distribute the Program or its derivative works. These actions are prohibited by law if you do not accept this License. Therefore, by modifying or distributing the Program (or any work based on the Program), you indicate your acceptance of this License to do so, and all its terms and conditions for copying, distributing or modifying the Program or works based on it.

6. Each time you redistribute the Program (or any work based on the Program), the recipient automatically receives a license from the original licensor to copy, distribute or modify the Program subject to these terms and conditions. You may not impose any further restrictions on the recipients' exercise of the rights granted herein. You are not responsible for enforcing compliance by third parties to this License.

7. If, as a consequence of a court judgment or allegation of patent infringement or for any other reason (not limited to patent issues), conditions are imposed on you (whether by court order, agreement or otherwise) that contradict the conditions of this License, they do not excuse you from the conditions of this License. If you cannot distribute so as to satisfy simultaneously your obligations under this License and any other pertinent obligations, then as a consequence you may not distribute the Program at all. For example, if a patent license would not permit royalty-free redistribution of the Program by all those who receive copies directly or indirectly through you, then the only way you could satisfy both it and this License would be to refrain entirely from distribution of the Program.

If any portion of this section is held invalid or unenforceable under any particular circumstance, the balance of the section is intended to apply and the section as a whole is intended to apply in other circumstances.

It is not the purpose of this section to induce you to infringe any patents or other property right claims or to contest validity of any such claims; this section has the sole purpose of protecting the integrity of the free software distribution system, which is implemented by public license practices. Many people have made generous contributions to the wide range of software distributed through that system in reliance on consistent application of that system; it is up to the author/donor to decide if he or she is willing to distribute software through any other system and a licensee cannot impose that choice.

This section is intended to make thoroughly clear what is believed to be a consequence of the rest of this License.

8. If the distribution and/or use of the Program is restricted in certain countries either by patents or by copyrighted interfaces, the original copyright holder who places the Program under this License may add an explicit geographical distribution limitation excluding those countries, so that distribution is permitted only in or among countries not thus excluded. In such case, this License incorporates the limitation as if written in the body of this License.

9. The Free Software Foundation may publish revised and/or new versions of the General Public License from time to time. Such new versions will be similar in spirit to the present version, but may differ in detail to address new problems or concerns.

Each version is given a distinguishing version number. If the Program specifies a version number of this License which applies to it and "any later version", you have the option of following the terms and conditions either of that version or of any later version published by the Free Software Foundation. If the Program does not specify a version number of this License, you may choose any version ever published by the Free Software Foundation.

10. If you wish to incorporate parts of the Program into other free programs whose distribution conditions are different, write to the author to ask for permission. For software which is copyrighted by the Free Software Foundation, write to the Free Software Foundation; we sometimes make exceptions for this. Our decision will be guided by the two goals of preserving the free status of all derivatives of our free software and of promoting the sharing and reuse of software generally.

No Warranty

11. BECAUSE THE PROGRAM IS LICENSED FREE OF CHARGE, THERE IS NO WARRANTY FOR THE PROGRAM, TO THE EXTENT PERMITTED BY APPLICABLE LAW. EXCEPT WHEN OTHERWISE STATED IN WRITING THE COPYRIGHT HOLDERS AND/OR OTHER PARTIES PROVIDE THE PROGRAM "AS IS" WITHOUT WARRANTY OF ANY KIND, EITHER EXPRESSED OR IMPLIED, INCLUDING, BUT NOT LIMITED TO, THE IM-

PLIED WARRANTIES OF MERCHANTABILITY AND FITNESS FOR A PARTICULAR PURPOSE. THE ENTIRE RISK AS TO THE QUALITY AND PERFORMANCE OF THE PROGRAM IS WITH YOU. SHOULD THE PROGRAM PROVE DEFECTIVE, YOU ASSUME THE COST OF ALL NECESSARY SERVICING, REPAIR OR CORRECTION.

12. IN NO EVENT UNLESS REQUIRED BY APPLICABLE LAW OR AGREED TO IN WRITING WILL ANY COPYRIGHT HOLDER, OR ANY OTHER PARTY WHO MAY MODIFY AND/OR REDISTRIBUTE THE PROGRAM AS PERMITTED ABOVE, BE LIABLE TO YOU FOR DAMAGES, INCLUDING ANY GENERAL, SPECIAL, INCIDENTAL OR CONSEQUENTIAL DAMAGES ARISING OUT OF THE USE OR INABILITY TO USE THE PROGRAM (INCLUDING BUT NOT LIMITED TO LOSS OF DATA OR DATA BEING RENDERED INACCURATE OR LOSSES SUSTAINED BY YOU OR THIRD PARTIES OR A FAILURE OF THE PROGRAM TO OPERATE WITH ANY OTHER PROGRAMS), EVEN IF SUCH HOLDER OR OTHER PARTY HAS BEEN ADVISED OF THE POSSIBILITY OF SUCH DAMAGES.

How to Apply These Terms to Your New Programs

If you develop a new program, and you want it to be of the greatest possible use to the public, the best way to achieve this is to make it free software which everyone can redistribute and change under these terms.

To do so, attach the following notices to the program. It is safest to attach them to the start of each source file to most effectively convey the exclusion of warranty; and each file should have at least the "copyright" line and a pointer to where the full notice is found.

```
one line to give the program's name and an idea of what it does.
Copyright (C) yyyy  name of author

This program is free software; you can redistribute it and/or
modify it under the terms of the GNU General Public License as
published by the Free Software Foundation; either version 2 of
the License, or (at your option) any later version.

This program is distributed in the hope that it will be useful,
but WITHOUT ANY WARRANTY; without even the implied warranty of
MERCHANTABILITY or FITNESS FOR A PARTICULAR PURPOSE.
See the GNU General Public License for more details.
```

You should have received a copy of the GNU General Public License
along with this program; if not, write to the Free Software
Foundation, Inc., 59 Temple Place - Suite 330, Boston, MA
02111-1307, USA.

Also add information on how to contact you by electronic and paper mail.

If the program is interactive, make it output a short notice like this when it starts
in an interactive mode:

```
Gnomovision version 69, Copyright (C) yyyy name of author
Gnomovision comes with ABSOLUTELY NO WARRANTY;
for details type 'show w'.
This is free software, and you are welcome to redistribute it
under certain conditions; type 'show c' for details.
```

The hypothetical commands 'show w' and 'show c' should show the appropriate
parts of the General Public License. Of course, the commands you use may be
called something other than 'show w' and 'show c'; they could even be mouse-
clicks or menu items—whatever suits your program.

You should also get your employer (if you work as a programmer) or your school,
if any, to sign a "copyright disclaimer" for the program, if necessary. Here is a
sample; alter the names:

```
Yoyodyne, Inc., hereby disclaims all copyright interest
in the program 'Gnomovision' (which makes passes at compilers)
written by James Hacker.

signature of Ty Coon, 1 April 1989
Ty Coon, President of Vice
```

This General Public License does not permit incorporating your program into
proprietary programs. If your program is a subroutine library, you may consider it
more useful to permit linking proprietary applications with the library. If this is
what you want to do, use the GNU Library General Public License instead of
this License.

Glossary

/bin/sh
The path to the standard shell on Linux (and Unix) systems.

/etc/conf.modules
File that specifies commands, options, and paths for modules. This file sets up any module aliases and parameters that might be required. (This file name will soon be changed to /etc/modules.conf for standardization reasons.)

/etc/crontab
File used to configure system jobs (task schedule).

/etc/fstab
File used to configure filesystems on a machine.

**/etc/group **
File used to assign users to specific (or shared) groups.

/etc/hosts
File that contains hosts found on your system.

/etc/httpd/conf/httpd.conf
The main httpd server configuration file.

/etc/inittab
File containing system configuration information, including virtual consoles.

/etc/lilo.conf
File used to configure LILO.

/etc/named.conf
File used to configure DNS.

/etc/passwd
File containing user information, such as user ID, user name, group ID, and password.

/etc/printcap
File used to configure printers.

/etc/rc.d/rc.local
Script used for local startup configuration.

/etc/rc.d/rc.sysinit

Script run at boot-time by the init process.

/etc/securetty

File used to specify the tty on which root is allowed to login.

/etc/sendmail.cf

Main configuration file for sendmail.

/etc/skel

Directory containing default user files used when you're creating new accounts.

/etc/smb.conf

Configuration file for Samba.

/etc/smbpasswd

File containing password information for Windows users who are connecting to the Samba server.

/etc/sysconfig

Directory containing script configuration files.

a.out

The old executable style of Linux and Unix systems. (The name comes from the default output file name of the C compiler.)

Apache

Popular Hypertext Transport Protocol (HTTP) server, based originally on the popular Web server NCSA httpd 1.3.

APM (Advanced Power Management)

System used to manage CPU calls, shutdown options, suspend options, and other power-related functions.

ARP (Address Resolution Protocol)

The protocol used to resolve IP addresses to MAC addresses on Ethernet networks.

autoprobe

A system's capability to make calls to a specific device, receiving identification and other information from the device automatically.

bash (Bourne Again Shell)

The GNU implementation of the Bourne/POSIX shell (/bin/sh).

BIND (Berkeley Internet Name Domain)

The standard, free, reference DNS server implementation used by the vast majority of sites on the Internet.

BIOS (Basic Input/Output System)

The code in a computer's ROM or Flash RAM that initializes the hardware and starts the boot process.

BSD (Berkeley Software Distribution)

The Unix derivative created by the University of California at Berkeley. (The portions of BSD not derived from AT&T code are open-source software.)

building

Term used for compiling, or creating programs, RPM files, database files, and so on.

bzip

Compression utility for files.

character-cell mode

Console-based menu system.

CIDR

Classless InterDomain Routing.

CISC (Complex Instruction Set Computing)

The CPU architecture used in the Intel 80x86 line of microprocessors. CISC has variable-length instructions that might require several clock cycles to complete.

clear
Tool used to clear all text from an xterm or console.

clone
A machine with the exact hardware and software configuration as another machine.

COFF (Common Object File Format)
The binary format used by some Unix systems, also used in a modified form by Windows NT, and introduced in Unix System V Release 3. Linux supports COFF executables of some other systems but does not use the format natively.

compile
To convert the source code of a program to machine code.

conf.modules
The file in /etc with configuration information for loadable kernel modules.

control-panel
The Red Hat menu used to configure Red Hat networking, users, and printing.

CPU
Central processing unit.

crackers
People who attempt to or succeed at breaking into computer systems unlawfully.

crontab
The file or files that specify commands to be run by the cron program at certain times. Also the command used to manipulate those files.

daemon
A program that runs in the background and whose parent process is **init**. Usually daemons provide some kind of system services.

device
A block or character special file that generally points to a piece of hardware.

DHCP (Dynamic Host Configuration Protocol)
A superset of bootp that is used to assign IP addresses to clients on a network. DHCP is used for dynamic hosts that can move, connect, and disconnect from networks.

dig
Tool used to query a name server for domain name packet information.

Disk Druid
Graphical tool used to format and partition a hard drive during Red Hat installation.

distribution
A collection of software built into a complete system. Examples of Linux distributions include Red Hat Linux, Caldera OpenLinux, SuSE Linux, Debian GNU/Linux, Stampede, and Slackware.

DNS (Domain Name Service)
The protocol used to resolve domain names to IP addresses.

dnsquery
Tool used to query a domain name server for a host using resolver.

domain
Name assigned to an IP address to identify a machine to an IP address.

dual-boot
Method in which a computer is set up to boot from two or more operating systems.

dynamic route
Route that is assigned "on the fly," meaning that no definitive route is set, and a route for a packet is assigned each time a packet is sent (not predetermined).

edquota
Tool used to edit disk quotas.

ELF (Executable and Linkable Format)
The binary format of Linux executables, as well as the standard binary format of many other Unix (and Unix-like) systems.

Elm
Text-based mail reader used on Unix systems. The interface is text-based, and commands are given by simple keystrokes as prompted by the mail reader.

Ethernet
The dominant LAN hardware protocol.

eth0
Ethernet device name.

ext2
Mount type associated with Linux filesystems.

FDDI (Fiber Distributed Data Interface)
A networking hardware layer that uses fiber-optic cable as the physical medium.

fdisk
The program that is used to manage partitions on a disk.

filesystem
Refers to the on-disk structures that store information such as file properties and the location of file data.

firewall
System used to monitor and control access to and from a network.

Free Software Foundation
See FSF.

fsck
The program that is used to check the consistency of filesystems.

FSF (Free Software Foundation)
Foundation established to promote the development and use of free software.

fstab
The file in /etc that contains mappings from device names to mount points.

FTP (File Transfer Protocol)
A protocol used to transfer files between two hosts.

GDM (GNOME Display Manager)
Tool used to replace default XDM (X Display Manager). GDM allows the user to log in to GNOME, KDE, or AnotherLevel.

GIMP
Linux tool used to manipulate graphics. Similar to Adobe Photoshop.

GMC (GNOME Midnight Commander)
GNOME file manager that allows such capabilities as drag and drop to the desktop features and file browsing similar to the Windows Explorer.

GNOME (GNU Network Object Model Environment)
A window environment based on CORBA.

GnoRPM
GUI tool that replaces glint as the package management tool.

GPL (General Product License)
License established to preserve the rights of free software and free-software authors.

group
Associates multiple users with one identification method, allowing files and services to be accessed by group permissions rather than by individual user permission.

groupdel
Tool used to delete all users in a group.

gzip
Compression utility for files.

hardware address (MAC address)
A vendor-assigned 6-byte number in firmware on Ethernet hardware that uniquely identifies the Ethernet controller on a network.

home
Directory dedicated to a user.

host name
Name assigned to identify your machine to a local network.

host
Tool used to look up the host for a domain name.

HTTP (Hypertext Transport Protocol)
The protocol used to transfer files for the World Wide Web.

I/O (Input/Output)
Often used to refer to a device's I/O address, which is the location in memory where the CPU can access the memory on the device.

IANA (Internet Assigned Numbers Authority)
Body that sets standards used on the Internet.

IBM (International Business Machines)
The company that created the IBM PC, which most x86-based systems are based on (and compatible with).

ICMP (Internet Control Message Protocol)
The control (non-data) message protocol of TCP/IP.

IDE (Integrated Drive Electronics)
The standard PC bus for hard drives and other disk devices.

ifconfig
Tool used to view and configure active network interfaces.

ifdown
Tool used to disable a specified network interface (such as eth0).

ifup

Tool used to enable a specified interface (such as eth0).

IMAP (Internet Message Access Protocol)

A protocol used to read electronic mail on a remote server.

inetd

Internet daemon that controls most of the network services that listen for incoming connections on your machine.

init

Tool used to access various runlevels.

initial ramdisk

Required when support is needed, such as SCSI support during boot. The ramdisk is noted in your /etc/lilo.conf file as an **initrd=** comment.

initrd

File used as the initial ramdisk used to boot a system that uses SCSI during the boot process.

inode

A filesystem structure that uniquely identifies a file and its properties (permissions, size, and so on).

insmod

Tool used to load a specific module manually.

IP forwarding

A routing system used to route packets originating from a separate host to another host on the network.

ipchains

Tool that specifies firewall policies to the Linux 2.2 kernel.

IPv6

The next generation of TCP/IP, which is more secure than the current generation (IPv4) and which uses 128-bit addresses (instead of the current 32-bit addresses).

IPX

Network protocol used primarily on NetWare.

IRQ

Hardware interrupt request.

ISA

Industry Standard Architecture PC bus interface.

ISDN (Integrated Services Digital Network)

Digital telephony service with 128K bandwidth.

iso9660

Mount type associated with CD-ROM devices.

ISP (Internet Service Provider)

Organization that charges fees for providing Internet access service and other Internet-related services.

kbdconfig

Tool to configure the system keyboard.

KDE

The K Desktop Environment.

kernel

The heart of an operating system. The kernel controls access to hardware, handles hardware events (such as interrupts), schedules timeslices for processes, and manages resources.

kernelcfg
GUI tool used to configure the Linux kernel.

kerneld
Daemon used, in versions up to Red Hat Linux 5.2, to handle kernel modules.

kickstart
Tool used to automate Red Hat Linux installation.

kmod
A kernel task that handles loading the kernel.

LDP (Linux Documentation Project)
Online Linux resource for information. See **http://www.linuxdoc.org/**.

LILO (Linux Loader)
A tool used to boot the kernel on x86 hardware.

lilo.conf
The file in /etc that describes kernels and other operating systems for LILO to boot.

linuxconf
Tool used to configure Linux networking, users, programs, and more.

lo
Loopback interface name.

login
Name used synonymously with username. To log in or gain access to a system with a username and password.

lpd
Print daemon.

lsmod
Tool used to tell you which modules are loaded.

MAC address
Protocol that has been replaced by bootp and DHCP, although it is still somewhat commonly used.

make config
Command used for text-based kernel configuration.

make menuconfig
Console-based tool used for kernel configuration.

make xconfig
GUI-based tool used for kernel configuration.

masquerading
Routing option set up to disguise internal network traffic as a single system.

MBR (master boot record)
Superblock of the hard disk that contains system boot information.

MDA (mail delivery agent)
Software that's responsible for receiving (and sending) mail for the user to and from the MTA.

minix
Modular Unix-like system developed by Andrew Tanenbaum.

mkfs
The program used to create filesystems.

modprobe
Tool used to automatically load a model and all its dependencies.

modular
Type of kernel whose drivers compile only what is required at boot time. Remaining drivers and support are installed as modules and are loaded only when needed.

module
Loadable kernel-object files that can be inserted and removed from a running kernel and that can contain device drivers, filesystem drivers, and other kernel code.

monolithic
Type of kernel whose system support is compiled directly in the kernel.

mount
Command used to mount filesystems and to view lists of mounted filesystems.

mountpoint
Directory where a filesystem or device is mounted.

mouseconfig
Menu-based tool used to configure the system mouse.

msdos
The MS-DOS-compatible filesystem.

MTA (mail transport agent)
System responsible for the physical sending and receiving of user and system mail.

MUA (mail user agent)
Responsible for providing the "front-end" interface to users to create and read mail.

name serve
Server dedicated to resolving DNS and host names via DNS.

netcfg
Tool used to configure networking.

netmask
A bitmask that is used to define an IP segment.

netstat
Tool used to report network information.

NetWare
Network-based operating system developed by Novell.

NFS (Network File System)
The native Unix filesystem-sharing protocol.

NIC (network interface card)
Adapter card used to connect a system to the network.

NIS (Network Information Service)
Formerly known as Yellow Pages, a protocol used to store shared configuration information (such as the passwd, group, and hosts files) on a server.

nmbd
Windows NetBIOS names for sending and receiving names of machines on the network.

nslookup
Tool used to query Internet name servers for IP and domain information.

ntpdate
Tool similar to rdate. The ntpdate tool is used to retrieve the date and time from the network by polling the Network Time Protocol Servers as specified in the command.

open-source software
See OSS.

operating system (OS)
A software program that controls the operations on a computer system.

OSS (open-source software)
Software whose source code is available to the public.

output
The text result from a console command.

PAM (Pluggable Authentication Modules)
System that enables ruleset implementation without having to recode individual services.

partition
A section of a disk. Under Linux, each partition on a disk shows up as a separate device.

passwd
Tool used to change (or set) a user password.

PCI (Peripheral Component Interconnect)
The 32- or 64-bit, 33MHz bus that was designed by Intel and that is used in most current PCs and workstations.

PCMCIA
Slot-style hardware used in laptops.

peripheral
Device attached externally to a computer.

Perl
Programming and scripting language developed by Larry Wall.

permissions
Access levels granted to a file, program, or directory, for a user or group. Can be changed with chmod.

Pine
Text-based mail reader used on Unix systems. The Pine mail reader is a little more user-friendly than Elm is. Pine uses key-combination menu-based options and a simpler text editor.

plug and play
Hardware that is software (not jumper) configurable.

PMS (Package Management System)
Package management system project led by Rik Faith. It was a predecessor to RPM (*see* RPM).

pointer
The arrow or other indicator that represents the location of your mouse, trackball, glide point, or other pointing device and that corresponds to the location on the screen. Quite often the shape, color, or size of the pointer will change to indicate that the mouse has a particular function on that specific area of the screen.

POP (Post Office Protocol)

A protocol used to retrieve electronic mail from a remote server. (Currently, Linux supports two POP protocols: POP2 and POP3. POP2 is obsolete, although it is still supported.)

ppp0

ppp interface name.

printtool

Tool used to configure printing.

prototype

Machine configured as a test, or base model, and used for cloning.

pwconv

Tool used to convert /etc/passwd to using shadow passwords.

pwunconv

Tool used to convert /etc/passwd from using shadow passwords.

query

A request sent by one program to another program or package for information.

RAM (Random Access Memory)

Memory used on a system for storing temporary data for programs and files.

RARP (Reverse ARP)

A protocol used to discover the IP address of a device given its MAC address.

rdate

The Red Hat Linux tool used to synchronize the system time with a specified machine. The rdate tool synchronizes only once when used.

rebuilding

Recompiling.

RIP (Routing Information Protocol)

A protocol used to dynamically reconfigure routing information.

RISC (Reduced Instruction Set Computing)

The CPU architecture used in the Alpha, Sparc, and other CPUs, and that has short, fixed-length instructions that perform simple tasks. More complex instructions must be built out of simpler instructions. This architecture allows the CPU to be simpler and generally faster than a CISC CPU, but at the cost of often needing to execute many more instructions than does a CISC CPU.

rmmod

Tool used to remove a loadable kernel module.

root

The superuser, whose user ID is 0. File permissions are ignored for root.

root directory

The / directory.

root window

The background of your screen. The root window doesn't have any of the standard characteristics of any other window, but it does have some unique applications. The root window is where you can customize your background images, among various other tasks.

route

The program that is used to manage the kernel's routing tables.

router

A system responsible for managing and relaying network packets.

routing table

The kernel's mapping of IP addresses to network interfaces. The routing table tells the kernel how to send IP traffic to its destination.

RPM (Red Hat Package Manager)

Program used to manage Red Hat Linux packages for system programs and tools.

Samba

Open-source tool that implements SMB (Server Message Block).

screen

Your whole desktop. The terms "screen" and "desktop" are often interchanged. Technically, the screen is the primary video display that you use to view your X Window System.

SCSI (Small Computer Systems Interface)

The bus used to connect disk drives and other peripherals on some PCs and on most workstations and other non-x86-based systems.

sendmail

Program responsible for mail transfer between servers.

services

Names associated with particular pairs of TCP/IP protocol and port numbers. Also the name of the file in /etc with mappings from those names to particular protocols and port numbers.

shadow passwords

A system used to move /etc/passwd information to a non-world-readable file, allowing options such as password aging.

shell

The command interpreter.

SMB (Server Message Block)

The standard filesystem and printer-sharing protocol of Lan Manager and Windows.

smbadduser

Tool used to add Windows Samba users to your system.

smbclient

Client-side program used to connect to an SMB server from Linux.

smbmount

Utility used to mount SMB shares.

smbpasswd

Utility used to add users to /etc/smbpasswd, allowing for Windows encrypted passwords.

smbprint

Script used for printing through SMB share.

smbrun

Script used to start the SMB server.

smbstatus

Tool used to print status information for the running SMB server.

smbtar
Script used for backing up Windows machines to your SMB server.

smbumount
Tool used to unmount the SMB service.

smbuser
Unix-to-NT user mapping.

SMP (symmetric multiprocessing)
Support for machines with more than one CPU.

sndconfig
Red Hat tool used to configure sound.

source code
Also known simply as *source;* the text files that contain instructions that are converted to machine code by a compiler.

spec file
A file containing the specification for a given package, file, or program for use by RPM.

SQL
Structured Query Language, used for databases.

Squid
Caching proxy server that caches data streams such as FTP, gopher, and HTTP.

static route
Preconfigured mandatory path for specified network requests and/or packets.

superuser
Also known as *root.* Special system user with privileged access to configure all parts of a Linux system.

supplementary group
An assigned group used in addition to the main user group.

swap
The process of paging memory to disk as virtual memory. Also used to refer to the spaces on disk used for paging.

SWAT
Web-based configuration tool for SMB.

switchdesk
Tool used to switch between installed desktops.

symbolic link
Also known as *symlink,* a directory entry that points to a path to another file.

SysLinux
Tool that boots the Linux kernel from a DOS filesystem.

System Commander
Commercial bootloader that you can purchase from a local software vendor.

tar
Compression utility used for files.

TCP (Transmission Control Protocol)
The connection-oriented protocol of TCP/IP.

TCP/IP (Transmission Control Protocol/ Internet Protocol)
The network protocol of the Internet, and the native networking protocol of Linux and Unix.

tcp_wrappers

A tool that uses the system files /etc/hosts.allow and /etc/hosts.deny to control who can and cannot access services managed by **inetd**.

terminal emulator

A window with just text that basically imitates a text terminal. An example of a terminal emulator is an xterm.

TeX

Special text formatting and typesetting program.

timeconfig

GUI tool used to configure system time.

tools

Software commands used to administer a program or computer services.

TOS

Type of service.

TTL (Time To Live)

A field in an IP packet that defines the number of routers the packet should pass through before being rejected. (The **traceroute** command works by repeatedly sending an ICMP echo packet, incrementing the TTL by one until the host is reached.)

UDP (User Datagram Protocol)

The stream-oriented, connectionless protocol of TCP/IP.

umask

File-creation mask used to set up default file permissions based on the umask setting subtracted from full file permissions of 777.

Unix

The operating system that was developed in the late 1960s and early 1970s at Bell Labs and that is the inspiration for Linux.

URL (Uniform Resource Locator)

A Web address such as **http://www.coriolis.com/**.

user

Individual with an account on a machine.

user ID

The number associated with individual user accounts. The system automatically sets this number when the account is created.

useradd

Tool used to add user accounts to a system. (Equivalent to **adduser**.)

userdel

Tool used to delete a system user.

vfat

Mount type associated with Windows partitions and filesystems.

virtual consoles

Multiple text-based logins located on separate virtual screens on your system.

virtual hosts

Apache feature allowing a single machine to host multiple domains.

visual bell

Visual alarm, such as a screen flash, used to specify a system beep without using the speaker.

vmlinuz

A compressed vmlinux kernel file, which is a play on vmunix, the standard kernel name on Unix systems. (Compressed files often have the last character changed to z or have a .z or .Z appended to the file name.)

window

A frame where any given application resides and is managed by the window manager. The active window is the window that you are currently using on your desktop. The active window is usually indicated by being on top, in focus, or highlighted compared to the inactive windows on the screen.

window manager

The main interface between the X Window System and the user. The window manager provides functionality such as window borders, menus, icons, desktops, and toolbars, and allows the user to customize them all.

X

The X Window System, originally developed at MIT as a client-server protocol for building graphical user interfaces.

xf86config

Text-based configuration tool that is used to configure the XF86Config file.

xhost

Tool used to grant X permission to host applications for other machines.

xntp3

Tool used to set up a continuously running synchronization daemon.

ypcat

Tool used to print the values of all keys in the specified NIS database.

ypmatch

Tool used to print the values of keys from an NIS map.

yppoll

Tool used to return the version and master server of the specified NIS map.

yppush

Tool used to notify the slave servers when master databases are changed.

ypwhich

Tool used to return the name of the NIS server used by the NIS client.

Index

Y